FEDERAL CLERICAL EXAM

LearningExpress

LEARNINGEXPRESS

NEW YORK

98-65391
CIP

Printed in the United States of America
9 8 7 6 5 4 3

ISBN 1-57685-101-X

Regarding the Information in this Book
We attempt to verify the information presented in our books prior to publication. It is always a good idea, however, to double-check such important information as minimum requirements, application and testing procedures, and deadlines with the hiring agency, as such information can change from time to time.

For Further Information
For information on LearningExpress, other LearningExpress products, or bulk sales, please call or write to us at:

LearningExpress™
900 Broadway
Suite 604
New York, NY 10003
212-995-2566

ISBN 1-57685-101-X

7 85555 85101 6

CONTENTS

LIST OF CONTRIBUTORS

The following individuals contributed to the content of this book:

Elizabeth Chesla is an adult educator and curriculum developer at Polytechnic University in New York who has also taught reading and writing at New York University School of Continuing Education and New York Institute of Technology in New York City.

Judith N. Meyers is director of the Two Together Tutorial Program of the Jewish Child Care Association in New York City and an Adult Basic Education Practitioner at City University of New York.

Carolyn Miller, M.A., is a freelance editor, writer, and teacher in San Francisco, California.

Judith F. Olson, M.A., is chairperson of the language arts department at Valley High School in West Des Moines, Iowa, where she also conducts test preparation workshops.

Jo Lynn Southard is a freelance writer and editor living in Portland, Maine.

Shirley Tarbell is a test development specialist and writer living in Portland, Maine.

C·H·A·P·T·E·R 1

GETTING A CLERICAL JOB WITH THE FEDERAL GOVERNMENT

CHAPTER SUMMARY

This chapter will introduce you to the numerous clerical careers available with the federal government and the benefits of working for Uncle Sam. You'll also learn about the most common entry-level positions and how to find and apply for the government clerical jobs that are right for you.

A messenger in Florida. A telephone operator in Montana. A secretary in South America. What do these diverse people have in common? They all work for the federal government in some of the 60 or so different clerical positions available to civilian employees. There's a whole army of people working for Uncle Sam, keeping the federal government running smoothly, in positions from accounting machine operator to teletypist and everything in between.

Every year hundreds of thousands of people apply to join the ranks of federal employees. That's not surprising—after all, a job with the federal government has a lot to offer, including a competitive salary, job security, government pension, and upward mobility. But competition is often intense, and the job search and application process can be daunting. Let's take a closer look at just what it means to work for the government, how the government hires its employees, and how you can get an edge in the job selection process.

WHY WORK FOR UNCLE SAM?

There are many good reasons to work for the U.S. government: lots of opportunities, good salary and benefits, job security, and more.

Number One Employer

The federal government is the largest single employer in the United States—and one of the largest in the world. Its nearly 3 million employees work in over 2,000 different occupations that are comparable to just about every job you can find in the private sector. Hundreds of thousands of positions open up each year from employee promotions and retirements alone, ensuring that even in times of budget cuts and downsizing, positions—and lots of them—will always be available with the federal government. And no matter how good or bad the economy, we'll always need the messengers, telephone operators, clerks, and secretaries who make sure the government runs smoothly.

Minimum Qualifications

All you need for a clerical career with the government is a high school diploma (or GED) and, for most positions, U.S. citizenship. If you are a male over 18, born after December 31, 1959, you must also be registered with (or exempt from) the Selective Service. Beyond the minimum requirements, your education, skills, experience, and location will determine what specific jobs you are eligible for with the federal government.

Worldwide Opportunities

With its diversity of jobs and geographic locations, the federal government offers flexibility in job opportunities that's unmatched in the private sector. While the bulk of federal civilian employees work in and around Washington, D.C., there are civilian government employees in every state and in just about every country on the globe.

Following the District of Columbia, California, New York, Texas, and Florida come in with the highest numbers of government employees. Atlanta, Baltimore, Chicago, Denver, Los Angeles/Long Beach, New York City, Philadelphia, San Antonio, and San Diego are among the cities with the largest government civilian employee populations.

But you don't have to live in a big city to find work with the federal government. In many small towns, a large percentage of civilians are federal employees. A look in the blue pages of your local phone book will show you just how many federal agencies there are in your area. Meanwhile, over 100,000 federal employees—approximately 3.8 percent of the civilian work force—work outside of the United States in foreign countries. Some of those people, of course, are clerical workers—no office can run without support staff!

Salaries

As a government employee, you'll earn a respectable income, even at the entry level. Positions that require a high school diploma or GED and little or no work experience often offer higher pay than comparable jobs in the private sector. While the same may not be true for all entry-level jobs, employees with relevant education or experience are far more likely than their private-sector counterparts to be promoted into higher-paying positions.

The table on this page offers some examples of entry-level salaries for various clerical positions with the federal government.

Benefits

It's hard to beat the benefits and security of working for the government. New employees of the federal government receive:

SAMPLE SALARIES

Job Title	Grade	Salary (1997)
Computer Operator	GS–0332	$16,647–$21,641
Messenger	GS–0302	$16,647–$21,641
Occupational Analyst	GS–0222	$15,256–$19,203
Salary and Wage Administrator	GS–0223	$15,256–$19,203
Secretary	GS–0318	$16,647–$21,641
Telephone Operator	GS–0381	$16,647–$21,641

For an explanation of grade, or pay level, see "Series and Grade System" below.

- 10 paid national holidays per year (plus Inauguration Day every four years)
- 13–26 days of annual leave per year
- 13 days of sick leave per year
- Regular cost of living adjustments (COLA)
- Death and disability insurance
- Group life insurance
- Health care (medical and dental benefits)
- Government pension

Special Employee Programs

Federal employees also enjoy the added benefit of special employee programs. Most agencies have their own programs, and there are also programs available to most or all federal employees, such as the Federal Employee Education and Assistance Fund (FEEAF). The FEEAF provides grants and scholarships to federal employees and their dependents without adding to the taxpayers' burden: all of the money comes from employee contributions.

Incentive Awards Program

If you're a federal employee and find an innovative way to reduce government costs or improve government operations, you can be rewarded with a big bonus—up to half a million dollars!—through the federal government's Incentive Awards Program.

Steady Hiring

Despite recent government cutbacks, experts foresee steady hiring in the government's future. The U.S. Department of Labor's *Occupational Outlook Handbook* (1994–1995) predicts a 10 percent increase in government employment in the next decade.

Job Security

One of the greatest benefits of being a federal employee is job security. Once you've completed the three-year probationary period, you become a career employee, eligible for full benefits and protected from layoffs by several layers of employees.

TYPES OF EMPLOYEES

Full-Time Positions

While the specific employee categories in the different agencies may vary, in general, there are four types of full-time employees working for the federal government:

- **Temporary.** These are positions that last for less than one year. There are no special privileges or benefits, but as a temporary employee, your foot is in the government door, and that's a great advantage: not only will you have insider knowledge of job openings, but if you do your job well, you'll have a terrific advantage over other candidates.

- **Term.** These positions are created and filled for a specific period of time for the completion of a specific project or study. They may last from one to three years, sometimes more, and term employees often receive health benefits but are usually not eligible for pension. Again, term employees can find out about job openings early and those who do their jobs well have an edge in competing for more permanent positions.
- **Career-conditional.** Most entry-level civilian employees start out in this three-year probationary position, during which they are evaluated and after which they become eligible for a full-time permanent position (career status). This three-year period is critical for those who wish for career status and includes most career benefits but with various restrictions. (Disability insurance, for example, is often excluded or limited for career-conditional employees.)
- **Career.** Most employees are at this full-time, full-benefit level, which they achieve after the three-year career-conditional probation period. These are usually the last positions to be affected by downsizing and layoffs.

Part-Tme and Work-Study Positions

There are also part-time and student work-study positions available with the federal government, but the parameters of these positions vary from agency to agency. In general, if you are at least 16, you can begin working part-time for the government so long as you are in good standing at your high school and remain in good standing until you graduate. Many agencies also have regular part-time positions.

Clerical and Administrative Support Positions

Just about every federal agency needs people to handle the day-to-day details of office work. These people fall into an entry-level category known as clerical and administrative support.

In general, clerical and administrative support personnel provide support to higher-level employees by performing such routine office work as:

- Answering telephones
- Typing correspondence
- Performing stenography (taking dictation in shorthand or on a machine)
- Working with mail and files
- Operating office machines (typewriters, copiers, fax machines, computers, mail processing equipment, etc.)
- Doing data entry

They may also complete research projects and prepare reports, or be given assignments that demand specialized skills, such as proficiency with a 10-key adding machine or experience with word processing or spreadsheet software.

"Clerical and administrative support" is a broad description of a job whose exact responsibilities can vary greatly, depending on the agency you work for. For example, take a look at the job description for a clerk (a GS-300 position) with the Internal Revenue Service:

Perform various clerical duties such as maintaining records, extracting, sorting, and filing tax returns and other related correspondence.

Note how the job responsibilities relate directly to the activities of the Internal Revenue Service. Here are two more job descriptions for clerks in the federal government:

Some Clerical and Administrative Jobs Covered by the Federal Clerical and Administrative Support Exam

Messenger
Information Receptionist
Mail and File Clerk
Correspondence Clerk
Clerk-Stenographer and Reporter
Work Unit Superviser
Secretary
Closed Microphone Reporter
Clerk-Typist
Office Automation Clerk and Assistant
Computer Operator
Computer Specialist
Computer Clerk and Assistant
Program Manager
Administrative Officer
Support Services Administrator
Management and Program Analyst
Management and Program Clerk and Assistant
Logistics Manager
Equipment Operator
Printing Clerk
Data Transcriber
Coder
Electric Accounting Machine Operator
Equal Opportunity Compliance Clerk
Equal Opportunity Assistant

Electric Accounting Machine Project Planner
Telephone Operator
Telecommunications Processor
Telecommunications
General Telecommunications
Communications Clerk
Miscellaneous Administration and Program Positions
Miscellaneous Clerk and Assistant Positions
Personnel Management Clerk
Personnel Clerk and Assistant
Military Personnel Clerk and Technician
Military Personnel Management Clerk
Personnel Staffing Clerk
Position Classification Clerk
Occupational Analysis Clerk
Salary and Wage Administration Clerk
Employee Relations Clerk
Labor Relations Clerk
Employee Development Clerk
Mediation Clerk
Labor Management Relations Examining Clerk
Contractor Industrial Relations Clerk
Wage and Hour Compliance Clerk
Equal Employment Opportunity Clerk
Federal Retirement Benefits Clerk

An Information Clerk (a GS-304 position) at the Mt. Baker-Snoqualmie National Forest in Washington State is expected to provide information to the public concerning opportunities, programs, and activities in the Forest, on adjacent public lands, and/or on National Park Service lands in the greater Puget Sound area (information is provided via personal contacts, telephone calls, and general correspondence); sell interpretive association items—i.e., maps, books, etc.; answer questions regarding the trailhead fee demonstration project; answer the telephone, Forest Service radio, and written inquiries; direct calls to the appropriate person and receive visitors; answer routine and repetitive inquiries and direct the more difficult and technical questions to the proper person for answers; type a variety of correspondence, reports, and forms, including technical material, tabular material, and other routine typing from rough drafts; post and file Manual and Handbook changes and supplements. Extensive communication skills are required for this position.

A Test Administrator (a GS-303 position) with the Office of Personnel Management will administer

Civil Service written examinations, which include tests for Federal employment eligibility and the Armed Services Vocational Aptitude Battery (ASVAB), at high schools; assure the adequacy of the test site (lighting, ventilation, furnishings, etc.) prior to test administration; instruct competitors on procedures and control time requirements; forward completed examinations to the appropriate office; safeguard test material, taking all steps necessary to insure the integrity of the testing process; collect applications and other documents from test applicants and forward these to the appropriate office for action; score ASVAB tests for in/out rating, notifying recruiters of results.

JOB PROSPECTS

There is an abundance of career opportunities for clerical and administrative support at all levels of government. Nearly half a million employees—about half of all civil service positions—fall into the GS-300 series, General Administration, Clerical, and Office Services Group. (Series and grades are explained below.) That's because clerks are needed in every government agency and facility and because there are so many different types of clerks working for the government.

The U.S. government employs entry level administrative assistants and clerks in offices and facilities all over the country. The Internal Revenue Service, for example, employs thousands of clerical and administrative support personnel in 11 different states. Other agencies, some of which are military, that employ clerical-related employees include:

- The National Park Service at Glacier National Park, MT
- Department of Labor in Dallas, TX
- Department of the Interior in Vernal, UT

The locations listed here are just some of the many cities in which these agencies employ administrative assistants.

SERIES AND GRADE SYSTEM OF CLASSIFICATION

In the federal government, civilian employees are organized—and paid—according to the kind of work they do (called the *series*) and the level of difficulty (called the *grade*) of their position. Salaries and wages, called *schedules*, are determined by these classifications. Each grade consists of several *steps*, or raises.

Because there are nearly a hundred government departments and independent agencies, there are many different job series and pay schedules within the federal government. Still, excluding postal workers, most entry-level employees fall into one of two main series and schedules:

- The General Schedule (GS), which includes most professional, technical, administrative, and clerical positions
- The Wage Grade (WG) series and schedule, which includes most federal blue collar workers

As a clerical worker, you would fall into the General Schedule category.

General Schedule Grade Levels

The General Schedule includes 15 grades for its positions, GS-1 through GS-15. GS 1–7 positions are generally entry-level positions; GS 8–12, mid-level; and GS 13–15, top-level. The grades also break down into professional and non-professional categories, with the professional grades requiring a bachelor's degree or higher. Nonprofessional grades are GS-1–4, GS-6, GS-

8, and GS-10, while professional grades are GS-5, GS-7, GS-9, and GS-11–12.

General Schedule Pay

For 1998, basic pay under the General Schedule or GS pay plan is as follows:

GS-1	$12,960
GS-2	$14,571
GS-3	$15,899
GS-4	$17,848
GS-5	$19,969
GS-6	$22,258
GS-7	$24,734
GS-8	$27,393
GS-9	$30,257
GS-10	$33.320
GS-11	$36,609
GS-12	$43,876
GS-13	$52,176
GS-14	$61,656
GS-15	$72,525

Specific job descriptions and series for each occupational group are available in the government's *Handbook of Occupational Groups and Series of Classes*, as well as in the *Position Classification Standards* volumes. The Office of Personnel Management's *Qualification Standards Handbook for General Schedule Positions* provides the minimum experience and education requirements for most federal GS jobs. These books, as well as Career Brochures describing different career paths within the federal government, should be on hand at Federal Employment Information Centers. (See the end of this chapter for a list of these centers.)

JOB TITLES TO LOOK FOR

If you're interested in being a clerk or administrative assistant, it's important to know, at least at the federal level, that many jobs that fit this description don't necessarily have the word "clerk" or "administrative assis-

tant" in their title. Thus, it's important that you read job announcements carefully. If you're looking just for "clerk" or "administrative assistant," you may miss out on excellent job opportunities.

At the federal level, there are 38 job series in GS-300, each of which have from several to several dozen individual job titles. Here are some of those job series:

GS-302—Messenger Series
GS-318—Secretary Series
GS-322—Clerk-Typist Series
GS-332—Computer Operation Series
GS-335—Computer Clerk and Assistant Series
GS-342—Support Services Administration Series
GS-350—Equipment Operator Series
GS-356—Data Transcriber Series
GS-382—Telephone Operating Series
GS-391—Telecommunications Series
GS-394—Communications Clerical Series

For a full listing of GS-300 job titles, consult the *Dictionary of Occupational Titles,* published by the U.S. Department of Labor's Employment and Training Commission.

HOW THE FEDERAL GOVERNMENT HIRES CIVILIAN EMPLOYEES

JOB VACANCY ANNOUNCEMENTS

When a civil servant job opens within a government agency, that agency will usually issue a *Competition Notice, Exam Announcement, Vacancy Announcement, Civil Service Announcement* or *Announcement* (five names for essentially the same thing). These announcements should list the following information:

- Open and close dates (filing period or application window)
- Job title
- Job number
- Geographic location
- Number of vacancies
- Hiring office/agency
- Salary
- Terms (part/full time)
- Benefits
- Job duties
- Job qualifications
- Criteria for evaluation or rating (education, experience, etc.)
- Any supplemental information required by candidate
- Who may apply (area of consideration or limits of consideration)
- How to apply
- Who to call for forms or with questions
- Where to mail completed forms
- Application deadline

Area of Consideration

If an agency wants to offer the position to a limited group of current or former employees, the job announcement will list the specific type of applicants to which the job is open (*area of consideration*). When the job is offered to external candidates, the position may still be restricted to persons within a certain geographical area, so read job announcements carefully to make sure you're eligible for consideration.

TWO HIRING SYSTEMS

Civilian employees are hired in one of two ways: through the Competitive Civil Service (CCS) or through the Excepted Service (ES). The CCS was once entirely under the jurisdiction of the Office of Personnel Man-

agement (OPM). Today, most agencies do their own recruitment, review, and hiring, but they still follow most of the procedures established for the CCS. Some agencies are not affiliated with the CCS and have independent hiring procedures; these are called *excepted agencies* and their hiring system is called the Excepted Service.

Competitive Civil Service

The Competitive Civil Service system is designed to give applicants fair and equal treatment and to ensure that federal applicants are hired based on objective criteria. Hiring has to be based solely on candidates' knowledge, skills, and abilities (which you'll sometimes see abbreviated as *KSA*) and not on any external factors such as race, religion, sex, and so on. Whereas employers in the private sector can hire employees for subjective reasons, federal employers must be able to justify their decisions with objective "evidence" that the candidate is qualified. Thus, applicants in the competitive service are scored through a special rating system that is made up of objective criteria such as level of education, number of years of experience, and test and interview scores.

Excepted Service

Agencies that hire through the Excepted Service are exceptions: They don't follow the CCS hiring process. The largest ES agency is the USPS, which by itself is one of the largest employers in the nation. Other ES agencies include the Foreign Service, the Federal Reserve System, the Tennessee Valley Authority, the Federal Bureau of Investigation, the Central Intelligence Agency, and the General Accounting Office.

Also in the ES category are work-study students, attorneys, chaplains, foreign language specialists, noncitizen positions, student trainers, confidential secretaries, and special assistants. While these jobs may be easier to apply for than CCS jobs because they often have a simpler hiring process, ES applicants are not subject to the benefit of ensured objectivity afforded those who go through the CCS, though hiring is still far more objective than in the private sector.

HOW APPLICANTS ARE RATED

In the CCS and in many ES agencies, applicants are usually rated on a scale of 1 to 100 according to the criteria outlined on the job vacancy announcement. Veterans receive preference of an additional 5 or 10 points, making 110 the highest possible score. (See "Veterans' Preferences" under "How to Apply" below.) This rating is often based on what the job application says about education and experience. Candidates are usually grouped into a "best qualified" or "qualified" list, which is reviewed by a personnel specialist who adds veterans' points as appropriate. Applicants who score under 70 are usually considered ineligible. Then, depending upon the position, candidates may be required to take an exam or series of exams.

Whereas in the private sector a favorable response to an initial interview can make or break your application process, in the government, the interview doesn't come until much farther into the process, after you've already received a ranking based on the information you provide in your application/resume and your performance on exams. Thus, it is critical that you treat the application process and initial tests very seriously. Don't just plan on winning the employer over in an interview.

MEETING THE REQUIREMENTS

Minimum requirements for clerical and administrative assistants vary from job to job, agency to agency. Overall, you must be a U.S. citizen or have applied for citizenship to apply for any government job.

For many entry level clerical and administrative assistant jobs in city and federal government, the typical minimum requirements are that you must:

- Be at least 18 years old
- Have a high school diploma or its equivalent

Although you don't need any experience to qualify for a GS-1 position, you'll need three months of office experience for a GS-2, and six months' experience for a GS-3 position. Those few months of experience can pay off, as you will see from the table General Schedule Pay.

KSAs and E & T

Although these jobs are termed entry level, some clerical/administrative assistant jobs demand a bit of preliminary knowledge or experience. You can acquire such hands-on skills as typing or using such office equipment an adding machine or word processor by working in a private sector company, or by taking classes with a business skills school.

The skills and experience you'll need to have are described in the job vacancy announcement. You're likely to encounter two acronyms in a job announcement or on an application that relate to your previous experience:

- E & T: Experience and training
- KSAs: Knowledge, skills, and abilities

Both of these acronyms mean about the same thing. You may be asked to describe your E & T (or KSAs) in an interview, on a job application, or in a cover letter to a personnel office (if applicable). Here's where you let your prospective employer know what prior experience you have gathered, the specific training you've completed, or skills and abilities you've honed that enable you to do the job.

Here is a sample of typical KSAs from a job vacancy announcement for an administrative assistant:

- Knowledge of administrative procedures and practices
- Effective communication
- How to collect, organize, evaluate data such as accounting, personnel, or purchasing
- Report writing
- How to prepare correspondence and administrative reports
- Utilize problem-solving techniques
- Work independently *and* work well with others
- Plan, organize, and coordinate multiple work assignments

Employee Registers/Eligibility Lists

If the position is one in which there are often regular openings or in which several vacancies are expected before the next job announcement, the agency will keep a list of eligible candidates called a *register* or *eligibility list*. With such a register, the agency doesn't have to keep opening for applications and can call on a list of candidates it already knows is qualified. This makes it all the more important that you be aware of application windows, because if an agency keeps a register, it may be some time before there's another filing period. Generally, however, registers are considered old after three years, and most registers have an average life span of one year.

FINDING JOB OPENINGS

Because of the diversity of jobs and sheer number of occupational titles in the federal government, you may find that there are many job titles for which you qualify. This is particularly true of clerical positions, where there are thousands of positions with similar requirements but different job titles. Unfortunately, you must apply to each job title and vacancy individually, but you may have many opportunities to become employed by the government.

As you scan job announcements, keep your eyes open and keep in mind that your experience and skills may qualify you for several job titles and several series. Be flexible—but also be realistic. Don't waste time applying to jobs that you are not qualified for. Unlike in the private sector, you can't convince an employer to hire you because you're a quick learner. You *must* meet the minimum qualification standards to be considered.

Unlike job openings in the private sector, government job openings aren't listed in the classified section of your city or local paper. You'll have to do some homework to find federal job vacancies since they won't be delivered to your door with the Sunday *Times*. But there are several excellent, easily accessible sources of government job information.

Job Listings Through the OPM

The Office of Personnel Management (OPM) updates a list of federal job vacancies daily. If you have a touch-tone phone, you can access this information 24 hours a day, 7 days a week by calling the OPM's automated telephone system, the Career America Connection, at 912-757-3000. While this service offers around-the-clock convenience, beware: It may take more than one phone call to find exactly the information you need. You can speak to an OPM representative during the hours of 8:00 a.m. to 4:30 p.m. Eastern Standard Time, and you can leave your name and address to have job announcements and application forms sent to you.

If you have a computer modem, you can access the same information through OPM's electronic bulletin board at 912-757-3100. This board can also be reached through the Internet (through Telnet only) at *fjob.mail.opm.gov*. You'll be able to scroll through information and won't risk running up a costly phone bill. If you don't have Internet access and cost is a concern, plan to call the bulletin board at night when long distance rates are lower.

The most user-friendly of the OPM resources, however, is its World Wide Web site at http://www.usajobs.opm.gov/. From this page you can search for jobs by region, state, zip code, country, and department.

The OPM also issues a publication called *Federal Exam Announcement* each quarter.

24-Hour Access to Job Information through the OPM

By telephone:
912-757-3000
By modem (electronic bulletin board):
912-757-3100
Through the Internet:
http://www.usajobs.opm.gov/

Federal Employment Information Centers

Federal Employment Information Centers (FEICs) are located all across the country. Most states have at least one FEIC, often located in the capital, and many states have several. The FEIC publishes local or regional federal government job listings in a *Federal Job Opportunity List* published every two weeks. These lists are also available at state unemployment offices. FEICs make job hunting easy by providing touch-screen computers that work much like ATMs. At the touch of a finger, you can print out job announcements that include who to contact for more information. There's a list of FEICs at the end of this chapter.

Contacting the Hiring Agency Directly

Because the OPM is no longer responsible for overseeing hiring in most agencies, you can also get detailed job information directly from each agency; they have their own personnel offices that publish their own job lists. Some agencies have job hotlines. You can also look in your local blue pages for names and addresses to contact.

On-Line Job Resources

America's Job Bank (AJB) is a computerized network that links up the 1,800 state employment services offices in the U.S. It offers access to over 250,000 jobs—about five percent of which are in government agencies—including entry level clerical and administrative support positions.

You can find AJB on the World Wide Web (http://www.ajb.dni.us/). In addition to the Internet, AJB is accessible via computer systems in high schools, colleges and universities, public libraries, and transition offices on military bases around the world.

Commercial Resources

The services provided by the OPM and FEICs are free, except for any long-distance charges for OPM calls. There are also a host of resources available from commercial sources.

The *Federal Jobs Digest* is a bi-weekly newspaper, published every other Monday, listing thousands of new government jobs both in the U.S. and oversees. The *Digest* includes job descriptions, salaries, and instructions regarding where and how to apply. A subscription to the *Digest* is available (call 1-800-824-500), and the *Digest* can also be found online at *http://www.job-sfed.com/fedjob4.html* as well as at newstands and libraries.

Federal Career Opportunities is a bi-weekly listing of national and overseas jobs available by subscription for $39. The publishers of *FCO* will also conduct a job search for you at $20 per search or $60 for a series of four searches. For more information, visit their site at *http://www.fedjobs.com.*

HOW TO APPLY

Applying for a job with the federal government can be a daunting task. The job lists are huge, and, as hiring continues to move out of the jurisdiction of the OPM and into the hands of the individual agencies, agencies can increasingly individualize the application process. Fortunately, the government has recently simplified the general application process a good deal.

Filing Period

All openings have a *filing period* or *application window*: a specific time period during which applications will be accepted. Be sure you are aware of the filing period so that you do not miss the deadline. It could be weeks or even years before there's another filing period for that specific job title and location.

Application Forms

The SF-71, once required for all federal job applicants, is no longer the only way to apply for a job with the government. Rather than filling out the lengthy SF-71, applicants can now use the Optional Application for Federal Employment (OF-612), a short and easy-to-use form. You can still use the SF-71 if you want, or, for an increasing number of jobs, you can use OPM Form 1203—an optical scan form that will quickly screen and rate your application.

Resume

You may also submit a resume instead of an OF-612 or SF-171. However, if your resume does not include the information that is requested on the OF-612 and in the job vacancy announcement, you *will not be considered* for the job. One vital piece of information people do not often include on resumes is their Social Security Number. The OPM also requests that your resume or application be brief; include *only* the relevant information.

Listed below are the items that your resume must include in order for you to be considered:

- **Job information**
  Job announcement number
  Job title
  Grade(s) for which you are applying
- **Personal information**
  Full name and mailing address (including ZIP code)
  Daytime and evening phone numbers (including area code)
  Social Security number
  Country of citizenship
  Veteran's preference, if applicable
- **Education**
  The name, city, state and ZIP code, if possible, of your high school, along with the date you earned your diploma or GED
  The name, city, state, and ZIP, if possible, of any colleges or universities you attended, as well as your major(s) and type and year of degree(s) received. If you did not receive a degree, show the total number of credits you earned and indicate whether those were earned in semester or quarter hours. (You do not need to send a copy of your college transcript unless the job vacancy announcement requests it.)

- **Work experience**

  Include the following information for all paid and unpaid work experience relating to the job vacancy you would like to fill:

  Job title

  Duties and accomplishments

  Name and address of employer

  Name and phone number of supervisor

  Dates employment began and ended (month and year)

  Number of hours per week

  Salary/wages

  Indicate whether your current supervisor may be contacted.

- **Other qualifications.**

  The OPM requests that you provide dates for these accomplishments, but do not send documentation unless it is specifically requested.

  List any job-related training courses you've taken (include course title and year)

  List job-related skills, such as foreign languages, computer software/hardware proficiency, machinery operability, and typing speed

  List current job-related certificates and licenses

  List job-related honors, awards, and special accomplishments, such as membership in a professional or honor society, leadership activities, publications, and performance awards.

How to Pitch Your Skills to the Job Announcement

Since your application often determines whether you get called for the next part of the selection process, it's important that your SF-71, OF-612, or resume highlight how your accomplishments fit into the job requirements. To help you match your application to the job announcement, request a Qualifications Information Statement. This statement specifies the exact job qualifications for the different grade levels, discusses hiring prospects, explains how education and experience will be rated, and tells you where and how to apply and what forms to use to apply. These forms are usually available for entry-level GS positions.

Some experts recommend that you also indicate the minimum grade level you will accept, keeping in mind that a step down in salary can get your foot in the door and be a stepping stone to regular promotions once you're in the system.

Remember that you will be rated primarily on related education and experience. Even volunteer experience counts, so list all that is relevant (but omit what is not). Look for key words in the job announcement (words like "teamwork," for example) and highlight duties and accomplishments that demonstrate to the agency that you have those qualities. The more concrete evidence you provide regarding your qualification, the higher you are likely to be ranked.

Veterans' Preferences and How to Apply

If you've served on active duty in the military, you may be eligible for veterans' preference: an addition of 5 points—or 10 points, if you are a disabled veteran—to your rating in the job selection process. To be eligible, either you must have been separated under honorable conditions, or, if you began serving after October 15, 1976, you must have a Campaign Badge, an Expeditionary Medal, or a service-connected disability.

To claim the 5-point preference, you need to attach proof of your eligibility: a copy of your DD-214, Certificate of Release or Discharge from Active Duty, or other eligible form. For the 10-point preference, you must attach Standard Form 15, the Application for 10-Point Veterans' Preference, and the eligibility proofs it requires. For more information regarding Veterans' Preference, call the OPM at 912-757-3000. Select "Federal Employment Topics" and then "Veterans."

NEXT STEPS

Filing your application is just the first step. As with any job application, there's more to it than that—and, this being the government, you may find there are more steps involved than there would be with a private employer.

Written Exam

For most clerical positions with the federal government, you will have to take the Clerical and Administrative Support Exam, which is the subject of the rest of this book. This exam has two parts, Verbal Abilities and Clerical Aptitude. The first of these attempts to find out if you have the basic communication abilities that will make you successful in an office. The questions in the Verbal Abilities section cover the following areas:

- Vocabulary
- Spelling
- Reading comprehension
- Grammar
- Word relations (analogies)

The section on Clerical Aptitude, as the name suggests, covers tasks good administrative assistants know how to do:

- Alphabetizing
- Arithmetic
- Name and number comparisons
- Number and letter matching

Accuracy is key in this section of the test.

The passing score on the exam may depend on the agency that is hiring you. In general, 70 is a minimum passing score, but many agencies will require scores of 75, 80, or even higher.

In the examination room, you will have to fill out a Qualifications and Availability Form (Form C). This form is reproduced at the end of this chapter.

Interviews

Interviews for government positions almost always come *after* your agency has already determined that you are otherwise qualified for the job. These interviews often serve more as a final checkpoint in the hiring process than a first step in the selection process as in the private sector. Most interviewers will go into detail about the type of work the job entails, the benefits of the position, and the procedures of the agency. They will also probably ask questions that will help them ascertain how motivated, cooperative, intelligent, and logical you are, as well as what kind of work habits, goals, and personal values you have.

Give yourself an edge in the interview by showing some knowledge of the agency and its business. During your application process, seek out others in the position you desire. Find out what their work is like and what qualities are valued. If you know something about the position and the agency, you'll demonstrate your interest and your motivation, two characteristics employers value highly.

You'll also be more likely to succeed if you're able to explain, comfortably, any gaps in your education or experience. Tell the truth; you'll be respected if you can admit to past failures or faults, especially if you can explain how you overcame, or plan to overcome, them.

Finally, you should be able to discuss your short and long-term career goals. Clearly, if your goals are congruent with the goals of the department, you're in a better position to be hired. Here again your research—talking to people already working with the department—and your overall awareness of the business of the agency will help.

Other Requirements

Before you're hired, Uncle Sam wants to make sure you're government material. That's why you will be asked to fill out a Declaration for Federal Employment (OF 306). This form is used to determine your "suitability" for working for the federal government and to authorize a background investigation. You must answer personal questions on subjects like loan defaults, felonies, and misdemeanors. Please note: Answering yes to questions does not automatically disqualify you, but your answers will be taken into consideration during the selection process.

You must also certify that all of the information you've provided is accurate and correct to the best of your knowledge, and your application will be checked. If investigators find you have falsified information in your application or resume, you may suffer one of three possible consequences: you won't be hired; you'll be fired; or you may be jailed or fined.

FEDERAL EMPLOYMENT INFORMATION CENTERS

The following is a state-by-state list of Federal Employment Information Centers. Various centers may have active staff, while some have a touch-screen computer screen, or kiosk, or a Career America Connection automated hotline system that gives job information specific to that state. Some centers have a combination of staff, kiosk, and hotline. A few centers are mail only. In the list below, centers with a Career America connection are designated CAC and those with a kiosk are designated K. If no phone is listed, you must go in person to the kiosk or write for information.

Alabama (CAC, K)
520 Wynn Dr., NW
Huntsville, AL 35816-3426
Phone: (205) 837-0894

Alaska (K)
Federal Building
222 West 7th Avenue, #22, Room #156
Anchorage, AK 99513-7572

Arizona (K)
VA Medical Center
650 E. Indian School Road
Building 21, Room #141
Phoenix, AZ 85012

Arkansas
(See San Antonio, TX.)

California (CAC)
211 Main Street, 2nd Floor, #235
San Francisco, CA 94120
Phone: 415-744-5627

Colorado (CAC, K)
12345 West Alameda Pkwy.
Lakewood, CO 80225
(303) 969-7050

Connecticut (K)
Federal Building, #133
450 Main Street, Hartford, CT 06103
(For additional information services, see
 Massachusetts)

Delaware
(See Philadelphia, PA)

District of Columbia (CAC)
Theodore Roosevelt Federal Building
1900 E Street NW, Room #1416
Washington, DC 20415
(202) 606-2700

Florida (CAC)
Downtown Jobs and Benefits Center
Florida Job Service Center
401 NW 2nd Ave., Suite N-214
Miami, FL 33130
(305) 536-6738

Georgia (CAC, K)
Richard B. Russell Federal Building
Main Lobby, #940A
75 Spring St. SW
Atlanta, GA 30303
(404) 331-4315

Hawaii, including Pacific overseas (CAC, K)
Federal Building, Room #5316
300 Ala Moana Blvd.
Honolulu, HI 96850
(808) 541-2791

Idaho
(See Washington.)

Illinois (CAC, K)
77 W. Jackson Blvd., # 530, 1st Floor Lobby
Chicago, IL 60604
(312) 353-6189

Indiana (K, CAC)
Minton-Capehart Federal Building, #339
575 N. Pennsylvania St.
Indianapolis, IN 46204
(313) 226-6950
(For additional information services, see
    Michigan. For Clark, Dearborn, and Floyd
    Counties, see Ohio.)

Iowa
(See Kansas City, MO. For Scott County, see
    Illinois.)

Kansas
(See Kansas City, MO.)

Kentucky
(See Ohio. For Henderson County, see Michigan.)

Louisiana (K)
Federal Building, 1st Floor Lobby
423 Canal St.
New Orleans, LA 70112
(For phone contact, see San Antonio, TX.)

Maine
(See Massachusetts.)

Maryland (K)
George H. Fallon Building, Lobby
Lombard St. and Hopkins Plaza
Baltimore, MD 21201
(For phone contact, see Philadelphia, PA.)

Massachusetts (K)
Thomas P. O'Neill, Jr., Federal Building
10 Causeway St.
Boston, MA 02222
(For phone contact, see Philadelphia, PA.)

Michigan (CAC, K)
477 Michigan Avenue, #565
Detroit, MI 48226
(313) 226-6950

Minnesota (CAC, K)
Bishop Henry Whipple Federal Building, #501
1 Federal Dr.
Ft. Snelling, MN 55111
(612) 725-3430

Mississippi
(See Alabama.)

Missouri (CAC, K)
Federal Building, #134
601 E. 12th St.
Kansas City, MO 64106
(816) 426-5702

Montana
(See Colorado.)

Nebraska
(See Kansas City, MO.)

New Hampshire
Thomas McIntyre Federal Building
1st Floor Lobby
80 Daniel Street
Portsmouth, NH 03801
(For additional information services, see
    Massachusetts.)

New Jersey (K)
Rodino Federal Building, 2nd Floor
970 Broad St.
Newark, NJ 07102
(For additional information services in Bergen,
    Essex, Hudson, Hunterdon, Middlesex, Morris,
    Passaic, Somerset, Sussex, Union, and Warren
    Counties, see New York City, NY. For
    additional information services in Atlantic,
    Burlington, Camden, Cape May, Cumberland,
    Gloucester, Mercer, Monmouth, Ocean, and
    Salem Counties, see Philadelphia, PA.)

New Mexico (K)
New Mexico State Job Service
501 Mountain Rd. NE, Lobby
Albuquerque, NM 87102

New York
(K) Jacob K. Javits Federal Building, Lobby
26 Federal Plaza
New York, NY 10278
or
(K) James Hanley Federal Building
100 S. Clinton St.
Syracuse, NY 13261

North Carolina (CAC, K)
4407 Bland Rd., #202
Raleigh, NC 27609
(919) 790-2822

North Dakota
(See Minnesota)

Ohio (CAC, K)
Federal Building, #509
200 West Second St.
Dayton, OH 45402
(513) 225-2720
(For Van Wert, Auglaize, Hardin, Marion,
   Crawford, Richland, Ashland, Wayne, Stark,
   Carroll, and Columbiana Counties and farther
   north, see Michigan.)

Oklahoma
(See San Antonio, TX.)

Oregon (K)
Federal Building, Room #376
1220 SW 3rd Avenue
Portland, OR 97204

Pennsylvania
(CAC, K) Federal Building, Room #168
228 Walnut St.
Harrisburg, PA 17108
(717) 782-4494
or
(CAC, K) William J. Green, Jr., Federal Building,
   2nd Floor
600 Arch St.
Phildelphia, PA 19106
(215) 597-7440
or
(K) Federal Building, 1st Floor Lobby
1000 Liberty Avenue
Pittsburgh, PA 15222
(For telephone, see Philadelphia listing.)

Puerto Rico (CAC, K)
U.S. Federal Building, #328
150 Carlos Chardon Avenue
San Juan, PR 00918
(787) 766-5242

Rhode Island
(See Massachusetts.)

South Carolina
(See North Carolina.)

South Dakota
(See Minnesota.)

Tennessee (K)
Naval Air Station, Transition Assistance Center
7800 3rd Ave., Building South, #239
Memphis, TN
(For mail or telephone, see Alabama listing.)

Texas
(K) 1100 Commerce St., 1st Floor Lobby, #6B10
Dallas, TX 75242
or
(CAC, K) Federal Building, 1st Floor Lobby
727 East Durango
San Antonio, TX 78217
(210) 805-2402

Utah
(See Colorado.)

Vermont (K)
Federal Building, 1st Floor Lobby
11 Elmwood Avenue
Burlington, VT 05401
(For additional information services, see
    Massachusetts.)

Virgin Islands
(See Puerto Rico.)

Virginia (CAC, K)
Federal Building, #500
200 Granby St.
Norfolk, VA 23510
(757) 441-3355

Washington (CAC, K)
Federal Building, #110
915 Second Avenue
Seattle, WA 98174
(206) 553-0888

Washington, DC
(See District of Columbia.)

West Virginia
(See Ohio.)

Wisconsin
(For Dane, Grant, Green, Iowa, Lafayette, Rock,
    Jefferson, Walworth, Milwaukee, Waukesha,
    Racine, and Kenosha Counties, see Illinois. For
    all other counties, see Minnesota.)

Wyoming
(See Colorado.)

U.S. OFFICE OF PERSONNEL MANAGEMENT
QUALIFICATIONS & AVAILABILITY FORM

FORM C

FORM APPROVED
OMB No. 3206-0040

PRINT YOUR RESPONSE IN THE BOXES AND BLACKEN IN THE APPROPRIATE OVALS.

USE A NO. 2 PENCIL

DO NOT FOLD, STAPLE, TEAR OR PAPER CLIP THIS FORM.
DO NOT SUBMIT PHOTOCOPIES OF THIS FORM.
We can process this form only if you:
- Use a number 2 lead pencil.
- Completely blacken each oval you choose.
- Completely erase any mistakes or stray marks.

EXAMPLES

CORRECT MARK   INCORRECT MARKS

1 YOUR NAME: _____

2 JOB APPLYING FOR: _____

3 ANNOUNCEMENT NUMBER: _____

FOLLOW THE DIRECTIONS ON THE
"FORM C INSTRUCTION SHEET"

4 OCCUPATION (OCC)

5 CASE NO. (CNO)

6 LOWEST GRADE (LAG)

7 EMPLOYMENT AVAILABILITY

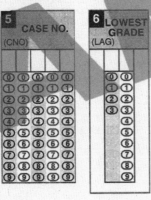

ARE YOU AVAILABLE FOR:

	YES	NO
A) full-time employment -40 hours per week?	Y	N (FTE)
B) part-time employment of		(PTE)
-16 or fewer hrs/week?	Y	N
-17 to 24 hrs/week?	Y	N
-25 to 32 hrs/week?	Y	N
C) temporary employment lasting		(TMP)
-less than 1 month?	Y	N
-1 to 4 months?	Y	N
-5 to 12 months?	Y	N

	YES	NO
D) jobs requiring travel away from home for		(TRV)
-1 to 5 nights/month?	Y	N
-6 to 10 nights/month?	Y	N
-11 plus nights/month?	Y	N
E) other employment questions (see directions)		(OEM)
Question 1?	Y	N
Question 2?	Y	N
Question 3?	Y	N
Question 4?	Y	N

8 (OSP) OCCUPATIONAL SPECIALTIES

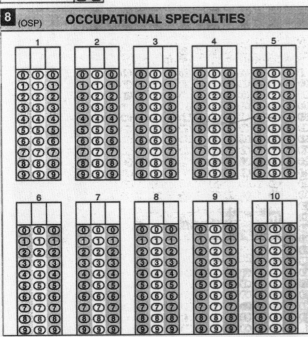

9 (GFP) GEOGRAPHIC AVAILABILITY

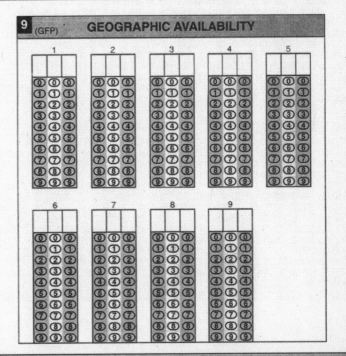

3137791

OPM FORM 1203-AW (7-92)

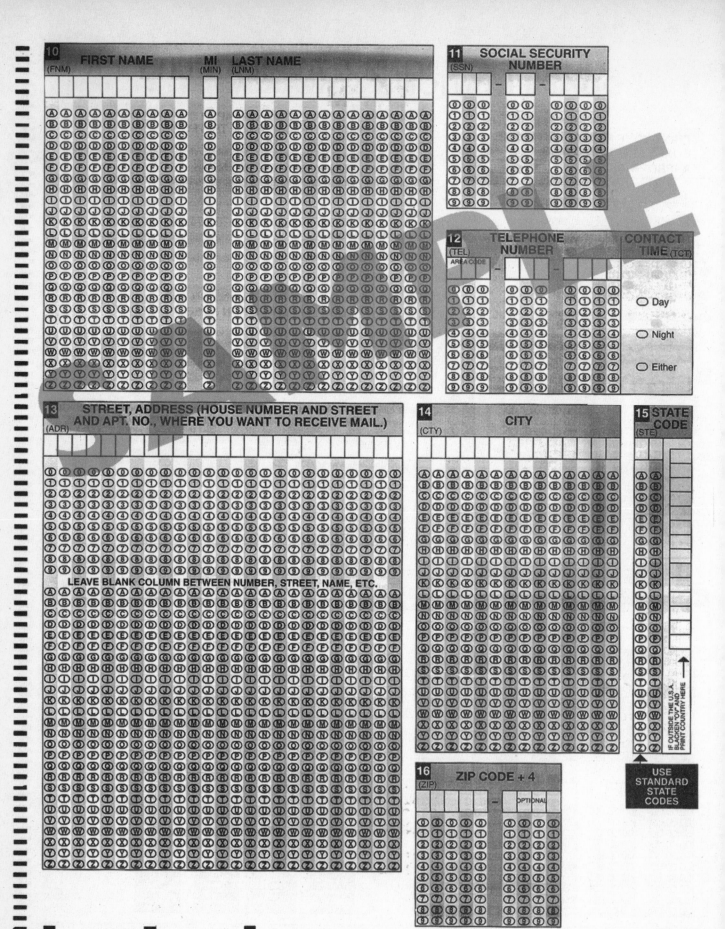

Page 2

OCCUPATIONAL QUESTIONS
17 (OCQ)

JOB PREFERENCE
18 (JBF)

LANGUAGES
19 (LNG)

DATE BLOCK
20 (SDF)

OTHER INFORMATION
21 (MSC)

SPECIAL KNOWLEDGE
22 (SPK)

23 VETERAN PREFERENCE CLAIM
(VET)

○ No preference claimed

○ 5 points preference claimed

10 POINT PREFERENCE- You must enclose a completed Standard Form 15.

○ 10 points preference claimed (award of a Purple Heart or noncompensable service-connected disability)

○ 10 points compensable disability preference claimed (disability rating of less than 30%)

○ 10 points other (wife, widow, husband, widower, mother preference claimed)

○ 10 points compensable disability preference claimed (disability rating of 30% or more)

24 BACKGROUND INFORMATION
(SB1)

	YES	NO
1. Are you a citizen of the United States?	Ⓨ	Ⓝ
2. During the last 10 years, were you fired from any job for any reason or did you quit after being told that you would be fired?	Ⓨ	Ⓝ
3. Are you now or have you ever been: (Answer the following questions.)		
a) convicted of or forfeited collateral for any felony?	Ⓨ	Ⓝ
b) convicted of or forfeited collateral for any firearms or explosive violation?	Ⓨ	Ⓝ
c) convicted, forfeited collateral, imprisoned, on probation, or on parole, during the last 10 years?	Ⓨ	Ⓝ
d) convicted by a court martial?	Ⓨ	Ⓝ
4. Are you currently under charges for any violation of law?	Ⓨ	Ⓝ

25 DATES OF ACTIVE DUTY - MILITARY SERVICE

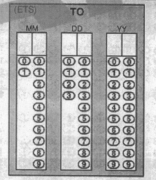

26 SIGNATURE/DATE

I certify that the information on this form is true and correct to the best of my knowledge. **NOTE:** A false statement on any part of your application may be grounds for not hiring you, or for firing you after you begin work. Also, you may be punished by fine or imprisonment (U.S. Code, title 18, section 1001).

Signature

Date signed

PRIVACY ACT

The Office of Personnel Management is authorized to rate applicants for Federal jobs under sections 1302, 3301, and 3304 of title 5 of the U.S. Code. Section 1104 of title 5 allows the Office of Personnel Management to authorize other Federal agencies to rate applicants for Federal jobs. We need the information you put on this form to see how well your education and work skills qualify you for a Federal job. We also need information on matters such as citizenship and military service to see whether you are affected by laws we must follow in deciding who may be employed by the Federal Government.

We must have your Social Security Number (SSN) to identify your records because other people may have the same name and birthdate. The Office of Personnel Management may also use your SSN to make requests for information about you from employers, schools, banks, and others who know you, but only as allowed by law or Presidential directive. The information we collect by using your SSN will be used for employment purposes and also for studies and statistics that will not identify you.

Information we have about you may also be given to Federal, State and local agencies for checking on law violations or for other lawful purposes. We may send your name and address to State and local Government agencies, Congressional and other public offices, and public international organizations, if they request names of people to consider for employment. We may also notify your school placement office if you are selected for a Federal job.

Giving us your SSN or any of the other information is voluntary. However, we cannot process your application, which is the first step toward getting a job, if you do not give us the information we request.

PUBLIC REPORTING BURDEN

The public reporting burden of information is estimated to vary from 20 minutes to 45 minutes to complete this form including time for reviewing instructions, gathering the data needed, and completing and reviewing entries. The average time to complete this form is 30 minutes. Send comments regarding the burden estimate or any other aspect of this collection of information, including suggestions for reducing this burden, to: US Office of Personnel Management, Office of Information Management, 1900 E Street, NW, CHP 500, Washington, DC 20415; and to the Office of Information and Regulatory Affairs, Office of Management and Budget, Paperwork Reduction Project 3206-0040, Washington, DC 20503.

OFFICE USE ONLY - DO NOT MARK BELOW

STOP

AVP	ASB	CDT			EIC	RAT

3137791

C·H·A·P·T·E·R 2

EASYSMART TEST PREPARATION SYSTEM

CHAPTER SUMMARY

Taking the Federal Clerical Exam can be tough. It demands a lot of preparation if you want to achieve a top score. Your career in clerical work for the federal government depends on your passing the exam. The EasySmart Test Preparation System, developed exclusively for LearningExpress by leading test experts, gives you the discipline and attitude you need to be a winner.

First, the bad news: Taking the Federal Clerical Exam is no picnic, and neither is getting ready for it. Your future as a federal clerical worker depends on your getting a passing score, but there are all sorts of pitfalls that can keep you from doing your best on this all-important exam. Here are some of the obstacles that can stand in the way of your success:

- Being unfamiliar with the format of the exam
- Being paralyzed by test anxiety
- Leaving your preparation to the last minute
- Not preparing at all!
- Not knowing vital test-taking skills: how to pace yourself through the exam, how to use the process of elimination, and when to guess

- Not being in tip-top mental and physical shape
- Messing up on test day by having to work on an empty stomach or shivering through the exam because the room is cold

What's the common denominator in all these test-taking pitfalls? One word: *control*. Who's in control, you or the exam?

Now the good news: The EasySmart Test Preparation System puts *you* in control. In just nine easy-to-follow steps, you will learn everything you need to know to make sure that *you* are in charge of your preparation and your performance on the exam. *Other* test-takers may let the test get the better of them; *other* test-takers may be unprepared or out of shape, but not *you*. *You* will have taken all the steps you need to take to get a high score on the Federal Clerical Exam.

Here's how the EasySmart Test Preparation System works: Nine easy steps lead you through everything you need to know and do to get ready to master your exam. Each of the steps listed below includes both reading about the step and one or more activities. It's important that you do the activities along with the reading, or you won't be getting the full benefit of the system. Each step tells you approximately how much time that step will take you to complete.

Step 1. Get Information	30 minutes
Step 2. Conquer Test Anxiety	20 minutes
Step 3. Make a Plan	50 minutes
Step 4. Learn to Manage Your Time	10 minutes
Step 5. Learn to Use the Process of Elimination	20 minutes
Step 6. Know When to Guess	20 minutes
Step 7. Reach Your Peak Performance Zone	10 minutes
Step 8. Get Your Act Together	10 minutes
Step 9. Do It!	10 minutes
Total	**3 hours**

We estimate that working through the entire system will take you approximately three hours, though it's perfectly OK if you work faster or slower than the time estimates assume. If you can take a whole afternoon or evening, you can work through the whole EasySmart Test Preparation System in one sitting. Otherwise, you can break it up, and do just one or two steps a day for the next several days. It's up to you—remember, *you're* in control.

STEP 1: GET INFORMATION

Time to complete: 30 minutes
Activities: Read Chapter 1, "Getting a Clerical Job with the Federal Government"
Knowledge is power. The first step in the EasySmart Test Preparation System is finding out everything you can about the Federal Cleical Exam. Once you have your information, the next steps in the EasySmart Test Preparation System will show you what to do about it.

Part A: Straight Talk About the Federal Clerical Exam
Why do you have to take this exam, anyway? Simply put, because you and others like you, as federal clerical workers, provide invaluable service in keeping the federal government running smoothly. Without its army of clerical workers, the government would swiftly grind to a halt.

It's important for you to remember that your score on the Federal Clerical Exam does not determine how smart you are or even whether you will make a good clerical worker. There are all kinds of things a written exam like this can't test: whether you are likely to show up late or call in sick a lot, whether you can keep your cool under the pressure of deadlines, whether you can be trusted with confidential information if that's part of your job. Those kinds of things are hard to evaluate, while whether you can fill in the right little circles on a bubble answer sheet is easy to evaluate.

This is not to say that filling in the right little circles is not important! The knowledge tested on written exam is knowledge you will need to do your job. And your opportunity to enter the field of federal clerical work depends on your passing this exam. And that's why you're here—using the EasySmart Test Preparation System to achieve control over the exam.

Part B: What's on the Test
If you haven't already done so, stop here and read Chapter 1 of this book, which gives you an overview of federal government hiring procedures, and take a quick look at Chapters 4 through 11 for an overview of the content of the test.

STEP 2: CONQUER TEST ANXIETY

Time to complete: 20 minutes
Activity: Take the Test Stress Test

Having complete information about the exam is the first step in getting control of the exam. Next, you have to overcome one of the biggest obstacles to test success: test anxiety. Test anxiety can not only impair your performance on the exam itself; it can even keep you from preparing! In Step 2, you'll learn stress management techniques that will help you succeed on your exam. Learn these strategies now, and practice them as you work through the exams in this book, so they'll be second nature to you by exam day.

COMBATING TEST ANXIETY

The first thing you need to know is that a little test anxiety is a good thing. Everyone gets nervous before a big exam—and if that nervousness motivates you to prepare thoroughly, so much the better. It's said that Sir Laurence Olivier, one of the foremost British actors of this century, threw up before every performance. His stage fright didn't impair his performance; in fact, it probably gave him a little extra edge—just the kind of edge you need to do well, whether on a stage or in an examination room.

On the next page is the Test Stress Test. Stop here and answer the questions on that page, to find out whether your level of test anxiety is something you should worry about.

Stress Management Before the Test

If you feel your level of anxiety getting the best of you in the weeks before the test, here is what you need to do to bring the level down again:

- **Get prepared.** There's nothing like knowing what to expect and being prepared for it to put you in control of test anxiety. That's why you're reading this book. Use it faithfully, and remind yourself that you're better prepared than most of the people taking the test.
- **Practice self-confidence.** A positive attitude is a great way to combat test anxiety. This is no time to be humble or shy. Stand in front of the mirror and say to your reflection, "I'm prepared. I'm full of self-confidence. I'm going to ace this test. I know I can do it." Say it into a tape recorder and play it back once a day. If you hear it often enough, you'll believe it.
- **Fight negative messages.** Every time someone starts telling you how hard the exam is or how it's almost impossible to get a high score, start telling them your self-confidence messages above. If the someone with the negative messages is *you*, telling yourself *you don't do well on exams, you just can't do this*, don't listen. Turn on your tape recorder and listen to your self-confidence messages.

(continued on page 6)

Test Stress Test

You only need to worry about test anxiety if it is extreme enough to impair your performance. The following questionnaire will provide a diagnosis of your level of test anxiety. In the blank before each statement, write the number that most accurately describes your experience.

0 = Never   1 = Once or twice   2 = Sometimes   3 = Often

_____ I have gotten so nervous before an exam that I simply put down the books and didn't study for it.

_____ I have experienced disabling physical symptoms such as vomiting and severe headaches because I was nervous about an exam.

_____ I have simply not showed up for an exam because I was scared to take it.

_____ I have experienced dizziness and disorientation while taking an exam.

_____ I have had trouble filling in the little circles because my hands were shaking too hard.

_____ I have failed an exam because I was too nervous to complete it.

_____ **Total: Add up the numbers in the blanks above.**

Your Test Stress Score

Here are the steps you should take, depending on your score. If you scored:
- **Below 3,** your level of test anxiety is nothing to worry about; it's probably just enough to give you that little extra edge.
- **Between 3 and 6,** your test anxiety may be enough to impair your performance, and you should practice the stress management techniques listed in this section to try to bring your test anxiety down to manageable levels.
- **Above 6,** your level of test anxiety is a serious concern. In addition to practicing the stress management techniques listed in this section, you may want to seek additional, personal help. Call your local high school or community college and ask for the academic counselor. Tell the counselor that you have a level of test anxiety that sometimes keeps you from being able to take the exam. The counselor may be willing to help you or may suggest someone else you should talk to.

- **Visualize.** Imagine yourself reporting for your first day as a federal clerical worker. Think of yourself answering phones, typing on a computer, and interacting with the public. Visualizing success can help make it happen—and it reminds you of why you're going to all this work in preparing for the exam.
- **Exercise.** Physical activity helps calm your body down and focus your mind. Besides, being in good physical shape can actually help you do well on the exam. Go for a run, lift weights, go swimming—and do it regularly.

Stress Management on Test Day

There are several ways you can bring down your level of test anxiety on test day. They'll work best if you practice them in the weeks before the test, so you know which ones work best for you.

- **Deep breathing.** Take a deep breath while you count to five. Hold it for a count of one, then let it out on a count of five. Repeat several times.
- **Move your body.** Try rolling your head in a circle. Rotate your shoulders. Shake your hands from the wrist. Many people find these movements very relaxing.
- **Visualize again.** Think of the place where you are most relaxed: lying on the beach in the sun, walking through the park, or whatever. Now close your eyes and imagine you're actually in that place. If you practice in advance, you'll find that you only need a few seconds of this exercise to experience a significant increase in your sense of well-being.

When anxiety threatens to overwhelm you right there during the exam, there are still things you can do to manage the stress level:

- **Repeat your self-confidence messages.** You should have them memorized by now. Say them quietly to yourself, and believe them!
- **Visualize one more time.** This time, visualize yourself moving smoothly and quickly through the test answering every question right and finishing just before time is up. Like most visualization techniques, this one works best if you've practiced it ahead of time.
- **Find an easy question.** Skim over the test until you find an easy question, and answer it. Getting even one circle filled in gets you into the test-taking groove.
- **Take a mental break.** Everyone loses concentration once in a while during a long test. It's normal, so you shouldn't worry about it. Instead, accept what has happened. Say to yourself, "Hey, I lost it there for a minute. My brain is taking a break." Put down your pencil, close your eyes, and do some deep breathing for a few seconds. Then you're ready to go back to work.

Try these techniques ahead of time, and see if they don't work for you!

STEP 3: MAKE A PLAN

Time to complete: 30 minutes

Activity: Construct a study plan

Maybe the most important thing you can do to get control of yourself and your exam is to make a study plan. Too many people fail to prepare simply because they fail to plan. Spending hours on the day before the exam poring over sample test questions not only raises your level of test anxiety, it also is simply no substitute for careful preparation and practice over time.

Don't fall into the cram trap. Take control of your preparation time by mapping out a study schedule. On the following pages are four sample schedules, based on the amount of time you have before you take the Federal Clerical Exam. If you're the kind of person who needs deadlines and assignments to motivate you for a project, here they are. If you're the kind of person who doesn't like to follow other people's plans, you can use the suggested schedules here to construct your own.

Even more important than making a plan is making a commitment. You can't review everything that's likely to be on the test in one night. You have to set aside some time every day for study and practice. Try for at least 20 minutes a day. Twenty minutes daily will do you much more good than two hours on Saturday.

Don't put off your study until the day before the exam. Start now. A few minutes a day, with half an hour or more on weekends, can make a big difference in your score.

SCHEDULE A: THE LEISURE PLAN

If you have six months or more in which to prepare, you're lucky! Make the most of your time.

Time	Preparation
Exam minus 6 months	Take the diagnostic exam in Chapter 3. Use your score to help you decide on <u>one</u> area to concentrate on this month, and read the corresponding chapter. When you get to that chapter in this plan, review it.
Exam minus 5 months	Read Chapters 4 and 5, and work through the exercises. Find other people who are preparing for the test and form a study group.
Exam minus 4 months	Read Chapters 6 and 7, and work through the exercises.
Exam minus 3 months	Read Chapters 8 and 9, and work through the exercises. Set aside some time every day for some serious reading of books and magazines.
Exam minus 2 months	Read Chapters 10 and 11, and work through the exercises. Practice your math skills in everyday situations.
Exam minus 1 month	Take the first practice test in Chapter 12. Use your score to help you decide where to concentrate your efforts. Review the relevant chapters, and get the help of a friend or teacher.
Exam minus 1 week	Take the second practice test in Chapter 13, and again review the areas that give you the most trouble.
Exam minus 1 day	Relax. Do something unrelated to the exam. Eat a good meal and go to bed at your usual time.

SCHEDULE B: THE JUST-ENOUGH-TIME PLAN

If you have three to five months before the exam, that should be enough time to prepare for the written test. This schedule assumes four months; stretch it out or compress it if you have more or less time.

Time	Preparation
Exam minus 4 months	Take the diagnostic test in Chapter 3. Then read Chapters 4 and 5, and work through the exercises.
Exam minus 3 months	Read Chapters 6 and 7, and work through the exercises. Start a program of serious reading to improve your reading comprehension.
Exam minus 2 months	Read Chapters 8, 9, 10, and 11, and work through the exercises. Work on your math skills in everyday situations.
Exam minus 1 month	Take the first practice test in Chapter 12. Use your score to help you decide where to concentrate your efforts this month. Review the relevant chapters, and get the help of a friend or teacher.
Exam minus 1 week	Take the second practice test in Chapter 13. See how much y ou're learned in the past months? Review the chapter on the <u>one</u> area that gives you the most trouble.
Exam minus 1 day	Relax. Do something unrelated to the exam. Eat a good meal and go to bed at your usual time.

SCHEDULE C: MORE STUDY IN LESS TIME

If you have one to three months before the exam, you still have enough time for some concentrated study that will help you imrove your score. This schedule is built around a two-month timeframe. If you have only one month, spend an extra couple of hours a week to get all these steps in. If you have three months, take some of the steps from Schedule B and fit them in.

Time	Preparation
Exam minus 8 weeks	Take the diagnostic test in Chapter 3. Evaluate your performance to find one or two areas you're weakest in. Choose one or two chapter(s) from among Chapters 4–11 to read in these two weeks. When you get to those chapters in this plan, review them.
Exam minus 6 weeks	Read Chapters 4–7, and work through the exercises.
Exam minus 4 weeks	Read Chapters 8–11, and work through the exercises.
Exam minus 2 weeks	Take the first practice test in Chapter 12. Then score it and read the answer explanations until you're sure you understand them. Review the areas where your score is lowest.
Exam minus 1 week	Take the second practice test in Chapter 13. Review Chapters 4–11, concentrating on the areas where a little work can help the most.
Exam minus 1 day	Relax. Do something unrelated to the exam. Eat a good meal and go to bed at your usual time.

SCHEDULE D: THE CRAM PLAN

If you have three weeks or less before the exam, you really have your work cut out for you. Carve half an hour out of your day, *every day,* for study. This schedule assumes you have the whole three weeks to prepare in; if you have less time, you'll have to compress the schedule accordingly.

Time	Preparation
Exam minus 3 weeks	Take the diagnostic test in Chapter 3. Read Chapters 4–7, and work through the exercises.
Exam minus 2 weeks	Read Chapters 8–11, and work through the exercises. Take the first practice test in Chapter 12.
Exam minus 1 week	Take the second practice test in Chapter 13. Evaluate your performance on the practice tests. Review the parts of Chapters 4–11 that you had the most trouble with. Get a friend or teacher to help you with the section you had the most difficulty with.
Exam minus 1 day	Relax. Do something unrelated to the exam. Eat a good meal and go to bed at your usual time.

STEP 4: LEARN TO MANAGE YOUR TIME

Time to complete: 10 minutes to read, many hours of practice!
Activities: Practice these strategies as you take the sample tests in this book
Steps 4, 5, and 6 of the EasySmart Test Preparation System put you in charge of your exam by showing you test-taking strategies that work. Practice these strategies as you take the sample tests in this book, and then you'll be ready to use them on test day.

First, you'll take control of your time on the exam. The Federal Clerical Exam has a time limit, which may give you more than enough time to complete all the questions—or may not. It's a terrible feeling to hear the examiner say, "Five minutes left," when you're only three-quarters of the way through the test. Here are some tips to keep that from happening to you.

- **Follow directions.** If the directions are given orally, lisen to them. If they're written on the exam booklet, read them carefully. Ask questions *before* the exam begins if there's anything you don't understand. If you're allowed to write in your exam booklet, write down the beginning time and the ending time of the exam.
- **Pace yourself.** Glance at your watch every few minutes, and compare the time to how far you've gotten in the subtest. When one-quarter of the time has elapsed, you should be a quarter of the way through the test, and so on. If you're falling behind, pick up the pace a bit.
- **Keep moving.** Don't dither around on one question. If you don't know the answer, skip the question and move on. Circle the number of the question in your test booklet in case you have time to come back to it later.
- **Keep track of your place on the answer sheet.** If you skip a question, make sure you skip on the answer sheet too. Check yourself every 5–10 questions to make sure the question number and the answer sheet number are still the same.
- **Don't rush.** Though you should keep moving, rushing won't help. Try to keep calm and work methodically and quickly.

STEP 5: LEARN TO USE THE PROCESS OF ELIMINATION

Time to complete: 20 minutes
Activity: Complete worksheet on Using the Process of Elimination
After time management, your next most important tool for taking control of your exam is using the process of elimination wisely. It's standard test-taking wisdom that you should always read all the answer choices before choosing your answer. This helps you find the right answer by eliminating wrong answer choices. And, sure enough, that standard wisdom applies to the Federal Clerical Exam, too—at least on the Verbal Abilities section. On the Clerical Aptitude section, you may not have time to go through a long process of elimination.

Let's say you're facing a reading comprehension question that goes like this:

When a suspect who is merely being questioned incriminates himself, he might later seek to have the case dismissed on the grounds of not having been apprised of his Miranda rights when arrested. So police officers must read suspects their Miranda rights upon taking them into custody.

1. When must police officers read Miranda rights to a suspect?
    a. while questioning the suspect
    b. before taking the suspect to the police station
    c. before releasing the suspect
    d. while placing the suspect under arrest

You should always use the process of elimination on a question like this, even if the right answer jumps out at you. Sometimes the answer that jumps out isn't right after all.

So you start with answer choice **a**–*while questioning the suspect*. This one is pretty easy to eliminate. The first sentence states that a suspect might incriminate himself while being questioned, so obviously his Miranda rights should be read to him before questioning begins. Mark an X next to choice **a** so you never have to look at it again.

On to the next–*before taking the suspect to the police station*. This looks like a possibility, although you can imagine situations in which a suspect might incriminate himself before being taken to the police station. Still, if no better answer comes along . . . . So put a question mark beside choice **b**, meaning "pretty good answer; I might use this one."

Choice **c** has the same problem as choice **a**–*before releasing the suspect* can cover a long time period, certainly long enough for the suspect to incriminate himself. So you place an X beside this answer choice, meaning "no good, I won't come back to this one."

Choice **d**–*while placing the suspect under arrest*. Look quickly back at the passage and your gaze is sure to light on the second sentence, the second half of which reads *upon taking them into custody*. This appears to be a restatement of choice **d**, the best answer yet, so put an asterisk beside it.

Now your question looks like this:

1. When must police officers read Miranda rights to a suspect?
  ✕ a. while questioning the suspect
  ? b. before taking the suspect to the police station
  ✕ c. before releasing the suspect
  * d. while placing the suspect under arrest

You've got just one asterisk, for a good answer. If you're pressed for time, you should simply mark answer **d** on your answer sheet. If you've got the time to be extra careful, you could compare your asterisk answer to your question-mark answer to make sure that it's better.

It's good to have a system for marking good, bad, and maybe answers. We're recommending this one:

× = bad
* = good
? = maybe

If you don't like these marks, devise your own system. Just make sure you do it long before test day—while you're working through the practice exams in this book—so you won't have to worry about it during the test.

Even when you think you're absolutely clueless about a question, you can often use process of elimination to get rid of one answer choice. If so, you're better prepared to make an educated guess, as you'll see in Step 6. More often, the process of elimination allows you to get down to only *two* possibly right answers. Then you're in a strong position to guess. And sometimes, even though you don't know the right answer, you find it simply by getting rid of the wrong ones, as you did in the example above.

Try using your powers of elimination on the questions in the worksheet Using the Process of Elimination beginning on the next page. The questions aren't about federal clerical work; they're just designed to show you how the process of elimination works. The answer explanations for this worksheet show one possible way you might use the process to arrive at the right answer.

The process of elimination is your tool for the next step, which is knowing when to guess.

STEP 6: KNOW WHEN TO GUESS

Time to complete: 20 minutes
Activity: Complete worksheet on Your Guessing Ability
Armed with the process of elimination, you're ready to take control of one of the big questions in test-taking: Should I guess? The first and main answer is Yes. Unless the exam has what's called a "guessing penalty," you have nothing to lose and everything to gain from guessing. The more complicated answer to the question depends both on the exam and on you—your personality and your "guessing intuition."

The Federal Clerical Exam both does and does not have a guessing penalty—the Clerical Aptitude section does and the Verbal Abilities section does not. Read on to find out what this means for you.

How the "Guessing Penalty" Works

There may be a "guessing penalty" on the Clerical Aptitude portion of the Federal Clerical Exam. A "guessing penalty" really only works against *random* guessing—filling in the little circles to make a nice pattern on your answer sheet. If you can eliminate one or more answer choices, as outlined above, you're better off taking a guess than leaving the answer blank, even on the sections that have a penalty.

(continued on page 16)

Using the Process of Elimination

Use the process of elimination to answer the following questions.

1. Ilsa is as old as Meghan will be in five years. The difference between Ed's age and Meghan's age is twice the difference between Ilsa's age and Meghan's age. Ed is 29. How old is Ilsa?
   a. 4
   b. 10
   c. 19
   d. 24

2. "All drivers of commercial vehicles must carry a valid commercial driver's license whenever operating a commercial vehicle." According to this sentence, which of the following people need NOT carry a commercial driver's license?
   a. a truck driver idling his engine while waiting to be directed to a loading dock
   b. a bus operator backing her bus out of the way of another bus in the bus lot
   c. a taxi driver driving his personal car to the grocery store
   d. a limousine driver taking the limousine to her home after dropping off her last passenger of the evening

3. Smoking tobacco has been linked to
   a. increased risk of stroke and heart attack
   b. all forms of respiratory disease
   c. increasing mortality rates over the past ten years
   d. juvenile delinquency

4. Which of the following words is spelled correctly?
   a. incorrigible
   b. outragous
   c. domestickated
   d. understandible

Answers

Here are the answers, as well as some suggestions as to how you might have used the process of elimination to find them.

1. **d.** You should have eliminated answer **a** off the bat. Ilsa can't be four years old if Meghan is going to be Ilsa's age in five years. The best way to eliminate other answer choices is to try plugging them in to the information given in the problem. For instance, for answer **b,** if Ilsa is 10, then Meghan must be 5. The difference in their ages is 5. The difference between Ed's age, 29, and Meghan's age, 5, is 24. Is 24 two times 5? No. Then answer **b** is wrong. You could eliminate answer **c** in the same way and be left with answer **d.**

2. **c.** Note the word *not* in the question, and go through the answers one by one. Is the truck driver in choice **a** "operating a commericial vehicle"? Yes, idling counts as "operating," so he needs to have a commercial driver's license. Likewise, the bus operator in answer **b** is operating a commercial vehicle; the question doesn't say the operator has to be on the street. The limo driver in **d** is operating a commercial vehicle, even if it doesn't have passenger in it. However, the cabbie in answer **c** is *not* operating a commercial vehicle, but his own private car.

3. **a.** You could eliminate answer **b** simply because of the presence of the word *all*. Such absolutes hardly ever appear in correct answer choices. Choice **c** looks attractive until you think a little about what you know—aren't *fewer* people smoking these days, rather than more? So how could smoking be responsible for a higher mortality rate? (If you didn't know that *mortality rate* means the rate at which people die, you might keep this choice as a possibility, but you'd still be able to eliminate two answers and have only two to choose from.) And choice **d** is plain silly, so you could eliminate that one, too. And you're left with the correct choice, **a.**

4. **a.** How you used the process of elimination here depends on which words you recognized as being spelled incorrectly. If you knew that the correct spellings were *outrageous, domesticated,* and *understandable,* then you were home free. Surely you knew that at least one of those words was wrong!

Here's how a "guessing penalty" works: Depending on the number of answer choices in a given exam, some proportion of the number of questions you get wrong is subtracted from the total number of questions you got right. For instance, since there are five answer choices in the Clerical Aptitude section, the "guessing penalty" is likely to be one-fourth of your wrong answers. Suppose you took a test of 100 questions. You answered 88 of them right and 12 wrong.

If there's no guessing penalty, your score is simply 88. But if there's a one-fourth point guessing penalty, the scorers take your 12 wrong answers and divide by 4 to come up with 3. Then they *subtract* that 3 from your correct-answer score of 88 to leave you with a score of 85. Thus, you would have been better off if you had simply not answered those 12 questions that you weren't sure of. Then your total score would still be 88, because there wouldn't be anything to subtract.

What You Should Do About the Guessing Penalty

That's how a guessing penalty works. The first thing this means for you is that marking your answer sheet at random doesn't pay. If you're running out of time on the Clerical Aptitude section, you should not use your remaining seconds to mark a pretty pattern on your answer sheet. Take those few seconds to try to answer one more question right.

But as soon as you get out of the realm of random guessing, the "guessing penalty" no longer works against you. If you can use the process of elimination to get rid of even one wrong answer choice, the odds stop being against you and start working in your favor.

When there are five answer choices, eliminating just one wrong answer makes your odds of choosing the correct answer one in four. That's the same as the one-out-of-four guessing penalty—even odds. If you eliminate two answer choices, your odds are one in three—better than the guessing penalty. In either case, you should go ahead and choose one of the remaining answer choices.

WHEN THERE IS NO GUESSING PENALTY

The Verbal Abilities section is not likely to have a guessing penalty. That means that, all other things being equal, you should always go ahead and guess, even if you have no idea what the question means. Nothing can happen to you if you're wrong. But all other things aren't necessarily equal. The other factor in deciding whether or not to guess, besides the exam and whether or not it has a guessing penalty, is you. There are two things you need to know about yourself before you go into the exam:

■ Are you a risk-taker?
■ Are you a good guesser?

Your risk-taking temperament matters most on exams with a guessing penalty. Without a guessing penalty, even if you're a play-it-safe person, guessing is perfectly safe. Overcome your anxieties, and go ahead and mark in an answer. But what if you're not much of a risk-taker, *and* you think of yourself as the world's worst guesser? Complete the worksheet Your Guessing Ability on the next page to get an idea of how good your intuition is.

STEP 7: REACH YOUR PEAK PERFORMANCE ZONE

Time to complete: 10 minutes to read; weeks to complete!
Activity: Complete the Physical Preparation Checklist
To get ready for a challenge like a big exam, you have to take control of your physical, as well as your mental, state. Exercise, proper diet, and rest will ensure that your body works with, rather than against, your mind on test day, as well as during your preparation.

(continued on page 20)

Your Guessing Ability

The following are ten really hard questions. You're not supposed to know the answers. Rather, this is an assessment of your ability to guess when you don't have a clue. Read each question carefully, just as if you did expect to answer it. If you have any knowledge at all of the subject of the question, use that knowledge to help you eliminate wrong answer choices. Use this answer grid to fill in your answers to the questions.

ANSWER GRID

1. ⓐ ⓑ ⓒ ⓓ   5. ⓐ ⓑ ⓒ ⓓ   9. ⓐ ⓑ ⓒ ⓓ
2. ⓐ ⓑ ⓒ ⓓ   6. ⓐ ⓑ ⓒ ⓓ   10. ⓐ ⓑ ⓒ ⓓ
3. ⓐ ⓑ ⓒ ⓓ   7. ⓐ ⓑ ⓒ ⓓ
4. ⓐ ⓑ ⓒ ⓓ   8. ⓐ ⓑ ⓒ ⓓ

1. September 7 is Independence Day in
   a India
   b. Costa Rica
   c. Brazil
   d. Australia

2. Which of the following is the formula for determining the momentum of an object?
   a. $p = mv$
   b. $F = ma$
   c. $P = IV$
   d. $E = mc^2$

3. Because of the expansion of the universe, the stars and other celestial bodies are all moving away from each other. This phenomenon is known as
   a. Newton's first law
   b. the big bang
   c. gravitational collapse
   d. Hubble flow

4. American author Gertrude Stein was born in
   a. 1713
   b. 1830
   c. 1874
   d. 1901

5. Which of the following is NOT one of the Five Classics attributed to Confucius?
   a. the I Ching
   b. the Book of Holiness
   c. the Spring and Autumn Annals
   d. the Book of History

6. The religious and philosophical doctrine that holds that the universe is constantly in a struggle between good and evil is known as
   a. Pelagianism
   b. Manichaeanism
   c. neo-Hegelianism
   d. Epicureanism

7. The third Chief Justice of the U.S. Supreme Court was
   a. John Blair
   b. William Cushing
   c. James Wilson
   d. John Jay

8. Which of the following is the poisonous portion of a daffodil?
   a. the bulb
   b. the leaves
   c. the stem
   d. the flowers

9. The winner of the Masters golf tournament in 1953 was
   a. Sam Snead
   b. Cary Middlecoff
   c. Arnold Palmer
   d. Ben Hogan

10. The state with the highest per capita personal income in 1980 was
    a. Alaska
    b. Connecticut
    c. New York
    d. Texas

Answers

Check your answers against the correct answers below.

1. c.	**5.** b.	**9.** d.
2. a.	**6.** b.	**10.** a.
3. d.	**7.** b.	
4. c.	**8.** a.	

How Did You Do?

You may have simply gotten lucky and actually known the answer to one or two questions. In addition, your guessing was more successful if you were able to use the process of elimination on any of the questions. Maybe you didn't know who the third Chief Justice was (question 7), but you knew that John Jay was the first. In that case, you would have eliminated answer **d** and therefore improved your odds of guessing right from one in four to one in three.

According to probability, you should get 2 1/2 answers correct, so getting either two or three right would be average. If you got four or more right, you may be a really terrific guesser. If you got one or none right, you may be a really bad guesser.

Keep in mind, though, that this is only a small sample. You should continue to keep track of your guessing ability as you work through the sample questions in this book. Circle the numbers of questions you guess on as you make your guess; or, if you don't have time while you take the practice tests, go back afterward and try to remember which questions you guessed at. Remember, on a test with five answer choices, your chances of getting a right answer is one in five. So keep a separate "guessing" score for the Clerical Aptitude portion of each exam. How many questions did you guess on? How many did you get right? If the number you got right is at least one-fifth of the number of questions you guessed on, you are at least an average guesser, maybe better—and you should always go ahead and guess on the real exam. If the number you got right is significantly lower than one-fifth of the number you guessed on, you should guess only selectively, when you can eliminate at least one wrong answer.

EXERCISE

If you don't already have a regular exercise program going, the time during which you're preparing for an exam is actually an excellent time to start one. And if you're already keeping fit—or trying to get that way—don't let the pressure of preparing for an exam fool you into quitting now. Exercise helps reduce stress by pumping wonderful good-feeling hormones called endorphins into your system. It also increases the oxygen supply throughout your body, including your brain, so you'll be at peak performance on test day.

A half hour of vigorous activity—enough to raise a sweat—every day should be your aim. If you're really pressed for time, every other day is OK. Choose an activity you like and get out there and do it. Jogging with a friend always makes the time go faster, or take a radio.

But don't overdo. You don't want to exhaust yourself. Moderation is the key.

DIET

First of all, cut out the junk. Go easy on caffeine and nicotine, and eliminate alcohol and any other drugs from your system at least two weeks before the exam. Promise yourself a binge the night after the exam, if need be.

What your body needs for peak performance is simply a balanced diet. Eat plenty of fruits and vegetables, along with protein and carbohydrates. Foods that are high in lecithin (an amino acid), such as fish and beans, are especially good "brain foods."

The night before the exam, you might "carbo-load" the way athletes do before a contest. Eat a big plate of spaghetti, rice and beans, or whatever your favorite carbohydrate is.

REST

You probably know how much sleep you need every night to be at your best, even if you don't always get it. Make sure you do get that much sleep, though, for at least a week before the exam. Moderation is important here, too. Extra sleep will just make you groggy.

If you're not a morning person and your exam will be given in the morning, you should reset your internal clock so that your body doesn't think you're taking an exam at 3 a.m. You have to start this process well before the exam. The way it works is to get up half an hour earlier each morning, and then go to bed half an hour earlier that night. Don't try it the other way around; you'll just toss and turn if you go to bed early without having gotten up early. The next morning, get up another half an hour earlier, and so on. How long you will have to do this depends on how late you're used to getting up. Use the Physical Preparation Checklist on page 23 to make sure you're in tip-top form.

STEP 8: GET YOUR ACT TOGETHER

Time to complete: 10 minutes to read; time to complete will vary
Activity: Complete Final Preparations worksheet
You're in control of your mind and body; you're in charge of test anxiety, your preparation, and your test-taking strategies. Now it's time to take charge of external factors, like the testing site and the materials you need to take the exam.

FIND OUT WHERE THE TEST IS AND MAKE A TRIAL RUN

The testing agency or OPM will notify you when and where your exam is being held. Do you know how to get to the testing site? Do you know how long it will take to get there? If not, make a trial run, preferably on the same day of the week at the same time of day. Make note, on the worksheet Final Preparations on page 24, of the amount of time it will take you to get to the exam site. Plan on arriving 10–15 minutes early so you can get the lay of the land, use the bathroom, and calm down. Then figure out how early you will have to get up that morning, and make sure you get up that early every day for a week before the exam.

GATHER YOUR MATERIALS

The night before the exam, lay out the clothes you will wear and the materials you have to bring with you to the exam. Plan on dressing in layers; you won't have any control over the temperature of the examination room. Have a sweater or jacket you can take off if it's warm. Use the checklist on the worksheet Final Preparations on page 23 to help you pull together what you'll need.

Don't Skip Breakfast

Even if you don't usually eat breakfast, do so on exam morning. A cup of coffee doesn't count. Don't do doughnuts or other sweet foods, either. A sugar high will leave you with a sugar low in the middle of the exam. A mix of protein and carbohydrates is best: cereal with milk and just a little sugar, or eggs with toast, will do your body a world of good.

STEP 9: DO IT!

Time to complete: 10 minutes, plus test-taking time
Activity: Ace the Federal Clerical Exam!
Fast forward to exam day. You're ready. You made a study plan and followed through. You practiced your test-taking strategies while working through this book. You're in control of your physical, mental, and emotional state. You know when and where to show up and what to bring with you. In other words, you're better prepared than most of the other people taking the Federal Clerical Exam with you. You're psyched.

Just one more thing. When you're done with the exam, you will have earned a reward. Plan a celebration. Call up your friends and plan a party, or have a nice dinner for two—whatever your heart desires. Give yourself something to look forward to.

And then do it. Go into the exam, full of confidence, armed with test-taking strategies you've practiced till they're second nature. You're in control of yourself, your environment, and your performance on the exam. You're ready to succeed. So do it. Go in there and ace the exam. And look forward to your future career as a federal clerical worker!

Physical Preparation Checklist

For the week before the test, write down 1) what physical exercise you engaged in and for how long and 2) what you ate for each meal. Remember, you're trying for at least half an hour of exercise every other day (preferably every day) and a balanced diet that's light on junk food.

Exam minus 7 days
Exercise: _____ for _____ minutes
Breakfast: _____
Lunch: _____
Dinner: _____
Snacks: _____

Exam minus 6 days
Exercise: _____ for _____ minutes
Breakfast: _____
Lunch: _____
Dinner: _____
Snacks: _____

Exam minus 5 days
Exercise: _____ for _____ minutes
Breakfast: _____
Lunch: _____
Dinner: _____
Snacks: _____

Exam minus 4 days
Exercise: _____ for _____ minutes
Breakfast: _____
Lunch: _____
Dinner: _____
Snacks: _____

Exam minus 3 days
Exercise: _____ for _____ minutes
Breakfast: _____
Lunch: _____
Dinner: _____
Snacks: _____

Exam minus 2 days

Exercise: _____ for _____ minutes

Breakfast: _____

Lunch: _____

Dinner: _____

Snacks: _____

Exam minus 1 day

Exercise: _____ for _____ minutes

Breakfast: _____

Lunch: _____

Dinner: _____

Snacks: _____

Final Preparations

Getting to the Exam Site

Location of exam site: _____

Date: _____

Depature time: _____

Do I know how to get to the exam site? Yes _____ No _____

If no, make a trial run.

Time it will take to get to exam site: _____

Things to lay out the night before

Clothes I will wear   _____

Sweater/jacket   _____

Watch   _____

Photo ID   _____

4 No. 2. pencils   _____

_____   _____

_____   _____

C · H · A · P · T · E · R 3

DIAGNOSTIC FEDERAL CLERICAL EXAM

CHAPTER SUMMARY

This is the first of three practice tests in this book based on the Clerical and Administrative Support Exam for federal clerical workers. Use this test to see how you would do if you were to take the exam today.

This diagnostic practice exam is of the same type as the real Clerical and Administrative Support Exam you will be taking. Like the real exam, it is divided into two parts:

- The **Verbal Abilities** section consists of 85 multiple-choice questions on:
  vocabulary
  grammar
  spelling
  word relations (analogies)
  reading comprehension
- The **Clerical Aptitude** section consists of 120 multiple-choice questions on:
  number and letter matching
  name and number comparison
  alphabetizing
  general math—addition, subtraction, multiplication, and division

You'll have just 50 minutes for both parts in the real exam. But for this first practice exam, do not worry too much about timing. Just take the test in as relaxed a manner as you can.

The answer sheet you should use for answering the questions is on the following page. Then comes the exam itself, and after that is the answer key. Except for the spelling questions, each answer in the Verbal Abil-

ities section is explained in the answer key. This key will help you to find out why the correct answers are correct and the incorrect answers wrong. The Clerical Aptitude section does not have answer explanations as none are needed; you can find why the answers are correct by looking back at the questions. The answer key is followed by a section on how to score your exam.

VERBAL ABILITIES

#				
1.	ⓐ	ⓑ	ⓒ	ⓓ
2.	ⓐ	ⓑ	ⓒ	ⓓ
3.	ⓐ	ⓑ	ⓒ	ⓓ
4.	ⓐ	ⓑ	ⓒ	ⓓ
5.	ⓐ	ⓑ	ⓒ	ⓓ
6.	ⓐ	ⓑ	ⓒ	ⓓ
7.	ⓐ	ⓑ	ⓒ	ⓓ
8.	ⓐ	ⓑ	ⓒ	ⓓ
9.	ⓐ	ⓑ	ⓒ	ⓓ
10.	ⓐ	ⓑ	ⓒ	ⓓ
11.	ⓐ	ⓑ	ⓒ	ⓓ
12.	ⓐ	ⓑ	ⓒ	ⓓ
13.	ⓐ	ⓑ	ⓒ	ⓓ
14.	ⓐ	ⓑ	ⓒ	ⓓ
15.	ⓐ	ⓑ	ⓒ	ⓓ
16.	ⓐ	ⓑ	ⓒ	ⓓ
17.	ⓐ	ⓑ	ⓒ	ⓓ
18.	ⓐ	ⓑ	ⓒ	ⓓ
19.	ⓐ	ⓑ	ⓒ	ⓓ
20.	ⓐ	ⓑ	ⓒ	ⓓ
21.	ⓐ	ⓑ	ⓒ	ⓓ
22.	ⓐ	ⓑ	ⓒ	ⓓ
23.	ⓐ	ⓑ	ⓒ	ⓓ
24.	ⓐ	ⓑ	ⓒ	ⓓ
25.	ⓐ	ⓑ	ⓒ	ⓓ
26.	ⓐ	ⓑ	ⓒ	ⓓ
27.	ⓐ	ⓑ	ⓒ	ⓓ
28.	ⓐ	ⓑ	ⓒ	ⓓ
29.	ⓐ	ⓑ	ⓒ	ⓓ
30.	ⓐ	ⓑ	ⓒ	ⓓ
31.	ⓐ	ⓑ	ⓒ	ⓓ
32.	ⓐ	ⓑ	ⓒ	ⓓ
33.	ⓐ	ⓑ	ⓒ	ⓓ
34.	ⓐ	ⓑ	ⓒ	ⓓ
35.	ⓐ	ⓑ	ⓒ	ⓓ
36.	ⓐ	ⓑ	ⓒ	ⓓ
37.	ⓐ	ⓑ	ⓒ	ⓓ
38.	ⓐ	ⓑ	ⓒ	ⓓ
39.	ⓐ	ⓑ	ⓒ	ⓓ
40.	ⓐ	ⓑ	ⓒ	ⓓ
41.	ⓐ	ⓑ	ⓒ	ⓓ
42.	ⓐ	ⓑ	ⓒ	ⓓ
43.	ⓐ	ⓑ	ⓒ	ⓓ
44.	ⓐ	ⓑ	ⓒ	ⓓ
45.	ⓐ	ⓑ	ⓒ	ⓓ
46.	ⓐ	ⓑ	ⓒ	ⓓ
47.	ⓐ	ⓑ	ⓒ	ⓓ
48.	ⓐ	ⓑ	ⓒ	ⓓ
49.	ⓐ	ⓑ	ⓒ	ⓓ
50.	ⓐ	ⓑ	ⓒ	ⓓ
51.	ⓐ	ⓑ	ⓒ	ⓓ
52.	ⓐ	ⓑ	ⓒ	ⓓ
53.	ⓐ	ⓑ	ⓒ	ⓓ
54.	ⓐ	ⓑ	ⓒ	ⓓ
55.	ⓐ	ⓑ	ⓒ	ⓓ
56.	ⓐ	ⓑ	ⓒ	ⓓ
57.	ⓐ	ⓑ	ⓒ	ⓓ
58.	ⓐ	ⓑ	ⓒ	ⓓ
59.	ⓐ	ⓑ	ⓒ	ⓓ
60.	ⓐ	ⓑ	ⓒ	ⓓ
61.	ⓐ	ⓑ	ⓒ	ⓓ
62.	ⓐ	ⓑ	ⓒ	ⓓ
63.	ⓐ	ⓑ	ⓒ	ⓓ
64.	ⓐ	ⓑ	ⓒ	ⓓ
65.	ⓐ	ⓑ	ⓒ	ⓓ
66.	ⓐ	ⓑ	ⓒ	ⓓ
67.	ⓐ	ⓑ	ⓒ	ⓓ
68.	ⓐ	ⓑ	ⓒ	ⓓ
69.	ⓐ	ⓑ	ⓒ	ⓓ
70.	ⓐ	ⓑ	ⓒ	ⓓ
71.	ⓐ	ⓑ	ⓒ	ⓓ
72.	ⓐ	ⓑ	ⓒ	ⓓ
73.	ⓐ	ⓑ	ⓒ	ⓓ
74.	ⓐ	ⓑ	ⓒ	ⓓ
75.	ⓐ	ⓑ	ⓒ	ⓓ
76.	ⓐ	ⓑ	ⓒ	ⓓ
77.	ⓐ	ⓑ	ⓒ	ⓓ
78.	ⓐ	ⓑ	ⓒ	ⓓ
79.	ⓐ	ⓑ	ⓒ	ⓓ
80.	ⓐ	ⓑ	ⓒ	ⓓ
81.	ⓐ	ⓑ	ⓒ	ⓓ
82.	ⓐ	ⓑ	ⓒ	ⓓ
83.	ⓐ	ⓑ	ⓒ	ⓓ
84.	ⓐ	ⓑ	ⓒ	ⓓ
85.	ⓐ	ⓑ	ⓒ	ⓓ

CLERICAL APTITUDE

1.	ⓐ ⓑ ⓒ ⓓ ⓔ	41.	ⓐ ⓑ ⓒ ⓓ ⓔ	81.	ⓐ ⓑ ⓒ ⓓ ⓔ
2.	ⓐ ⓑ ⓒ ⓓ ⓔ	42.	ⓐ ⓑ ⓒ ⓓ ⓔ	82.	ⓐ ⓑ ⓒ ⓓ ⓔ
3.	ⓐ ⓑ ⓒ ⓓ ⓔ	43.	ⓐ ⓑ ⓒ ⓓ ⓔ	83.	ⓐ ⓑ ⓒ ⓓ ⓔ
4.	ⓐ ⓑ ⓒ ⓓ ⓔ	44.	ⓐ ⓑ ⓒ ⓓ ⓔ	84.	ⓐ ⓑ ⓒ ⓓ ⓔ
5.	ⓐ ⓑ ⓒ ⓓ ⓔ	45.	ⓐ ⓑ ⓒ ⓓ ⓔ	85.	ⓐ ⓑ ⓒ ⓓ ⓔ
6.	ⓐ ⓑ ⓒ ⓓ ⓔ	46.	ⓐ ⓑ ⓒ ⓓ ⓔ	86.	ⓐ ⓑ ⓒ ⓓ ⓔ
7.	ⓐ ⓑ ⓒ ⓓ ⓔ	47.	ⓐ ⓑ ⓒ ⓓ ⓔ	87.	ⓐ ⓑ ⓒ ⓓ ⓔ
8.	ⓐ ⓑ ⓒ ⓓ ⓔ	48.	ⓐ ⓑ ⓒ ⓓ ⓔ	88.	ⓐ ⓑ ⓒ ⓓ ⓔ
9.	ⓐ ⓑ ⓒ ⓓ ⓔ	49.	ⓐ ⓑ ⓒ ⓓ ⓔ	89.	ⓐ ⓑ ⓒ ⓓ ⓔ
10.	ⓐ ⓑ ⓒ ⓓ ⓔ	50.	ⓐ ⓑ ⓒ ⓓ ⓔ	90.	ⓐ ⓑ ⓒ ⓓ ⓔ
11.	ⓐ ⓑ ⓒ ⓓ ⓔ	51.	ⓐ ⓑ ⓒ ⓓ ⓔ	91.	ⓐ ⓑ ⓒ ⓓ ⓔ
12.	ⓐ ⓑ ⓒ ⓓ ⓔ	52.	ⓐ ⓑ ⓒ ⓓ ⓔ	92.	ⓐ ⓑ ⓒ ⓓ ⓔ
13.	ⓐ ⓑ ⓒ ⓓ ⓔ	53.	ⓐ ⓑ ⓒ ⓓ ⓔ	93.	ⓐ ⓑ ⓒ ⓓ ⓔ
14.	ⓐ ⓑ ⓒ ⓓ ⓔ	54.	ⓐ ⓑ ⓒ ⓓ ⓔ	94.	ⓐ ⓑ ⓒ ⓓ ⓔ
15.	ⓐ ⓑ ⓒ ⓓ ⓔ	55.	ⓐ ⓑ ⓒ ⓓ ⓔ	95.	ⓐ ⓑ ⓒ ⓓ ⓔ
16.	ⓐ ⓑ ⓒ ⓓ ⓔ	56.	ⓐ ⓑ ⓒ ⓓ ⓔ	96.	ⓐ ⓑ ⓒ ⓓ ⓔ
17.	ⓐ ⓑ ⓒ ⓓ ⓔ	57.	ⓐ ⓑ ⓒ ⓓ ⓔ	97.	ⓐ ⓑ ⓒ ⓓ ⓔ
18.	ⓐ ⓑ ⓒ ⓓ ⓔ	58.	ⓐ ⓑ ⓒ ⓓ ⓔ	98.	ⓐ ⓑ ⓒ ⓓ ⓔ
19.	ⓐ ⓑ ⓒ ⓓ ⓔ	59.	ⓐ ⓑ ⓒ ⓓ ⓔ	99.	ⓐ ⓑ ⓒ ⓓ ⓔ
20.	ⓐ ⓑ ⓒ ⓓ ⓔ	60.	ⓐ ⓑ ⓒ ⓓ ⓔ	100.	ⓐ ⓑ ⓒ ⓓ ⓔ
21.	ⓐ ⓑ ⓒ ⓓ ⓔ	61.	ⓐ ⓑ ⓒ ⓓ ⓔ	101.	ⓐ ⓑ ⓒ ⓓ ⓔ
22.	ⓐ ⓑ ⓒ ⓓ ⓔ	62.	ⓐ ⓑ ⓒ ⓓ ⓔ	102.	ⓐ ⓑ ⓒ ⓓ ⓔ
23.	ⓐ ⓑ ⓒ ⓓ ⓔ	63.	ⓐ ⓑ ⓒ ⓓ ⓔ	103.	ⓐ ⓑ ⓒ ⓓ ⓔ
24.	ⓐ ⓑ ⓒ ⓓ ⓔ	64.	ⓐ ⓑ ⓒ ⓓ ⓔ	104.	ⓐ ⓑ ⓒ ⓓ ⓔ
25.	ⓐ ⓑ ⓒ ⓓ ⓔ	65.	ⓐ ⓑ ⓒ ⓓ ⓔ	105.	ⓐ ⓑ ⓒ ⓓ ⓔ
26.	ⓐ ⓑ ⓒ ⓓ ⓔ	66.	ⓐ ⓑ ⓒ ⓓ ⓔ	106.	ⓐ ⓑ ⓒ ⓓ ⓔ
27.	ⓐ ⓑ ⓒ ⓓ ⓔ	67.	ⓐ ⓑ ⓒ ⓓ ⓔ	107.	ⓐ ⓑ ⓒ ⓓ ⓔ
28.	ⓐ ⓑ ⓒ ⓓ ⓔ	68.	ⓐ ⓑ ⓒ ⓓ ⓔ	108.	ⓐ ⓑ ⓒ ⓓ ⓔ
29.	ⓐ ⓑ ⓒ ⓓ ⓔ	69.	ⓐ ⓑ ⓒ ⓓ ⓔ	109.	ⓐ ⓑ ⓒ ⓓ ⓔ
30.	ⓐ ⓑ ⓒ ⓓ ⓔ	70.	ⓐ ⓑ ⓒ ⓓ ⓔ	110.	ⓐ ⓑ ⓒ ⓓ ⓔ
31.	ⓐ ⓑ ⓒ ⓓ ⓔ	71.	ⓐ ⓑ ⓒ ⓓ ⓔ	111.	ⓐ ⓑ ⓒ ⓓ ⓔ
32.	ⓐ ⓑ ⓒ ⓓ ⓔ	72.	ⓐ ⓑ ⓒ ⓓ ⓔ	112.	ⓐ ⓑ ⓒ ⓓ ⓔ
33.	ⓐ ⓑ ⓒ ⓓ ⓔ	73.	ⓐ ⓑ ⓒ ⓓ ⓔ	113.	ⓐ ⓑ ⓒ ⓓ ⓔ
34.	ⓐ ⓑ ⓒ ⓓ ⓔ	74.	ⓐ ⓑ ⓒ ⓓ ⓔ	114.	ⓐ ⓑ ⓒ ⓓ ⓔ
35.	ⓐ ⓑ ⓒ ⓓ ⓔ	75.	ⓐ ⓑ ⓒ ⓓ ⓔ	115.	ⓐ ⓑ ⓒ ⓓ ⓔ
36.	ⓐ ⓑ ⓒ ⓓ ⓔ	76.	ⓐ ⓑ ⓒ ⓓ ⓔ	116.	ⓐ ⓑ ⓒ ⓓ ⓔ
37.	ⓐ ⓑ ⓒ ⓓ ⓔ	77.	ⓐ ⓑ ⓒ ⓓ ⓔ	117.	ⓐ ⓑ ⓒ ⓓ ⓔ
38.	ⓐ ⓑ ⓒ ⓓ ⓔ	78.	ⓐ ⓑ ⓒ ⓓ ⓔ	118.	ⓐ ⓑ ⓒ ⓓ ⓔ
39.	ⓐ ⓑ ⓒ ⓓ ⓔ	79.	ⓐ ⓑ ⓒ ⓓ ⓔ	119.	ⓐ ⓑ ⓒ ⓓ ⓔ
40.	ⓐ ⓑ ⓒ ⓓ ⓔ	80.	ⓐ ⓑ ⓒ ⓓ ⓔ	120.	ⓐ ⓑ ⓒ ⓓ ⓔ

VERBAL ABILITIES

Read the directions carefully, and then choose the best answer from the four choices.

1. *Homogeneous* means most nearly
   a. plain
   b. native
   c. dissimilar
   d. alike

2. *Insipid* means most nearly
   a. crafty
   b. tasteless
   c. delirious
   d. unbearable

For questions 3 and 4, choose the answer that is most clearly and correctly expressed.

3. a. On February 27, 1998, the city fire department responded to a blaze that breaks out at the Icarus Publishing Co. warehouse.
   b. On February 27, 1998, the city fire department responded to a blaze that will break out at the Icarus Publishing Co. warehouse.
   c. On February 27, 1998, the city fire department responded to a blaze that is breaking out at the Icarus Publishing Co. warehouse.
   d. On February 27, 1998, the city fire department responded to a blaze that had broken out at the Icarus Publishing Co. warehouse.

4. a. In many popular movies today, the heroes are more heavily armed than the villains.
   b. In many popular movies today, the heroes are more heavy armed than the villains.
   c. In many popular movies today, the heroes are heavier armed than the villains.
   d. In many popular movies today, the heroes are more heavier armed than the villains.

5. ELECTRICIAN is related to WIRE as NEUROLOGIST is related to
   a. vein
   b. nerve
   c. muscle
   d. organ

6. SQUARE is related to RECTANGLE as NOVEL is related to
   a. plot
   b. movie
   c. magazine
   d. book

7. TAILOR is related to SUIT as EDIT is related to
   a. agent
   b. manuscript
   c. writer
   d. opinion

8. *Ominous* means most nearly
   a. ordinary
   b. gracious
   c. quarrelsome
   d. threatening

One easy way for secretaries to recharge their self-esteem is to keep a "performance file," which is a collection of information that highlights talents, skills, and interests. The performance file is also proof of tasks completed, evidence of character, and interest in future growth. The file should contain an educational and employment history, memberships and awards in the community, letters of recommendation, and promotions.

9. The paragraph best supports the statement that
   a. performance files help secretaries earn promotions
   b. secretaries gain personal benefits by maintaining performance files
   c. education and employment are the most important part of performance
   d. self-esteem is enhanced when supervisors recognize a secretary's talents

For questions 10–12, choose the correctly spelled word.

10. a. iluminate
   b. illumenate
   c. illumanate
   d. illuminate

11. a. marjinal
   b. marginnal
   c. marginal
   d. marginel

12. a. althogh
   b. although
   c. allthough
   d. allthogh

Secretaries who want to advance within an organization should let their supervisors know what their goals are. If they see a particular job that interests them, they should write a letter to the pertinent office manager formally expressing their interest.

13. The paragraph best supports the statement that secretaries should
   a. improve their letter-writing skills before they seek other jobs
   b. arrange formal meetings with office managers to discuss their goals
   c. apply for new jobs within the company if they are unhappy in their current jobs
   d. let their supervisors know that they are interested in advancement

14. BINDING is related to BOOK as FRAME is related to
   a. criminal
   b. display
   c. picture
   d. artist

15. FRACTURE is related to BONE as BREACH is related to
   a. wave
   b. mountain
   c. birth
   d. contract

16. RULER is related to LENGTH as SCALE is related to
   a. weight
   b. girth
   c. depth
   d. speed

For questions 17 and 18, choose the correctly spelled word.

17. a. mechinical
    b. mechanical
    c. mechenical
    d. machanical

18. a. enquirry
    b. inquirry
    c. inquiry
    d. enquery

19. *Recluse* means most nearly
    a. hermit
    b. prophet
    c. fool
    d. intellectual

For questions 20–23, choose the answer that is most clearly and correctly expressed.

20. a. That fine circus elephant now belongs to my sister and I.
    b. That fine circus elephant now belongs to my sister and me.
    c. That fine circus elephant now belongs to my sister and mine.
    d. That fine circus elephant now belongs to my sister and myself.

21. a. The person that made these delicious candied figs has my vote.
    b. The person whom made these delicious candied figs has my vote.
    c. The person who made these delicious candied figs has my vote.
    d. The person whose made these delicious candied figs has my vote.

22. a. When we arrive in Singapore, it is raining.
    b. When we arrived in Singapore, it were raining.
    c. When we arrived in Singapore, it will be raining.
    d. When we arrive in Singapore, it was raining.

23. a. If you don't stop playing that video games, your mind will become warped.
    b. If you don't stop playing those video games, your mind will become warped.
    c. If you don't stop playing them video games, your mind will become warped.
    d. If you don't stop playing this video games, your mind will become warped.

24. OAR is related to CANOE as FOOT is related to
    a. cane
    b. shoe
    c. skateboard
    d. motorcycle

25. KNIFE is related to CUT as NETTLE is related to
    a. sting
    b. bruise
    c. contusion
    d. concussion

26. *Nevertheless* means most nearly
    a. consequently
    b. therefore
    c. however
    d. unfortunately

27. *Defray* means most nearly
    a. pay
    b. defend
    c. cheat
    d. disobey

For questions 28–30, choose the correctly spelled word.

28. a. termenate
b. terrminate
c. termanate
d. terminate

29. a. persecuted
b. pursecuted
c. presecuted
d. perrsecuted

30. a. psycology
b. pyschology
c. psychology
d. psychollogy

31. *Placid* means most nearly
a. flabby
b. wise
c. obedient
d. peaceful

32. *Statute* means most nearly
a. replica
b. ordinance
c. collection
d. hypothesis

Many office professionals today have an interest in replacing the currently used keyboard, known as the QWERTY keyboard, with a keyboard that can keep up with technological changes and make offices more efficient. The best choice is the Dvorak keyboard. Studies have shown that people using the Dvorak keyboard can type 20 to 1,000 percent faster and cut their error rate in half. Dvorak puts vowels and other frequently used letters right under the fingers (on the home row) where typists make 70 percent of their keystrokes.

33. The paragraph best supports the statement that the Dvorak keyboard
a. is more efficient than the QWERTY
b. has more vowel keys than the QWERTY
c. is favored by more typists than the QWERTY
d. is, on average, 100 percent faster than the QWERTY

34. CATASTROPHE is related to MISHAP as MIRACLE is related to
a. religion
b. good fortune
c. compassion
d. morality

35. MIRROR is related to REFLECT as LAMP is related to
a. illuminate
b. sunlight
c. fire
d. guide

The ability to use desktop computer equipment and software to create high-quality printing such as newsletters, business cards, letterhead, and brochures is called desktop publishing, or DTP. The most important part of any DTP project is planning. Know your intended audience, the message you want to communicate, and what form your message will take before you begin.

36. The paragraph best supports the statement that
  a. DTP is one way to become acquainted with a new business audience
  b. computer software is continually being refined to produce more high-quality printing
  c. the planning stage of a DTP project should include talking with the intended audience
  d. the first stage of any proposed DTP project should be organization

Although many office professionals are using messaging systems such as E-mail and computer fax modems, the stand-alone fax machine is still favored by a majority of office workers. The stand-alone fax is preferred because it is compatible worldwide.

37. The paragraph best supports the statement, implied in the passage, that
  a. computer fax modems are losing favor with office workers
  b. most office workers favor computer fax modems over other messaging systems
  c. E-mail messaging systems are not compatible throughout the world
  d. the stand-alone fax is the latest in a series of new messaging systems

For questions 38–40, choose the correctly spelled word.

38. a. repremand
  b. repramand
  c. reprimand
  d. repremmand

39. a. ilusion
  b. ilussion
  c. illusian
  d. illusion

40. a. buffalo
  b. bufallo
  c. buffalow
  d. bufello

41. *Spurious* means most nearly
  a. prevalent
  b. false
  c. melancholy
  d. actual

For questions 42 and 43, choose the answer that is most clearly and correctly expressed.

42. a. I am trying to become more skilled at weaving before winter arrived.
  b. I am trying to become more skilled at weaving before winter will have arrived.
  c. I am trying to become more skilled at weaving before winter will arrive.
  d. I am trying to become more skilled at weaving before winter arrives.

43. a. We have saw more of these strange pods since those people moved in next door.

b. We have been seeing more of these strange pods since those people moved in next door.

c. We have been seen more of these strange pods since those people moved in next door.

d. We have see more of these strange pods since those people moved in next door.

44. *Domain* means most nearly

a. entrance

b. rebellion

c. territory

d. formation

In order to balance both career and family, many secretaries are now job sharing. For job sharing to be successful, partners must be carefully matched to each other. They must be able to prepare and implement a program that includes strong organizational skills, consistent procedures, cooperation, and solid communication methods.

45. The paragraph best supports the statement that job sharing

a. is one way to learn cooperation and communication

b. will not work if the partners have a great deal of tension between them

c. is one way secretaries can meet the demands of both job and family

d. is a partnership that is now operating in most office settings

Due to downsizing and new technologies, the role of the traditional secretary is declining. At the same time, secretaries and administrative assistants are becoming much more important to businesses of all sizes. Although traditional jobs such as typist, stenographer, and data entry specialist have declined by about 33 percent, there has been a sharp increase in jobs such as clerical supervisor and medical and legal secretary.

46. The paragraph best supports the statement that

a. secretaries are less important now than they once were

b. many traditional secretaries have been promoted to clerical supervisors

c. due to downsizing, about 33 percent of all typists have recently become unemployed

d. advances in technology have contributed to the changing role of the secretary

47. JUDGE is related to INJUSTICE as PRIEST is related to

a. clergyman

b. excommunication

c. sacrilege

d. violation

48. ETERNAL is related to TEMPORAL as ALWAYS is related to

a. never

b. endless

c. soon

d. frequently

.   One good way to get ideas and suggestions for improving the workplace is to conduct a problem-solving meeting. Each meeting should identify a single situation, perhaps a problem that needs a resolution. Based on a clear statement of the problem, brainstorm possible solutions. List all of these on a board. After all the ideas have been listed, develop an action plan, and then have individuals accept responsibilities for the plan.

49. The paragraph best supports the statement that problem-solving meetings
   a. should list all of the problems in the workplace
   b. should be limited to solving one problem at a time
   c. are one way to get irresponsible people to improve
   d. are one way to improve employee morale

50. *Escalate* means most nearly
   a. intensify
   b. inaugurate
   c. justify
   d. terminate

51. *Disparage* means most nearly
   a. endorse
   b. finalize
   c. restrict
   d. criticize

For question 52, choose the answer that is most clearly and correctly expressed.

52. a. The main problem Jim had will be too many parking tickets.
   b. The main problem Jim had were too many parking tickets.
   c. The main problem Jim had will have been too many parking tickets.
   d. The main problem Jim had was too many parking tickets.

   There are many myths about gossip, backbiting, and even back *stabbing* among secretaries and other office workers, but the truth is that office workers get along with one another just as well as world leaders do—and therein lies the problem. Just as in the larger world, many of the issues that cause conflict in the office center around control, so as one goes about one's job, the first thing one should remember is to focus on the work itself, rather than on the office hierarchy.

53. The paragraph best supports the statement that
   a. secretaries and other office workers get along with one another, just as world leaders do
   b. one should focus on one's work while keeping a close eye on the office hierarchy
   c. one can reduce conflict in one's office by concentrating on one's work rather than on who's on top
   d. there is not as much gossip, backbiting, and back stabbing among office workers as there is purported to be

Understand that your boss has problems, too. This is easy to forget. When someone has authority over you, it's hard to remember that they're just human. They have children at home who misbehave, dogs or cats or parakeets that need to go to the vet, deadlines to meet, bosses of their own—sometimes even bad ones—overseeing their work. If your boss *occasionally* acts unreasonable, try to keep in mind that it might have nothing to do with you. Of course of his or her behavior is *consistently* abusive, you'll have to do something about it. But occasional mood swings are something we're all entitled to.

54. The paragraph best supports the idea that
   a. on your job, you should remember your boss is human and forgive occasional bad behavior
   b. if you forgive your boss's occasional bad behavior, he or she will likely forgive yours
   c. unreasonable behavior is not to be tolerated, whether in your boss or in your fellow employees
   d. unreasonable behavior is natural in some employers and must be forgiven if one is to keep one's job

55. *Methodical* means most nearly
   a. erratic
   b. deliberate
   c. humble
   d. deformed

56. *Urbane* means most nearly
   a. sentimental
   b. foolish
   c. sophisticated
   d. vulgar

57. *Rationale* means most nearly
   a. explanation
   b. regret
   c. denial
   d. anticipation

For questions 58–61, choose the answer that is most clearly and correctly expressed.

58. a. I don't like fish as well as my sister does.
   b. I don't like fish as well as my sister.
   c. Fish isn't liked by me as well as my sister.
   d. My sister likes it, but I don't like fish as well.

59. a. After renting him the room, a cat was discovered to belong to Mr. Morris.
   b. A cat belonging to Mr. Morris was discovered by Alvin after renting him a room.
   c. After renting him the room, Alvin discovered that Mr. Morris owned a cat.
   d. After renting him a room, Mr. Morris was discovered by Alvin to own a cat.

60. a. Though often romanticized in movies, the lives of criminals are, in reality, bleak and unrewarding.
   b. In reality, the lives of criminals are bleak and unrewarding; however, it is often romanticized in movies.
   c. Movies often romanticize the life of the criminal; however, in reality, they are bleak and unrewarding.
   d. In reality bleak and unrewarding, movies often romanticize the lives of criminals.

61.
a. Some people say jury duty is a nuisance that just takes up their precious time and that we don't get paid enough.
b. Some people say jury duty is a nuisance that just takes up your precious time and that one doesn't get paid enough.
c. Some people say jury duty is a nuisance that just takes up one's precious time and that one doesn't get paid enough.
d. Some people say jury duty is a nuisance that just takes up our precious time and that they don't get paid enough.

There is a great deal of room in the secretarial field for variety and creativity, and also for advancement. A secretary can, with the right training, be anything he or she wants to be, from corporate administrative assistant in a multinational conglomerate in Chicago to office manager of a small veterinary clinic in Idaho.

62. The paragraph best supports the statement that a secretary
a. needs to continually update his or her training in order to advance
b. can have a creative job if he or she works hard enough
c. will have a mediocre job if he or she does not get the right training
d. can choose the job that suits him or her because there is such variety in the field

In the old days, a secretary typed, filed, answered phones, fetched the boss's coffee, and did little else. These days she or he must have extensive knowledge of computer programs including word processors, spreadsheets, and even operating systems. The secretary may be called upon to generate spreadsheets, charts, and graphs; do desktop publishing using a variety of graphics and drawing software; prepare graphics for presentation at committee meetings, board meetings, and stockholder meetings; and even create databases.

63. The paragraph best supports the statement that secretaries today
a. must have more skill than they needed in the past
b. are more intelligent than they were in the past
c. are more apt to be men than they were in the past
d. are more highly paid than they were in the past

64. VEIL is related to BRIDE as UNIFORM is related to
a. army
b. khaki
c. war
d. soldier

65. SALVE is related to BURN as SPLINT is related to
a. bruise
b. fracture
c. puncture
d. abrasion

For questions 66 and 67, choose the answer that is most clearly and correctly expressed.

66. a. The evidence had been improperly gathered, the case was dismissed.
b. Because the evidence had been improperly gathered, the case was dismissed.
c. Because the evidence had been improperly gathered. The case was dismissed.
d. The evidence had been improperly gathered the case was dismissed.

67. a. Doctor Falkenrath believes that neither immorality nor amorality is a spiritual defect.
b. Doctor Falkenrath believes that neither immorality nor amorality are a spiritual defect.
c. Doctor Falkenrath believes that immorality and amorality are not a spiritual defect.
d. Doctor Falkenrath believes that both immorality and amorality is not spiritual defects.

Sometimes subspecialty courses are part of the secretarial degree; sometimes they are courses one can take on one's own at the same or another school. Whether one goes for a certificate, diploma, or degree in secretarial training, one may want to branch out into subjects completely different from secretarial courses, as these can make a secretarial career more rewarding and creative.

68. The paragraph best supports the statement that
a. secretaries are more well-rounded and creative than most people give them credit for
b. a secretarial degree by itself is worthless

c. one can have more job satisfaction if one has a broad education
d. while in school, one should take courses in as many subjects as possible

For question 69, choose the correctly spelled word.

69. a. primier
b. premeer
c. premeir
d. premier

Job candidates should remember that any job search is a two-way street. Just as applicants will undergo a background check by the company or organization they wish to work for, so they should do a background check on the prospective employer. They should research the job and the company or organization to make sure it meets *their* needs.

70. The paragraph best supports the statement that
a. job applicants are too easily intimidated into not doing a background check on the prospective employer
b. as a job applicant, it is as important to think of one's own needs as those of the prospective employer
c. some employers will try to keep a job applicant from checking too closely into the company or organization background
d. job applicants should inform prospective employers that they are scrutinizing the company or organization they're applying to

The resume is the means by which most employers obtain a written history of the skills, knowledge, and work experience of potential job candidates. Its aim is to get the applicant an interview, not to get him or her a job. Employers don't hire on the basis of a resume, but unless one prepares a good resume, one may never get a chance to pitch oneself to the people one wants to work for.

71. The paragraph best supports the statement that
   a. presenting a well-written resume won't necessarily land one a job, but it is an important step in the job-hunting process
   b. a well-written resume alone will not guarantee a job interview
   c. a well-written resume is important, but not as important as a good interview in the job-hunting process
   d. employers trust resumes more than they do interviews, because the information the applicant gives is in writing

For questions 72–74, choose the correctly spelled word.

72. a. relience
   b. reliance
   c. relliance
   d. relience

73. a. melancholy
   b. melancholly
   c. melencholy
   d. melancoly

74. a. regretabble
   b. regretable
   c. regrettable
   d. regretabel

For questions 75 and 76, choose the answer that is most clearly and correctly expressed.

75. a. If you steal the artichokes from Petra's garden. You'll be sorry.
   b. If you steal the artichokes, from Petra's garden, you'll be sorry.
   c. If you steal the artichokes from Petra's garden, you'll be sorry.
   d. If you steal, the artichokes from Petra's garden, you'll be sorry.

76. a. We ate the popcorn and watch the movie.
   b. While watching the movie, the popcorn was eaten.
   c. Popcorn, while watching the movie, was eaten.
   d. We ate the popcorn while we watched the movie.

77. BROCCOLI is related to VEGETABLE as DALMATIAN is related to
   a. breed
   b. companion
   c. spotted
   d. canine

At times administrative assistants become privy to confidential information about their organization. Similarly, administrative assistants may—especially if they are in a position of authority—be trusted with a personal confidence. Although they may be tempted, they should not violate confidentiality in either case, as they can seriously damage the organization for which they work, its customers or clients, or their own coworkers.

78. The main idea of the paragraph is that
   a. although one might be tempted, one should not solicit confidential information from one's employer
   b. one should never violate a personal confidence
   c. one should not violate confidences one receives on the job, as this might harm the employer or others
   d. secretaries and administrative assistants are often in the unique position of learning secrets about their employers

While violating legitimate confidentiality is always ill-advised, a secretary should not cover up serious breaches of ethics, whether by coworkers, boss, or the organization itself. "I was just doing my job" is not an acceptable excuse for ethics violations anymore.

79. The paragraph best supports the idea that, if one is asked by one's employer to do something that violates one's own ethics, one should
   a. resign from one's job
   b. refuse to do whatever it is
   c. report one's employer to the authorities
   d. comply with the request

80. INSECT is related to BEETLE as RODENT is related to
   a. mammal
   b. pest
   c. rat
   d. infestation

81. HORRIFYING is related to SCARY as MALEVOLENT is related to
   a. ugly
   b. blasphemous
   c. spiteful
   d. remorseful

82. *Refrain* means most nearly
   a. secure
   b. glimpse
   c. persevere
   d. desist

83. *Animosity* means most nearly
   a. readiness
   b. compassion
   c. hostility
   d. impatience

For questions 84 and 85, choose the correctly spelled word.

84. a. blasphemy
   b. blasfemy
   c. blassphemy
   d. blasphamy

85. a. prescripsion
   b. prescription
   c. prascription
   d. prescripption

CLERICAL APTITUDE

1. Add:

    14
   +55

a. 65
b. 69
c. 75
d. 79
e. none of these

2. Subtract:

    59
   −15

a. 54
b. 49
c. 44
d. 40
e. none of these

3. Divide:

14 | 70

a. 6
b. 5
c. 4
d. 3
e. none of these

4. Multiply:

    15
   ×16

a. 225
b. 235
c. 239
d. 240
e. none of these

5. Subtract:

    37
   −17

a. 26
b. 25
c. 31
d. 20
e. none of these

For questions 6–10, choose the suggested answer that contains numbers and letters all of which appear in that question.

6.   G   4   6   T   7   H   5   P

7.   2   F   H   R   T   6   7   5

8.   H   7   6   V   8   2   F   G

9.   F   6   H   T   5   7   8   V

10.   V   4   6   2   F   P   S

Suggested Answers
a. = 6, 8, F, G
b. = 4, 6, S, V
c. = 4, 7, H, P
d. = 2, 5, R, T
e. = none of these

In questions 11–15, choose the correct place for the name in the box.

11. Hutchinson, W. J.

   a. →

     Hutchins, A. P.

   b. →

     Hutchins, P.T.

   c. →

     Hutchinson, L.A.

   d. →

     Hutchinson, M. O.

   e. →

12. Leslie, Paula

   a. →

     Leslie, Amy

   b. →

     Leslie, Dana

   c. →

     Leslie, Jane

   d. →

     Leslie, Mary

   e. →

13. Medlin, Faith

   a. →

     Medlin, Vera

   b. →

     Medvid, Rachel

   c. →

     Medvid, Stella

   d. →

     Medwid, Bea

   e. →

14. Perry, Anson

   a. →

     Parry, Charles

   b. →

     Parry, Quentin

   c. →

     Parry, Stephen

   d. →

     Perry, Craig

   e. →

15. Reuter, Valerie

   a. →

     Reuter, Byron

   b. →

     Reuter, Marjorie

   c. →

     Reuther, Bruce

   d. →

     Reuther, Odetta

   e. →

16. Divide:

$9 \overline{)72}$

   a. 8

   b. 9

   c. 7

   d. 6

   e. none of these

17. Multiply:

     12

   $\times 16$

   a. 174

   b. 176

   c. 172

   d. 181

   e. none of these

18. Add:

$$\begin{array}{r} 42 \\ +11 \\ \hline \end{array}$$

   a. 55
   b. 54
   c. 51
   d. 43
   e. none of these

19. Divide:

$$90 \,|\, \overline{180}$$

   a. 2
   b. 3
   c. 4
   d. 5
   e. none of these

20. Multiply:

$$\begin{array}{r} 3 \\ \times 18 \\ \hline \end{array}$$

   a. 42
   b. 44
   c. 50
   d. 55
   e. none of these

In questions 21–25, compare the three names and numbers, and select the answer from the five choices below.

   a. if ALL THREE names or numbers are exactly ALIKE
   b. if only the FIRST and SECOND names or numbers are exactly ALIKE
   c. if only the FIRST and THIRD names or numbers are exactly ALIKE
   d. if only the SECOND and THIRD names or numbers are exactly ALIKE
   e. if ALL THREE names or numbers are DIFFERENT

21. 6936917   6936917   6939617

22. Clair N. Viney   Clair N. Viney   Claire N. Viney

23. 6945037   6945037   6945037

24. Benjamin Hubert   Benjamin Hurbert   Benjamin Huburt

25. 8476092   8470692   8476092

For questions 26–30, choose the suggested answer that contains numbers and letters all of which appear in that question.

26. 6   7   P   S   D   L   8   4

27. G   8   J   5   S   D   7   2

28. 4   S   6   P   8   2   K   G

29. 6   5   J   8   K   7   P   S

30. J   D   4   7   L   S   8   2

Suggested Answers
   a. = 4, 7, L, S
   b. = 4, 6, J, P
   c. = 2, 8, D, G
   d. = 5, 8, K, P
   e. = none of these

31. Add:

    17
    +13

a. 27
b. 30
c. 32
d. 28
e. none of these

32. Subtract:

    47
    −13

a. 26
b. 30
c. 34
d. 38
e. none of these

33. Multiply:

    17
    ×8

a. 145
b. 149
c. 153
d. 156
e. none of these

34. Add:

    32
    +54

a. 76
b. 82
c. 84
d. 88
e. none of these

35. Subtract:

    34
    −18

a. 10
b. 13
c. 16
d. 15
e. none of these

In questions 36–40, choose the correct place for the name in the box.

36. | Knapp, N. |

a. →
   Knapp, N. J.
b. →
   Knapp, N. T.
c. →
   Knapp, Norman
d. →
   Knapp, P. K.
e. →

37. | Miner, Brian |

a. →
   Miner, Alan
b. →
   Miner, Carl
c. →
   Miner, Cathy
d. →
   Miner, Denice
e. →

38. Levin, Shari

a. →

Levin, Eugene

b. →

Levin, G. P.

c. →

Levin, S. P.

d. →

Levin, S. R.

e. →

39. Thron, Mavis

a. →

Throne, Albert

b. →

Throne, Caitlin

c. →

Throne, Gregory

d. →

Throne, Lanny

e. →

40. West, Melvin

a. →

West, Colin

b. →

West, Edward

c. →

West, Harold

d. →

West, John

e. →

For questions 41–45, choose the suggested answer that contains numbers and letters all of which appear in that question.

41. 5 2 V T 3 R K 9

42. W 9 R 3 6 T G 2

43. 2 6 D K G 5 T 9

44. V 5 9 3 6 T G D

45. 3 2 R T 5 D 9 K

Suggested Answers

a. = 2, 5, G, K
b. = 3, 6, D, V
c. = 2, 3, T, W
d. = 5, 9, R, T
e. = none of these

In questions 46–50, compare the three names and numbers, and select the answer from the five choices beneath.

a. if ALL THREE names or numbers are exactly ALIKE

b. if only the FIRST and SECOND names or numbers are exactly ALIKE

c. if only the FIRST and THIRD names or numbers are exactly ALIKE

d. if only the SECOND and THIRD names or numbers are exactly ALIKE

e. if ALL THREE names or numbers are DIFFERENT

46. Betty Lou Winn   Betty Lou Wink   Betty Lou Winn

47. 9378120   9387120   9371820

48. Marc Caffery   Marc Caffery   Marc Caffrey

49. 6830274   6830274   6830274

50. Elizabeth R. Holmes   Elizabeth R. Holmer   Elizabeth R. Holmer

51. Divide:

8)‾32‾

  a. 6

  b. 4

  c. 8

  d. 7

  e. none of these

52. Add:

   17

 +15

  a. 25

  b. 27

  c. 30

  d. 32

  e. none of these

53. Subtract:

   47

 −28

  a. 16

  b. 17

  c. 19

  d. 21

  e. none of these

54. Divide:

12)‾36‾

  a. 3

  b. 4

  c. 2

  d. 5

  e. none of these

55. Multiply:

   4

 ×8

  a. 24

  b. 32

  c. 28

  d. 30

  e. none of these

In questions 56–60, choose the correct place for the name in the box.

56. | Howard, Scott |

  a. →

    Howard, Arlene

  b. →

    Howard, Richard

  c. →

    Howard, Steven

  d. →

    Howard, Thomas

  e. →

57. | Lolley, James |

  a. →

    Lolley, Janice

  b. →

    Lolley, Karen

  c. →

    Lolley, Mark

  d. →

    Lolly, Aaron

  e. →

58. Miller, Joseph

a. →
Miller, Harold

b. →
Miller, Lance

c. →
Miller, Nero

d. →
Miller, Samuel

e. →

59. Parrat, P.R.

a. →
Parra, A. S.

b. →
Parra, T. T.

c. →
Parrat, G. Y.

d. →
Parrat, S. A.

e. →

60. Labonty, Oren

a. →
Labonte, Michael

b. →
Labonte, Peter

c. →
Labonte, Steven

d. →
Labonty, Lawrence

e. →

In questions 61–65, compare the three names and numbers, and select the answer from the five choices beneath.

a. if ALL THREE names or numbers are exactly ALIKE

b. if only the FIRST and SECOND names or numbers are exactly ALIKE

c. if only the FIRST and THIRD names or numbers are exactly ALIKE

d. if only the SECOND and THIRD names or numbers are exactly ALIKE

e. if ALL THREE names or numbers are DIFFERENT

61. J. Philip Mills   J. Phillip Mills   J. Phillip Mills

62. Nathan B. Penta   Nathan B. Penta   Nathan B. Penta

63. 0984739   0984379   0984379

64. Ellen Sailor   Ellen Sallor   Ellen Saller

65. 7492894   7942894   7498294

66. Subtract:

34
−23

a. 17
b. 12
c. 9
d. 8
e. none of these

67. Divide:
7 |̄35

a. 6
b. 5
c. 7
d. 8
e. none of these

68. Multiply:

$$\begin{array}{r} 27 \\ \times 19 \\ \hline \end{array}$$

a. 513

b. 519

c. 528

d. 539

e. none of these

69. Add:

$$\begin{array}{r} 23 \\ +5 \\ \hline \end{array}$$

a. 20

b. 22

c. 25

d. 28

e. none of these

70. Divide:

$12\,\overline{)72}$

a. 9

b. 8

c. 7

d. 6

e. none of these

In questions 71–75, choose the correct place for the name in the box.

71. | Medford, Neil |

a. →

Medcalf, Merle

b. →

Medford, Larry

c. →

Medford, Patty

d. →

Medford, Sarah

e. →

72. | Philbrick, O. O. |

a. →

Philbrick, O. R.

b. →

Philbrick, O. S.

c. →

Philbrick, O. V.

d. →

Philbrick, O. W.

e. →

73. | Ronfeldt, Karen |

a. →

Ronfeldt, Jason

b. →

Ronfeldt, Mary

c. →

Ronfelt, Jeremy

d. →

Ronfelt, Meryl

e. →

74. | Dennison, Nils P. |

a. →

Denison, Neil

b. →

Denison, Paul

c. →

Dennison, Nils

d. →

Dennison, Nils S.

e. →

75. | Engels, Patrick |

a. →

Engels, Abel

b. →

Engels, Darrin

c. →

Engels, Frank

d. →

Engels, Micha

e. →

For questions 76–80, choose the suggested answer that contains numbers and letters all of which appear in that question.

76. D 8 7 R B L 6 9

77. 9 W 5 9 7 D B R

78. W 7 4 H P 6 D 8

79. P 7 L R 5 D 8 9

80. P L H 7 W 6 9 8

Suggested Answers

{
a. = 7, 8, P, R
b. = 7, 9, B, L
c. = 4, 6, D, H
d. = 5, 7, D, W
e. = none of these
}

In questions 81–85, compare the three names and numbers, and select the answer from the five choices beneath.

a. if ALL THREE names or numbers are exactly ALIKE

b. if only the FIRST and SECOND names or numbers are exactly ALIKE

c. if only the FIRST and THIRD names or numbers are exactly ALIKE

d. if only the SECOND and THIRD names or numbers are exactly ALIKE

e. if ALL THREE names or numbers are DIFFERENT

81. H.J. Terrano   J.H. Terrano   H.J. Terrano

82. Rusty Bachman   Rusty Bachman   Rusty Bachman

83. 8927843   8927843   9827843

84. Sylvia Harnish   Sylvie Harnish   Sylvia Harnish

85. 3748204   3784204   3784204

In questions 86–90, choose the correct place for the name in the box.

86. | Griffon, May |

a. →

Griffon, Mary

b. →

Griffon, Merle

c. →

Griffon, Mina

d. →

Griffon, Morris

e. →

87. | Klotz, Morris |

   a. →
     Klot, D. K.

   b. →
     Kloth, Emily

   c. →
     Klotz, Patrick

   d. →
     Klotz, Rodney

   e. →

88. | Napolitano, Beverly |

   a. →
     Napolitano, Diana

   b. →
     Napolitano, Jennifer

   c. →
     Napolitano, Joyce

   d. →
     Napolitano, Maria

   e. →

89. | Dorsey, Randy |

   a. →
     Dorsett, Mike

   b. →
     Dorsett, Raymond

   c. →
     Dorsey, Marsha

   d. →
     Dorsey, Toby

   e. →

90. | Grimaldi, Victor |

   a. →
     Grimaldi, David

   b. →
     Grimaldi, Martin

   c. →
     Grimaldi, Omar

   d. →
     Grimaldi, Patty

   e. →

For questions 91–95, choose the suggested answer that contains numbers and letters all of which appear in that question.

91. Y Z 9 6 7 F D 8

92. 4 9 Z H 8 A Y 5

93. 4 G 8 9 6 H Z D

94. H 8 Z D 4 7 A 9

95. 6 Z 9 8 F H 5 Y

Suggested Answers
{
  a. = 4, 7, A, Z
  b. = 4, 8, D, G
  c. = 6, 9, F, Y
  d. = 5, 9, A, H
  e. = none of these

In questions 96–100, compare the three names and numbers, and select the answer from the five choices beneath.

a. if ALL THREE names or numbers are exactly ALIKE
b. if only the FIRST and SECOND names or numbers are exactly ALIKE
c. if only the FIRST and THIRD names or numbers are exactly ALIKE
d. if only the SECOND and THIRD names or numbers are exactly ALIKE
e. if ALL THREE names or numbers are DIFFERENT

96. 8903281   8093281   8908231

97. 9387272   9387722   9387272

98. Justin P. Norris   Justin P. Norris   Justin P. Norris

99. Marilyn Stresser   Marilyn Strasser   Marilyn Strasser

100. Agnes F. Batson   Agnes F. Batson   Agnes E. Batson

101. Multiply:

    18
    ×3

a. 57
b. 56
c. 54
d. 55
e. none of these

102. Add:

    9
    +3

a. 11
b. 12
c. 13
d. 14
e. none of these

103. Subtract:

    78
    −5

a. 73
b. 75
c. 63
d. 61
e. none of these

104. Multiply:

    17
    ×17

a. 289
b. 253
c. 247
d. 240
e. none of these

105. Add:

    51
    +8

a. 60
b. 58
c. 57
d. 59
e. none of these

In questions 106–110, choose the correct place for the name in the box.

106. Dudley, B. D.

　a. →

　　Dudley, B. F.

　b. →

　　Dudley, B. H.

　c. →

　　Dudley. B. J.

　d. →

　　Dudley, B. L.

　e. →

107. Reilly, Janice

　a. →

　　Reilly, Blanche

　b. →

　　Reilly, Dorothy

　c. →

　　Reilly, Mary Alice

　d. →

　　Reilly, Patrice

　e. →

108. Weymouth, Wayne

　a. →

　　Weymouth, Quentin

　b. →

　　Weymouth, Ross

　c. →

　　Weymouth, Tommy Lee

　d. →

　　Weymouth, William

　e. →

109. Bruce, Cynthia

　a. →

　　Bruce, Cindy

　b. →

　　Bruce, Debbie

　c. →

　　Bruce, Edith

　d. →

　　Bruce, Ethel

　e. →

110. Iverson, Roger

　a. →

　　Iverson, Ralph

　b. →

　　Iverson, Renny

　c. →

　　Iverson, Richard

　d. →

　　Iverson, Rick

　e. →

In questions 111–115, compare the three names and numbers, and select the answer from the five choices beneath.

a. if ALL THREE names or numbers are exactly ALIKE

b. if only the FIRST and SECOND names or numbers are exactly ALIKE

c. if only the FIRST and THIRD names or numbers are exactly ALIKE

d. if only the SECOND and THIRD names or numbers are exactly ALIKE

e. if ALL THREE names or numbers are DIFFERENT

111. 5478960 · 5478960 · 5479860

112. 7782938 · 7782983 · 7782838

113. P. Arthur Geason · P. Arthur Gleason · P. Arthur Geason

114. Zelda Newcomb · Zelda Newcomb · Zelda Newcomb

115. 2749028 · 7249028 · 7249028

For questions 116–120, choose the suggested answer that contains numbers and letters all of which appear in that question.

116. T 6 1 F 3 S 7 J

117. 6 F 4 3 J T R 7

118. S J 7 F K 6 3 1

119. 3 4 R L T J 7 1

120. 3 1 F J S R 4 7

Suggested Answers
{
a. = 3, 6, F, R
b. = 1, 4, J, L
c. = 1, 3, S, T
d. = 3, 7, F, K
e. = none of these
}

ANSWERS

VERBAL ABILITIES

Answer explanations are given for all questions except spelling. If you are not sure why the designated answer is correct for a spelling question, consult a dictionary.

1. **d.** *Homogeneous* means of the same or a similar kind; *alike* means similar to.

2. **b.** *Insipid* means without flavor or zest; *tasteless* means lacking in flavor.

3. **d.** The sentence requires that the verb be in the past tense, *had broken out*. The other choices represent a shift in tense from the past, *responded*.

4. **a.** The missing phrase modifies the verb *are armed*, so you need the correct comparative form of the adverb, *more heavily*.

5. **b.** An *electrician* works with wires; a *neurologist* works with nerves to treat neurological disorders. Although neurologists may be incidentally involved with the other parts of the body (choices **a, c,** and **d**), the other parts are not their main focus of treatment.

6. **d.** A *square* is a type of rectangle; a *novel* is a type of book. The other choices are incorrect, because, although a novel may have a plot, it is not a type of plot (choice **a**). Although a novel may be made into a movie it is not a type of movie (choice **b**). Finally, although a novel and a magazine have some characteristics in common, a novel is not a type of magazine (choice **c**).

7. **b.** To *tailor* a suit is to alter it; to *edit* a manuscript is to alter it. The other choices are incorrect because they cannot be altered by editing.

8. **d.** *Ominous* means foreshadowing evil; *threatening* means dangerous or menacing.

9. **b.** The first two sentences imply that a performance file is a benefit to a secretary. Choice **a** is wrong because the paragraph does not indicate that maintaining the file would result in a promotion. Choice **c** is wrong because even though education and employment are mentioned, the paragraph does not say that these are most important. Choice **d** is not mentioned.

10. **d.**

11. **c.**

12. **b.**

13. **d.** The first sentence states that secretaries should tell their supervisors of their interests. Choice **a** is not mentioned. Choice **b** is incorrect because a letter is recommended, but a formal meeting is not. Choice **c** is attractive, but it is not stated in the paragraph.

14. **c.** A *binding* surrounds a book; a *frame* surrounds a picture. Choices **a** and **d** are wrong because a frame obviously does not surround a criminal or an artist and because these choices involve people, as the original pair of words does not. Choice **b** is wrong because, although a frame may surround a display, the word *display* is more vague than the words *book* or *picture*.

15. **d.** To *fracture* a bone is to break it; to *breach* a contract is to break it. None of the other choices mean to break something.

16. **a.** A *ruler* measures length; a *scale* measures weight. The other choices are wrong, as scale does not measure girth (choice **b**), depth (choice **c**), or speed (choice **d**).

17. **b.**

18. **c.**

19. a. A *recluse* is a person who lives withdrawn or shut up from the world, a *hermit* is a person who has withdrawn from society.

20. b. The correct form of the pronoun is the objective case, *me*. Remove the phrase *my sister and* to see that the other choices are incorrect.

21. c. The correct pronoun is *who*, not *that* (choice **a**), because it refers to a person rather than a thing. The correct form is the subject form, *who*, not the object form, *whom* (choice **b**) or the possessive form, *whose* (choice **d**, because *who* has done something, *made candied figs*.

22. a. The verbs *arrive* and *is* agree in tense. In the other sentences, the verbs do not agree.

23. b. The pronoun *those* agrees in number with the noun *games* to which it refers.

24. c. An *oar* propels a canoe; a *foot* propels a skateboard. A foot does not propel any of the other choices.

25. a. A *knife* causes a cut; a *nettle* causes a sting. A nettle does not cause any of the other choices.

26. c. *Nevertheless* means nonetheless or in spite of; *however* means nevertheless or yet.

27. a. To *defray* means to provide for the payment of something; to *pay* means to give money in exchange for goods or services.

28. d.

29. a.

30. c.

31. d. *Placid* means serenely free of disturbance; calm; *peaceful* means tranquil.

32. b. A *statute* is a law; an *ordinance* is a rule or law.

33. a. The end of the first sentence and the second sentence indicate that Dvorak is more efficient. Choice **b** is wrong because the vowels are placed differently on the two keyboards, but there is no indication that Dvorak has more vowels. Choice **c** is incorrect because the paragraph does not say

how typists feel about either keyboard. The third sentence indicates that choice **d** is incorrect.

34. b. A *mishap* is a lesser form of *catastrophe*, just as *good fortune* is a lesser form of *miracle*. The other choices involve words that are loosely related to *miracle*, perhaps, but do not involve a difference in degree.

35. a. The purpose of a *mirror* is to *reflect*. The purpose of a *lamp* is to *illuminate*. Choices **b** and **c** can be ruled out immediately–the purpose of a *lamp* is definitely not *sunlight* or *fire*. A *lamp* may *guide* one's steps (choice **d**), but that is not the sole purpose for which it is made.

36. d. The second sentence states the importance of planning, which means organization. Choice **a** is not mentioned. Choice **b** may be true, but it is not indicated in the paragraph. Choice **c** is wrong because the paragraph states that the intended audience should be known, but it does not say that this includes talking.

37. c. This answer is implied: the stand-alone fax is favored because it has worldwide compatibility over systems such as E-mail, which, by implication, do not have this feature. Choice **a** is not mentioned. Choice **b** is clearly wrong because stand-alone faxes are favored. Choice **d** is not mentioned.

38. c.

39. d.

40. a.

41. b. Something that is *spurious* is not genuine; something that is *false* is also not genuine.

42. d. The appropriate tense for the verb is the present tense, *arrives*. The other choices represent a shift in tense.

43. b. The verbal form *been seeing* fits with the verb *have*.

44. c. A *domain* is an area governed by a ruler; a *territory* is an area for which someone is responsible.

45. c. The answer is implied by the information in the first sentence. Choice **a** makes sense but this is not mentioned in the paragraph. Choice **b** is incorrect because tension isn't mentioned, and if job-sharers are not carefully matched, this does not mean there is tension between them—there could be many other factors. There is no indication in the paragraph that choice **d** is true.

46. d. The first sentence and the third sentence point to the relationship between technology and the changing role of the secretary. Choice **a** is incorrect because the second sentence indicates that the opposite is true. Choice **b** is not mentioned. Choice **c** is incorrect because there is no indication that typists have not found other jobs.

47. c. A *judge* who is guilty of *injustice* commits a serious transgression directly related to his or her profession, just as does a *priest* who is guilty of *sacrilege*. In the other choices, the words are loosely related to the word *priest*, but do not involve a transgression directly related to a profession.

48. a. *Eternal* and *temporal* are antonyms, and *always* and *never* are antonyms. None of the other choices is the opposite of *always*.

49. b. The answer is clearly stated in the second sentence. Choice **a** is incorrect because even though the meetings should identify problems, they should not list all problems in the workplace. Choices **c** and **d** are not mentioned.

50. a. To *escalate* is to increase in extent; to *intensify* is to make larger or stronger.

51. d. To *disparage* is to talk about something or someone in a negative manner; to *criticize* is to find fault with.

52. d. The verb *was* agrees with its subject, *problem*, and is in the past tense.

53. c. Choice **c** is stated in the last sentence. Choice **a** is not correct because the passage does *not* imply

that office workers get along nor does it imply that world leaders get along; it merely states office workers get along *just as well as* world leaders do, and the passage calls this a *problem*, implying that probably neither group gets along well. Choice **b** is incorrect because the passage says the opposite. Choice **d** is incorrect because the passage does not say that there's not much backbiting, merely that backbiting is not unique to secretaries and office workers.

54. a. The third sentence and the final sentence of the passage clearly indicate that choice **a** is correct. Choices **b** and **d** do not appear in the passage, and choice **c** is contradicted, especially by the final sentence.

55. b. *Methodical* means careful or in a planned manner; *deliberate* means careful or slow.

56. c. To be *urbane* is to show the refined manners of high society; to be *sophisticated* is to show worldly knowledge or refinement.

57. a. A *rationale* is a reason for something; an *explanation* is a clarification or definition or something.

58. a. This sentence is clearest. In choice **b**, the speaker likes his/her sister better than fish (which we hope is true, but which is not the most reasonable choice). Choice **c** is just plain confusing. Choice **d** has an unclear pronoun reference: *it* probably refers to *fish*, but who can tell?

59. c. In choice **a** there is a misplaced modifier; the cat seems to be renting the room. In choice **b**, it's unclear whether the pronoun *he* refers to the cat or to Mr. Morris. Choice **d** implies that Mr. Morris rented himself a room.

60. a. This is the only clear answer. In choices **b** and **c**, the pronouns *it* and *they* do not agree with the words they refer to. In choice **d**, the first phrase seems to refer to *movies* when it should refer to *the lives of criminals*.

61. c. The other choices are unclear because they contain unnecessary shifts in person, from *people* to *their* and *we* in choice **a**, to *your* and *one* in choice **b**, and to *our* and *they* in choice **d**.

62. d. The first sentence states there is variety in the secretarial field; the second emphasizes that a secretary can *be anything he or she wants to be*. Choices **a** and **c** are incorrect because, although training is mentioned in the passage, it is not emphasized. Choice **b** is incorrect because hard work is not mentioned in the passage.

63. a. Choice **a** is emphasized in the second sentence of the passage, which speaks of the extensive knowledge of computer programs secretaries today must have. The other choices are not mentioned in the passage.

64. d. A *veil* is worn by a bride; a *uniform* is worn by a soldier. Choice **a** is incorrect because the word *bride* denotes one person and therefore the word that completes the second set must denote one person. Choices **b** and **c** are incorrect because, although a uniform may be khaki-colored and may be worn **in** war, the uniform is not worn **by** khaki or **by** *war*.

65. b. A *salve* is used to treat a burn; a *splint* is used to treat a fracture. The other choices are incorrect, because a splint is not specifically associated with any of them.

66. b. Choices **a** and **d** are run-on sentences; choice **c** contains a sentence fragment.

67. a. The verb *is* agrees with its noun *neither*.

68. c. In the final sentence the passage mentions *variety and creativity*, which are directly related to *job satisfaction*. Choices **a** and **b** are neither stated nor implied in the passage. The passage advises a variety of courses, but does not necessarily advise a great number of courses, as in choice **d**.

69. d.

70. b. The passage states that secretaries should research prospective employers to make sure the job *will meet their needs*. Choices **a**, **c**, and **d** are not mentioned in the passage.

71. a. In the final sentence, the passage says that without a good resume *one may never get a chance to pitch oneself* to the prospective employer, obviously implying that the resume is an important step. Choices **b**, **c**, and **d** are not emphasized in the passage.

72. b.

73. a.

74. c.

75. c. This version is punctuated correctly. In choice **a**, the first sentence is a subordinate clause and therefore a fragment. In choice **b**, there is a superfluous comma before the prepositional phrase. In choice **d** there is a superfluous comma between the verb and its object.

76. d. In choice **a**, the lack of agreement in tense makes the sentence unclear as to time; in choice **b** it is unclear who ate the popcorn; choice **c** contains a misplaced modifier, implying that the popcorn watched the movie.

77. d. *Broccoli* is within the classification *vegetable*; *Dalmatian* is within the classification *canine*. Choice **a** is wrong, because, although a *Dalmatian* is a *breed* of dog, the word is not as specific as the word *canine* or as the word *vegetable*. Choice **b** is wrong because *companion* is not a classification of anything specific. Choice **c** is wrong because *spotted* is an adjective, whereas the correct answer must be a noun because the original pair are nouns.

78. c. Choice **c** is the main idea of the passage. The idea of soliciting confidences (choice **a**) is not mentioned. Choices **b** and **d** are in the passage but are much more narrow than choice **c** and therefore neither is the best answer.

79. **b.** Choice **b** is the main idea of the passage. Choices **a** and **c**, though reasonable courses of action, are not mentioned. Choice **d** is contradicted in the passage.

80. **c.** The classification *insect* includes the *beetle*; the classification *rodent* includes the *rat*. The answer is not **a** or **b** because classification and item are in reverse order (*insect is to beetle* puts classification first and item second; whereas, *rodent is to mammal* and *rodent is to pest* would both put item first and classification second). The answer is not **d** because *infestation* is not a living thing as the other choices are.

81. **c.** To be *horrifying* is more extremely negative than to merely be *scary*; to be *malevolent* is more extremely destructive than to merely be *spiteful*. Choice **a** is not correct because being *ugly* is not necessarily the same as being *malevolent*. Choice **b** is not correct, because to be *blasphemous* is not the same as to be *malevolent*. Choice **d** is incorrect because the definitions of *malevolent* and *remorseful* are not close at all.

82. **d.** To *refrain* is to hold back from doing something; to *desist* is to cease doing something.

83. **c.** *Animosity* is a strong dislike for something; *hostility* is antagonism.

84. **a.**

85. **b.**

CLERICAL APTITUDE

No answer explanations are given in this section. Once you know the correct answer, you should be able to go back to the question and see why it is right. Most mistakes in this section are the result of having to work quickly.

1. b.
2. c.
3. b.
4. d.
5. d.
6. c.
7. d.
8. a.
9. e.
10. b.
11. e.
12. e.
13. a.
14. d.
15. c.
16. a.
17. e.
18. e.
19. a.
20. e.
21. b.
22. b.
23. a.
24. e.
25. c.
26. a.
27. c.
28. e.
29. d.
30. a.

31. b.
32. c.
33. e.
34. e.
35. c.
36. a.
37. b.
38. e.
39. a.
40. e.
41. d.
42. c.
43. a.
44. b.
45. d.
46. c.
47. e.
48. b.
49. a.
50. d.
51. b.
52. d.
53. c.
54. a.
55. b.
56. c.
57. a.
58. b.
59. d.
60. e.
61. d.
62. a.
63. d.
64. e.
65. e.
66. e.
67. b.
68. a.

69. d.
70. d.
71. c.
72. a.
73. b.
74. d.
75. e.
76. b.
77. d.
78. c.
79. a.
80. e.
81. c.
82. a.
83. b.
84. c.
85. d.
86. b.
87. c.
88. a.
89. d.
90. e.
91. c.
92. d.
93. b.
94. a.
95. c.
96. e.
97. c.
98. a.
99. d.
100. b.
101. c.
102. b.
103. a.
104. a.
105. d.
106. a.

107. c.
108. d.
109. b.
110. e.
111. b.
112. e.
113. c.

114. a.
115. d.
116. c.
117. a.
118. d.
119. b.
120. e.

SCORING

In order to figure your total score on this exam, you'll need to figure your score for the Verbal Abilities and Clerical Aptitude sections separately. For the Verbal Abilities section, simply count up the number you got right. Questions you didn't answer or got wrong don't count.

1. Number of questions right: _____

For the Clerical Aptitude section, the scoring is a little more complicated. First, count up your right answers. Then count your wrong answers separately. Do not count questions you skipped. In order to figure the penalty for your wrong answers, divide your number of wrong answers by four, and then subtract the result from your total number of right answers.

2. Number of questions right: _____

3. Number of questions wrong: _____

4. Divide number 3 by 4: _____

5. Subtract number 4 from number 2: _____

Now you have your total raw score for both the Verbal Abilities and Clerical Aptitude sections. Add them together, and then divide by 205 to determine your total percentage score.

6. Add numbers 1 and 5 together: _____

7. Divide number 6 by 205: _____

The table on this page will help you check your math by giving you percentage equivalents for some possible scores. Use this percentage score to compare your score on this diagnostic exam to your scores on the practice exams later in this book. This percentage score may not be equivalent to the kind of score that will be reported to you on your Notification of Results when you take the real Clerical and Administrative Support Exam.

Number of questions right	Approximate percentage
205	100%
190	93%
176	86%
161	79%
145	71%
131	64%
116	57%
102	50%

On the real exam, you will need a score of at least 80 to pass; however, you should strive for the best score you can achieve, since your potential employer may well use exam scores to help him or her decide who to interview.

What's much more important than your total score, for now, is how you did on each of the kinds of question on the exam. You need to diagnose your strengths and weaknesses so that you can concentrate your efforts as you prepare for the exam. As you probably noticed, the various kinds of questions are all mixed up together on the exam. So take out your completed answer sheet and compare it to the table on the next page. Find out which kinds of questions you did well on and which kinds gave you more trouble. Then you can plan to spend more of your preparation time on the chapters of this book that correspond to the questions you found hardest and less time on the chapters in areas in which you did well.

Even if you got a perfect score on a particular kind of question, you'll want to spend at least some time on the relevant chapter, and you should spend a lot of time with the chapters on the question types that gave you the most difficulty. After you work through those chapters, take the first practice exam in Chapter 12 to see how much you've improved.

VERBAL ABIILITIES

Question Type	Question Numbers	Chapter
Vocabulary	1–2, 8, 19, 26–27, 31–32, 41, 44, 50–51, 55–57, 82–83	Chapter 4, Vocabulary and Spelling
Spelling	10–12, 17–18, 28–30, 38–40, 69, 72–74, 84–85	Chapter 4, Vocabulary and Spelling
Grammar	3–4, 20–23, 42–43, 52, 58–61, 66–67, 75–76	Chapter 5, Grammar
Reading Comprehension	9, 13, 33, 36–37, 45–46, 49, 53–54, 62–63, 68, 70–71, 78–79	Chapter 6, Reading Comprehension
Word Relations (Analogies)	5–7, 14–16, 24–25, 34–35, 47–48, 64–65, 77, 80–81	Chapter 7, Word Relations

CLERICAL APTITUDE

Question Type	Question Numbers	Chapter
Name and Number Comparisons	21–25, 46–50, 61–65, 81–85, 96–100, 111–115	Chapter 8, Name and Number Comparisons
Alphabetizing	11–15, 36–40, 56–60, 71–75, 86–90, 106–110	Chapter 9, Alphabetizing
Arithmetic	1–5, 16–20, 31–35, 51–55, 66–70, 101–105	Chapter 10, Arithmetic
Number & Letter Matching	6–10, 26–30, 41–45, 76–80, 91–95, 116–120	Chapter 11, Number and Letter Matching

C·H·A·P·T·E·R

VOCABULARY AND SPELLING 4

CHAPTER SUMMARY

Vocabulary and spelling are both tested on the Federal Clerical Exam. This chapter provides tips and exercises to help you improve your score in both areas.

A person's vocabulary is seen as a measure of an ability to express ideas clearly and precisely. For almost any job, you must know the working vocabulary of the profession or have the tools for acquiring that vocabulary quickly. Spelling is regarded as a measure of a person's accuracy in presenting information. Most civil servants have to be able to write correctly in order to communicate clearly. In addition, accurate spelling and a wide and flexible vocabulary are seen as the marks of thoughtful and well-educated people.

VOCABULARY

Many civil service exams test vocabulary. There are three basic kinds of questions.

- Synonyms and antonyms: Identifying words that mean the same or the opposite of given words

- Context: Determining the meaning of a word or phrase by noting how it is used in a sentence or paragraph
- Word parts: Choosing the meaning suggested by a part of the word, such as a prefix or suffix

SYNONYM AND ANTONYM QUESTIONS

A word is a *synonym* of another word if it has the same or nearly the same meaning as the other word. *Antonyms* are words with opposite meanings. Test questions often ask you to find the synonym or antonym of a word. If you're lucky, the word will be surrounded by a sentence that helps you guess what the word means. If you're less lucky, you'll just get the word, and then you'll have to figure out what the word means without any help.

Questions that ask for synonyms and antonyms can be tricky because they require you to recognize the meaning of several words that may be unfamiliar—not only the words in the questions but also the answer choices. Usually the best strategy is to *look* at the structure of the word and to *listen* for its sound. See if a part of a word looks familiar. Think of other words you know that have similar key elements. How could those words be related?

Synonym Practice

Try your hand at identifying the word parts and related words in these sample synonym questions. Circle the word that means the same or about the same as the underlined word. Answers and explanations appear right after the questions.

1. a set of <u>partial</u> prints
   a. identifiable
   b. incomplete
   c. visible
   d. enhanced

2. <u>substantial</u> evidence
   a. inconclusive
   b. weighty
   c. proven
   d. alleged

3. <u>corroborated</u> the statement
   a. confirmed
   b. negated
   c. denied
   d. challenged

4. <u>ambiguous</u> questions
   a. meaningless
   b. difficult
   c. simple
   d. vague

Answers to Synonym Questions

The explanations are just as important as the answers, because they show you how to go about choosing a synonym if you don't know the word.

1. **b.** *Partial* means *incomplete*. The key part of the word here is *part*. A partial print is only part of the whole.
2. **b.** *Substantial* evidence is *weighty*. The key part of the word here is *substance*. Substance has weight.
3. **a.** *Corroboration* is *confirmation*. The key part of the word here is the prefix *co-*, which means *with* or *together*. Corroboration means that one statement fits with another.
4. **d.** *Ambiguous* questions are *vague* or uncertain. The key part of this word is *ambi-*, which means *two* or *both*. An ambiguous question can be taken two ways.

Antonym Practice

The main danger in answering questions with antonyms is forgetting that you are looking for *opposites* rather than synonyms. Most questions will include one or more synonyms as answer choices. The trick is to keep your mind on the fact that you are looking for the opposite of the word. If you're allowed to mark in the books or on the test papers, circle the word *antonym* or *opposite* in the directions to help you remember.

Otherwise, the same tactics that work for synonym questions work for antonyms as well: try to determine the meaning of part of the word or to remember a context where you've seen the word before.

Circle the word that means the *opposite* of the underlined word in the sentences below. Answers are immediately after the questions.

5. <u>zealous</u> pursuit
   a. envious
   b. eager
   c. idle
   d. comical

6. <u>inadvertently</u> left
   a. mistakenly
   b. purposely
   c. cautiously
   d. carefully

7. <u>exorbitant</u> prices
   a. expensive
   b. unexpected
   c. reasonable
   d. outrageous

8. <u>compatible</u> workers
   a. comfortable
   b. competitive

   c. harmonious
   d. experienced

9. <u>belligerent</u> attitude
   a. hostile
   b. reasonable
   c. instinctive
   d. ungracious

Answers to Antonym Questions

Be sure to read the explanations as well as the right answers.

5. **c.** *Zealous* means *eager*, so *idle* is most nearly opposite. Maybe you've heard the word *zeal* before. One trick in this question is not to be misled by the similar sounds of *zealous* and *jealous*. The other is not to choose the synonym, *eager*.

6. **b.** *Inadvertently* means *by mistake*, so *purposely* is the antonym. The key element in this word is the prefix *in-*, which usually means *not, the opposite of*. As usual, one of the answer choices (a) is a synonym.

7. **c.** The key element here is *ex-*, which means *out of* or *away from*. *Exorbitant* literally means "out of orbit." The opposite of an *exorbitant* or *outrageous* price would be a *reasonable* one.

8. **b.** The opposite of *compatible* is *competitive*. Here you have to distinguish among three words that contain the same prefix, *com-*, and to let the process of elimination work for you. The other choices are too much like synonyms.

9. **b.** The key element in this word is the root *belli-*, which means *warlike*. The synonym choices, then, are *hostile* and *ungracious*; the antonym is *reasonable*.

CONTEXT QUESTIONS

Context is the surrounding text in which a word is used. Most people use context to help them determine the meaning of an unknown word. A vocabulary question that gives you a sentence around the vocabulary word is usually easier to answer than one with little or no context. The surrounding text can help you as you look for synonyms for the specified words in the sentences.

The best way to take meaning from context is to look for key words in sentences or paragraphs that convey the meaning of the text. If nothing else, the context will give you a means to eliminate wrong answer choices that clearly don't fit. The process of elimination will often leave you with the correct answer.

Context Practice

Try these sample questions. Circle the word that best describes the meaning of the underlined word in the sentence. Answers are immediately after the questions.

10. The clerks in the store were <u>appalled</u> by the wild and uncontrolled behavior of the angry customer.
    a. horrified
    b. amused
    c. surprised
    d. dismayed

11. Despite the fact that he appeared to have financial resources, the client claimed to be <u>destitute</u>.
    a. wealthy
    b. ambitious
    c. solvent
    d. impoverished

12. Though she was <u>distraught</u> over the disappearance of her child, the woman was calm enough to give the officer her description.
    a. punished
    b. distracted
    c. composed
    d. anguished

13. The unrepentant embezzler expressed no <u>remorse</u> for his actions.
    a. sympathy
    b. regret
    c. reward
    d. complacency

Some tests may ask you to fill in the blank by choosing a word that fits the context. In the following questions, circle the word that best completes the sentence.

14. Professor Washington was a very_____ man known for his reputation as a scholar.
    a. stubborn
    b. erudite
    c. illiterate
    d. disciplined

15. His_____was demonstrated by his willingness to donate large amounts of money to worthy causes.
    a. honesty
    b. loyalty
    c. selfishness
    d. altruism

Answers to Context Questions

Check to see whether you were able to pick out the key words that help you define the target word, as well as whether you got the right answer.

10. a. The key words *wild* and *uncontrolled* signify *horror* rather than the milder emotions described by the other choices.

11. d. The key words here are *financial resources,* but this is a clue by contrast. The introductory *Despite the fact* signals that you should look for the opposite of the idea of having financial resources.

12. d. The key words here are *though* and *disappearance of her child,* signalling that you are looking for an opposite of *calm* in describing how the mother spoke to the officer. The only word strong enough to match the situation is *anguish.*

13. b. *Remorse* means *regret* for one's action. The part of the word here to beware of is the prefix *re-.* It doesn't signify anything in this word, though it often means *again* or *back.* Don't be confused by the two choices which also contain the prefix *re-.* The strategy here is to see which word sounds better in the sentence. The key words are *unrepentant* and *no,* indicating that you're looking for something that shows no repentance.

14. b. The key words here are *professor* and *scholarly.* Even if you don't know the word *erudite,* the other choices don't fit the description of the professor.

15. d. The key words here are *large amounts of money to worthy causes.* They give you a definition of the word you're looking for. Again, even if you don't know the word *altruism,* the other choices seem inappropriate to describe someone so generous.

For Non-Native Speakers of English

Be very careful not to be confused by the *sound* of words that may mislead you. Be sure you look at the word carefully, and pay attention to the structure and appearance of the word as well as its sound. You may be used to hearing English words spoken with an accent. The sounds of those words may be misleading in choosing a correct answer.

QUESTIONS ABOUT WORD PARTS

Some tests may ask you to find the meaning of a part of a word: roots, which are the main part of the word; prefixes, which go before the root word; or suffixes, which go after. Any of these elements can carry meaning or change the use of a word in a sentence. For instance, the suffix *-s* or *-es* can change the meaning of a noun from singular to plural: *boy, boys.* The prefix *un-* can change the meaning of a root word to its opposite: *necessary, unnecessary.* Even if your test doesn't include word parts, knowing about them will help you answer other kinds of vocabulary questions.

To identify most parts of words, the best strategy is to think of words you already know which carry the same root, suffix, or prefix. Let what you know about those words help you to see the meaning in words that are less familiar.

Word Part Practice

Circle the word or phrase below that best describes the meaning of the underlined portion of the word. Answers appear after the questions.

16. <u>pro</u>active
    a. after
    b. forward
    c. toward
    d. behind

17. <u>re</u>cession
   a. against
   b. see
   c. under
   d. back

18. <u>con</u>temporary
   a. with
   b. over
   c. apart
   d. time

19. etymo<u>logy</u>
   a. state of
   b. prior to
   c. study of
   d. quality of

20. vanda<u>lize</u>
   a. to make happen
   b. to stop

   c. to fill
   d. to continue

Answers to Word Part Questions

Even if the word in the question was unfamiliar, you might have been able to guess the meaning of the prefix or suffix by thinking of some other word that has the same prefix or suffix.

16. b. Think of *propeller:* a propeller sends an airplane *forward.*

17. d. Think of *recall:* manufacturers *recall* or *bring back* cars that are defective; people *recall* or *bring back* past events in memory.

18. a. Think of *congregation:* a group of people gather *with* each other in a house of worship.

19. c. Think of *biology:* the *study of* life.

20. a. Think of *scandalize:* to *make* something shocking *happen.*

WORDS THAT ARE EASILY CONFUSED

Vocabulary tests of any kind often contain words that are easily confused with each other. A smart test taker will be aware of these easily mixed up words or phrases:

accept: to receive willingly	**except:** exclude or leave out
complement: to complete	**compliment:** to say something flattering
council: a group that makes decisions	**counsel:** to give advice
contemptuous: having an attitude of contempt	**contemptible:** worthy of contempt
continuous: without interruption	**continual:** from time to time
emigrate: to move from	**immigrate:** to move to
ingenious: something clever	**ingenuous:** guileless or naive
oral: pertaining to the mouth	**verbal:** pertaining to language
persecute: to oppress someone	**prosecute:** to bring a legal action against someone

How to Answer Vocabulary Questions

- The key to answering vocabulary questions is to **notice and connect** what you do know to what you may not recognize.
- **Know your word parts.** You can recognize or make a good guess at the meanings of words when you see some suggested meaning in a root word, prefix, or suffix.
- **Note directions very carefully.** Remember when you are looking for opposites rather than synonyms.
- **Use a process of elimination.** Think of how the word makes sense in the sentence.
- **Don't be confused by words that sound like other words,** but may have no relation to the word you need.

A List of Word Parts

On the next page are some of the word elements seen most often in vocabulary tests. Simply reading them and their examples five to ten minutes a day will give you the quick recognition you need to make a good association with the meaning of an unfamiliar word.

SPELLING

Generally spelling tests are in a multiple-choice format. You will be given several possible spellings for a word and asked to identify the one that is correct. Thus, you must be able to see very fine differences between word spellings. The best way to prepare for a spelling test is to have a good grasp of the spelling fundamentals and be able to recognize when those rules don't apply.

Remember that English is full of exceptions in spelling. You have to develop a good eye to spot the errors.

Even though there are so many variant spellings for words in English, civil service tests generally are looking to make sure that you know and can apply the basic rules. Here are some of those rules to review:

- *i* before *e*, except after *c*, or when *ei* sounds like *a*
  Examples: piece, receive, neighbor
- *gh* can replace *f* or be silent
  Examples: enough, night
- Double the consonant when you add an ending
  Examples: forget/forgettable, shop/shopping
- Drop the *e* when you add *ing*
  Example: hope/hoping
- The spelling of prefixes and suffixes generally doesn't change
  Examples: project, propel, proactive

SPELLING PRACTICE

Here are some examples of how spelling would appear on a civil service test. Choose the word that is spelled correctly in the following sentences. This time there's no answer key. Instead, use your dictionary to find the right answers.

21. We went to an _____ of early Greek art.
    a. exibition
    b. exhibition
    c. excibition
    d. exebition

word element	meaning	example
ama	love	amateur
ambi	both	ambivalent, ambidextrous
aud	hear	audition
belli	war	belligerent, bellicose
bene	good	benefactor
cid/cis	cut	homicide, scissor
cogn/gno	know	knowledge, recognize
curr	run	current
flu/flux	flow	fluid, fluctuate
gress	to go	congress, congregation
in	not, in	ingenious
ject	throw	inject, reject
luc/lux	light	lucid, translucent
neo	new	neophyte
omni	all	omnivorous
pel/puls	push	impulse, propeller
pro	forward	project
pseudo	false	pseudonym
rog	ask	interrogate
sub	under	subjugate
spec/spic	look, see	spectator
super	over	superfluous
temp	time	contemporary, temporal
un	not, opposite	uncoordinated
viv	live	vivid

22. We will _____ go to the movies tonight.
   a. probly
   b. probbaly
   c. probely
   d. probably

23. We took _____ of pictures on our vacation.
   a. allot
   b. alot
   c. a lot
   d. alott

24. The high scorer had the greatest number of
_____ answers.
   a. accurate
   b. acurate
   c. accuret
   d. acccurit

25. He was warned not to use
_____ force.
   a. exessive
   b. excesive
   c. excessive
   d. excesive

USING SPELLING LISTS

Some test makers will give you a list to study before you take the test. If you have a list to work with, here are some suggestions.

- Divide the list into groups of three, five, or seven to study. Consider making flash cards of the words you don't know.
- Highlight or circle the tricky elements in each word.
- Cross out or discard any words that you already know for certain. Don't let them get in the way of the ones you need to study.
- Say the words as you read them. Spell them out in your mind so you can "hear" the spelling.

Here's a sample spelling list. These words are typical of the words that appear on exams. If you aren't given a list by the agency that's testing you, study this one.

achievement	doubtful	ninety
allege	eligible	noticeable
anxiety	enough	occasionally
appreciate	enthusiasm	occurred
asthma	equipped	offense
arraignment	exception	official
autonomous	fascinate	pamphlet
auxiliary	fatigue	parallel
brief	forfeit	personnel
ballistics	gauge	physician
barricade	grieve	politics
beauty	guilt	possess
beige	guarantee	privilege
business	harass	psychology
bureau	hazard	recommend
calm	height	referral
cashier	incident	recidivism
capacity	indict	salary
cancel	initial	schedule
circuit	innocent	seize
colonel	irreverent	separate
comparatively	jeopardy	specific
courteous	knowledge	statute
criticism	leisure	surveillance
custody	license	suspicious
cyclical	lieutenant	tentative
debt	maintenance	thorough
definitely	mathematics	transferred
descend	mortgage	warrant

How to Answer Spelling Questions

- **Sound out the word in your mind.** Remember that long vowels inside words usually are followed by single consonants: *sofa, total.* Short vowels inside words usually are followed by double consonants: *dribble, scissors.*
- **Give yourself auditory (listening) clues when you learn words.** Say *"Wed-nes-day"* or *"lis-ten"* or *"bus-i-ness"* to yourself so that you remember to add letters you do not hear.
- **Look at each part of a word.** See if there is a root, prefix or suffix that will always be spelled the same way. For example, in *uninhabitable*, *un-*, *in-*, and *-able* are always spelled the same. What's left is *habit*, a self-contained root word that's pretty easy to spell.

MORE PRACTICE IN VOCABULARY AND SPELLING

Here is a second set of practice exercises with samples of each kind of question covered in this chapter. Answers to all questions except spelling questions are at the end of the chapter. For spelling questions, use a dictionary.

Circle the word that means the same or nearly the same as the underlined word.

26. convivial company
    a. lively
    b. dull
    c. tiresome
    d. dreary

27. conspicuous behavior
    a. secret
    b. outrageous
    c. visible
    d. boorish

28. meticulous record-keeping
    a. dishonest
    b. casual
    c. painstaking
    d. careless

29. superficial wounds
    a. life-threatening
    b. bloody
    c. severe
    d. shallow

30. impulsive actions
    a. cautious
    b. imprudent
    c. courageous
    d. cowardly

Circle the word that is most nearly opposite in meaning to the underlined word.

31. amateur athlete
    a. professional
    b. successful
    c. unrivaled
    d. former

32. lucid opinions
    a. clear
    b. strong
    c. hazy
    d. heartfelt

33. traveling <u>incognito</u>
   a. unrecognized
   b. alone
   c. by night
   d. publicly

34. <u>incisive</u> reporting
   a. mild
   b. sharp
   c. dangerous
   d. insightful

35. <u>tactful</u> comments
   a. rude
   b. pleasant
   c. complimentary
   d. sociable

Using the context, choose the word that means the same or nearly the same as the underlined word.

36. Though he had little time, the student took <u>copious</u> notes in preparation for the test.
   a. limited
   b. plentiful
   c. illegible
   d. careless

37. Though flexible about homework, the teacher was <u>adamant</u> that papers be in on time.
   a. liberal
   b. casual
   c. strict
   d. pliable

38. The condition of the room after the party was <u>deplorable</u>.
   a. regrettable
   b. pristine
   c. festive
   d. tidy

Choose the word that best completes the following sentences.

39. Her position as a(n) _____ teacher took her all over the city.
   a. primary
   b. secondary
   c. itinerant
   d. permanent

40. Despite her promise to stay in touch, she remained _____ and difficult to locate.
   a. steadfast
   b. stubborn
   c. dishonest
   d. elusive

Choose the word or phrase closest in meaning to the underlined part of the word.

41. <u>uni</u>verse
   a. one
   b. three
   c. under
   d. opposite

42. <u>re</u>entry
  a. back
  b. push
  c. against
  d. forward

43. <u>bene</u>fit
  a. bad
  b. suitable
  c. beauty
  d. good

44. educat<u>ion</u>
  a. something like
  b. state of
  c. to increase
  d. unlike

45. urban<u>ite</u>
  a. resident of
  b. relating to
  c. that which is
  d. possessing

Circle the correct spelling of the word that fits in the blank.

46. The information was _____
to the action.
  a. irelevent
  b. irrevelent
  c. irrelevant
  d. irrevelent

47. He made no _____ to take
the job.
  a. comittment
  b. commitment
  c. comitment
  d. comittmint

48. He made an income _____
to meet his needs.
  a. adaquate
  b. adequate
  c. adiquate
  d. adequet

49. We went to eat at a fancy new _____.
  a. restarant
  b. restaraunt
  c. restaurant
  d. resteraunt

50. The vote was _____ to elect
the chairman.
  a. unannimous
  b. unanimous
  c. unanimus
  d. unaminous

ADDITIONAL RESOURCES

One of the best resources for any adult student is the public library. Many libraries have sections for adult learners or for those preparing to enter or change careers. Those sections contain skill books and review books on a number of subjects, including spelling and vocabulary. Here are some books you might consult:

- *504 Absolutely Essential Words* by Murray Bromberg et al. (Barron's)
- *All About Words: An Adult Approach to Vocabulary Building* by Maxwell Nurnberg and Morris Rosenblum (Mentor Books)
- *Checklists for Vocabulary Study* by Richard Yorkey (Longman)

- *Vocabulary and Spelling in 20 Minutes a Day* by Judith Meyers (LearningExpress, order information at the back of this book)
- *Word Watcher's Handbook* by Phyllis Martin (St. Martin's)
- *Spelling Made Simple* by Stephen V. Ross (Doubleday)
- *Spelling the Easy Way* by Joseph Mersand and Francis Griffith (Barron's)
- *Word Smart Revised* by Adam Robinson (The Princeton Review)

ANSWERS TO PRACTICE QUESTIONS

26. a.	**33.** d.	**40.** d.
27. c.	**34.** a.	**41.** a.
28. c.	**35.** a.	**42.** a.
29. d.	**36.** b.	**43.** d.
30. b.	**37.** c.	**44.** b.
31. a.	**38.** a.	**45.** a.
32. c.	**39.** c.	

C·H·A·P·T·E·R

GRAMMAR

5

CHAPTER SUMMARY

This chapter reviews the sentence-level writing skills often tested on multiple-choice exams, including complete sentences, capitalization, punctuation, subject-verb agreement, verb tenses, pronouns, and confusing word pairs. It also shows you how to choose the answer that is most clearly written.

Knowing how to use written language is vital, not just for the exam, but for your federal clerical career. Almost every federal clerical job involves at least some writing. So the Federal Clerical Exam will include questions that test your grammar and your ability to tell a well-written sentence from a poorly written one.

COMPLETE SENTENCES

The sentence is the basic unit of written language. Most writing is done using complete sentences, so it's important to distinguish sentences from fragments. A sentence expresses a complete thought, while a fragment requires something more to express a complete thought.

Look at the following pairs of word groups. The first in each pair is a sentence fragment; the second is a complete sentence.

COMPLETE SENTENCES

Fragment	Complete Sentence
The dog walking down the street.	The dog was walking down the street.
Exploding from the bat for a home run.	The ball exploded from the bat for a home run.

These examples show that a sentence must have a subject and a verb to complete its meaning. The first fragment has a subject, but not a verb. *Walking* looks like a verb, but it is actually an adjective describing *dog*. The second fragment has neither a subject nor a verb. *Exploding* looks like a verb, but it too is an adjective describing something not identified in the word group.

Now look at the next set of word groups. Mark those that are complete sentences.

1.

   a. We saw the tornado approaching.
   b. When we saw the tornado approaching.

2.

   a. Before the house was built in 1972.
   b. The house was built in 1972.

3.

   a. Since we are leaving in the morning.
   b. We are leaving in the morning.

If you chose **1.a.**, **2.b.**, and **3.b.**, you were correct. You may have noticed that the groups of words are the same, but the fragments have an extra word at the beginning. These words are called subordinating conjunctions. If a group of words that would normally be a complete sentence is preceded by a subordinating conjunction, something more is needed to complete the thought.

- When we saw the tornado approaching, we headed for cover.
- Before the house was built in 1972, the old house was demolished.
- Since we were leaving in the morning, we went to bed early.

Here is a list of words that can be used as subordinating conjunctions.

after	that
although	though
as	unless
because	until
before	when
if	whenever
once	where
since	wherever
than	while

If you can tell when a group of words isn't a sentence, then you can tell when one or more sentences have been run together, sometimes with a comma in between. Some tests will ask you to find run-on sentences. Each of the sentences below is a run-on sentence. Can you find where to put a period and begin a new sentence?

1. We went to the beach, we had a good time.
2. Without exception, the prisoners conformed to the new ruling they kept their cells clean.
3. The defense needed time to examine the new evidence, the lawyer asked for an extension.

If you noticed that a new sentence begins after *beach* in the first sentence, after *ruling* in the second, and after *evidence* in the third, you were right. Generally, you can tell whether you're looking at a run-on by covering the second half of the sentence and asking yourself whether the first half by itself is a sentence. Then cover the first half. Is the second half a sentence by itself? If your answer to the first and/or second question is *no*, then the sentence is fine. If you answered both questions *yes*—both halves of the sentence could be sentences by themselves—then you've got a run-on, unless there happens to be a semicolon (;) between the two halves.

Some of the questions on a civil service exam may test your ability to distinguish a sentence from a fragment or a run-on. Check for a subject and a verb, as well as for subordinating conjunctions. Check yourself with the following sample questions. The answers are at the end of this chapter.

1. Which of the following groups of words is a complete sentence?
   a. The treasure buried beneath the floorboards beside the furnace.
   b. After we spent considerable time examining all of the possibilities before making a decision.
   c. In addition to the methods the doctor used to diagnose the problem.
   d. The historical account of the incident bore the most resemblance to fact.

2. Which of the following groups of words is a complete sentence?
   a. This was fun to do.
   b. We looking.
   c. Before the door opened.
   d. If we ever see you again.

3. Which of the following groups of words is a run-on?
   a. Whenever I see the moon rise, I am awed by the deep orange color.
   b. The special services unit completed its work and made its report to the chief.
   c. Unless we hear from the directors of the board before the next meeting, we will not act on the new proposal.
   d. We slept soundly we never heard the alarm.

CAPITALIZATION

You may encounter questions that test your ability to capitalize correctly. Here is a quick review of the most common capitalization rules.

- Capitalize the first word of a sentence. If the first word is a number, write it as a word.
- Capitalize the pronoun *I*.
- Capitalize the first word of a quotation: I said, "What's the name of your dog?" Do not capitalize the first word of a partial quotation: He called me "the worst excuse for a student" he had ever seen.
- Capitalize proper nouns and proper adjectives.

See the table on the next page.

The following passage contains no capitalized words. Circle those letters that should be capitalized.

when I first saw the black hills on january 2, 1995, i was shocked by their beauty. we had just spent new year's day in sioux falls, south dakota and had headed west toward our home in denver, colorado. as we traveled along interstate 90, i could see the black hills rising slightly in the distance. president calvin coolidge had called them "a wondrous sight to behold." i understood why. after driving through the badlands and stopping at wall drug in wall, south

CAPITALIZATION

Category	Example (Proper nouns)
days of the week, months of the year	Friday, Saturday; January, February
holidays, special events	Christmas, Halloween; Two Rivers Festival, Dilly Days
names of individuals	John Henry, George Billeck
names of structures, buildings	Lincoln Memorial, Principal Building
names of trains, ships, aircraft	Queen Elizabeth, Chicago El
product names	Corn King hams, Dodge Intrepid
cities and states	Des Moines, Iowa; Juneau, Alaska
streets, highways, roads	Grand Avenue, Interstate 29, Deadwood Road
landmarks, public areas	Continental Divide, Grand Canyon, Glacier National Park
bodies of water	Atlantic Ocean, Mississippi River
ethnic groups, languages, nationalities	Asian-American, English, Arab
official titles	Mayor Daley, President Johnson
institutions, organizations, businesses	Dartmouth College, Lions Club, Chrysler Corporation
proper adjectives	English muffin, Polish sausage

dakota, we liked the way the evergreen-covered hills broke the barren monotony of the landscape. my oldest daughter said, "dad, look! there's something that's not all white." we could see why the lakota sioux regarded them as a native american holy ground. we saw mount rushmore and custer state park, the home of the largest herd of buffalo in north america. we also drove the treacherous spearfish canyon road. fortunately, our jeep cherokee had no trouble with the ice and snow on the winding road.

Check your circled version against the corrected version of the passage below.

When I first saw the Black Hills on January 2, 1995, I was shocked by their beauty. We had just spent New Year's Day in Sioux Falls, South Dakota and had headed west toward our home in Denver, Colorado. As we traveled along Interstate 90, I could see the Black Hills rising slightly in the distance. President Calvin Coolidge had called them "a wondrous sight to behold." I understood why. After driving through the Badlands and stopping at Wall Drug in Wall, South Dakota, we liked the way the evergreen-covered hills broke the barren monotony of the landscape. My oldest daughter said, "Dad, look! There's something that's not all white." We could see why the Lakota Sioux regarded them as a Native American holy ground. We saw Mount Rushmore and Custer State Park, the home of the largest herd of buffalo in North America. We also drove the treacherous Spearfish Canyon Road. Fortunately, our Jeep Cherokee had no trouble with the ice and snow on the winding road.

Now try these sample questions. Choose the option that is capitalized correctly. Answers are at the end of the chapter.

4.
- a. This year we will celebrate christmas on Tuesday, December 25 in Manchester, Ohio.
- b. This year we will celebrate Christmas on Tuesday, December 25 in manchester, Ohio.
- c. This year we will celebrate Christmas on Tuesday, December 25 in Manchester, Ohio.
- d. This year we will celebrate christmas on Tuesday, December 25 in manchester, Ohio.

5.
- a. Abraham Adams made an appointment with Mayor Burns to discuss the building plans.
- b. Abraham Adams made an appointment with Mayor Burns to discuss the Building Plans.
- c. Abraham Adams made an appointment with mayor Burns to discuss the building plans.
- d. Abraham Adams made an appointment with mayor Burns to discuss the Building Plans.

6.
- a. Ms. Abigal Dornburg, M.D., was named head of the review board for Physicians Mutual.
- b. Ms. Abigal Dornburg, M.D., was named Head of the Review Board for Physicians Mutual.
- c. Ms. Abigal Dornburg, m.d. Was named head of the review board for Physicians mutual.
- d. Ms. Abigal dornburg, M.D., was named head of the review board for Physicians Mutual.

PUNCTUATION

PERIODS
Here is a quick review of the rules regarding the use of a period.

- Use a period at the end of a sentence that is not a question or an exclamation.
- Use a period after an initial in a name: Millard K. Furham.
- Use a period after an abbreviation, unless the abbreviation is an acronym.
  Abbreviations: Mr., Ms., Dr., A.M., General Motors Corp., Allied Inc.
  Acronyms: NASA, AIDS
- If a sentence ends with an abbreviation, use only one period. (We brought food, tents, sleeping bags, etc.)

COMMAS
Using commas correctly can make the difference between presenting information clearly and distorting the facts. The following chart demonstrates the neces-

sity of commas in written language. How many people are listed in the sentence?

COMMAS AND MEANING

Number undetermined	My sister Diane John Carey Melissa and I went to the fair.
Four people	My sister Diane, John Carey, Melissa, and I went to the fair.
Five people	My sister, Diane, John Carey, Melissa, and I went to the fair.
Six people	My sister, Diane, John, Carey, Melissa, and I went to the fair.

Here is a quick review of the most basic rules regarding the use of commas.

- Use a comma before *and, but, or, for, nor,* and *yet* when they separate two groups of words that could be complete sentences.
  Example: The coaches laid out the game plan, and the team executed it to perfection.
- Use a comma to separate items in a series.
  Example: The student driver stopped, looked, and listened when she got to the railroad tracks.
- Use a comma to separate two or more adjectives modifying the same noun.
  Example: The hot, black, rich coffee tasted great after an hour in below-zero weather. [Notice that there is no comma between *rich* (an adjective) and *coffee* (the noun *rich* describes)].
- Use a comma after introductory words, phrases, or clauses in a sentence.

Examples: Usually, the class begins with a short writing assignment. [Word]
Racing down the street, the yellow car ran a stoplight. [Phrase]
After we found the source of the noise, we relaxed and enjoyed the rest of the evening. [Clause]

- Use a comma after a name followed by Jr., Sr., or some other abbreviation.
  Example: The class was inspired by the speeches of Martin Luther King, Jr.
- Use a comma to separate items in an address.
  Example: The car stopped at 1433 West G Avenue, Orlando, Florida 36890.
- Use a comma to separate a day and a year, as well as after the year.
  Example: I was born on July 21, 1954, during a thunderstorm.
- Use a comma after the greeting of a friendly letter and after the closing of any letter.
  Example: Dear Uncle Jon,
  Sincerely yours,
- Use a comma to separate contrasting elements in a sentence.
  Example: Your essay needs strong arguments, not strong opinions, to convince me.
- Use commas to set off appositives (words or phrases that explain or identify a noun).
  Example: My cat, a Siamese, is named Ron.

The following passage contains no commas or periods. Add commas and periods as needed.

Dr Newton Brown Jr a renowned chemist has held research positions for OPEC Phillips Petroleum Inc Edward L Smith Chemical Designs and R J Reynolds Co His thorough exhaustive research is recognized in academic circles as well as in the business community as the most well-designed reliable data available Unfortunately on July 6 1988 he retired after a brief but serious illness He lives in a secluded retirement community at 2401 Beach Sarasota Springs Florida

Check your version against the corrected version below.

Dr. Newton Brown, Jr., a renowned chemist, has held research positions for OPEC, Phillips Petroleum Inc., Edward L. Smith Chemical Designs, and R. J. Reynolds Co. His thorough, exhaustive research is recognized in academic circles, as well as in the business community, as the most well-designed, reliable data available. Unfortunately, on July 6, 1988, he retired after a brief, but serious illness. He lives in a secluded retirement community at 2401 Beach, Sarasota Springs, Florida.

APOSTROPHES

Apostrophes communicate important information in written language. Here is a quick review of the two most important rules regarding the use of apostrophes.

- Use an apostrophe to show that letters have been omitted from a word to form a contraction.

Examples: do not = don't; national = nat'l; I will = I'll; it is = it's

- Use an apostrophe to show possession. (Exception: Possessive pronouns don't take an apostrophe: *its, yours, ours, theirs.*

Check yourself with these sample test questions. Choose which of the four options is punctuated correctly. Answers are at the end of the chapter.

7.

 a. Although it may seem strange, my partners purpose in interviewing Dr. E. S. Sanders Jr. was to eliminate him as a suspect in the crime.

 b. Although it may seem strange my partner's purpose in interviewing Dr. E. S. Sanders, Jr. was to eliminate him, as a suspect in the crime.

 c. Although it may seem strange, my partner's purpose in interviewing Dr. E. S. Sanders, Jr., was to eliminate him as a suspect in the crime.

 d. Although it may seem strange, my partner's purpose in interviewing Dr. E. S. Sanders, Jr. was to eliminate him, as a suspect in the crime.

APOSTROPHES TO SHOW POSSESSION		
Singular nouns (add 's)	**Plural nouns ending in s (add ')**	**Plural nouns not ending in s (add 's)**
boy's	boys'	men's
child's	kids'	children's
lady's	ladies'	women's

8.

a. After colliding with a vehicle at the intersection of Grand, and Forest Ms. Anderson saw a dark hooded figure crawl through the window, reach back and grab a small parcel, and run north on Forest.

b. After colliding with a vehicle at the intersection of Grand, and Forest, Ms. Anderson saw a dark hooded figure crawl through the window, reach back and grab a small parcel, and run north on Forest.

c. After colliding with a vehicle at the intersection of Grand and Forest Ms. Anderson saw a dark, hooded figure crawl through the window, reach back and grab a small parcel, and run north on Forest.

d. After colliding with a vehicle at the intersection of Grand and Forest, Ms. Anderson saw a dark, hooded figure crawl through the window, reach back and grab a small parcel, and run north on Forest.

9.

a. When we interviewed each of the boys and the fathers, we determined that the men's stories did not match the boy's versions.

b. When we interviewed each of the boys and the fathers, we determined that the men's stories did not match the boys' versions.

c. When we interviewed each of the boys and the fathers, we determined that the mens' stories did not match the boys' versions.

d. When we interviewed each of the boys' and the fathers', we determined that the men's stories did not match the boys' versions.

VERBS

SUBJECT-VERB AGREEMENT

In written language a subject must agree with its verb in number. In other words, if a subject is singular, the verb must be singular. If the subject is plural, the verb must be plural. If you are unsure whether a verb is singular or plural, apply this simple test. Fill in the blanks in the two sentences below with the matching form of the verb. The verb form that best completes the first sentence is singular. The verb form that best completes the second sentence is plural.

> One person _____. [Singular]
> Two people _____. [Plural]

Look at these examples using the verbs *speak* and *do*. Try it yourself with any verb that confuses you.

> One person *speaks*.   One person *does*.
> Two people *speak*.   Two people *do*.

Pronoun Subjects

Few people have trouble matching noun subjects and verbs, but pronouns are sometimes difficult for even the most sophisticated speakers of English. Some pronouns are always singular, others are always plural, still others can be both singular and plural.

These pronouns are always singular.

each	everyone
either	no one
neither	nobody
anybody	one
anyone	somebody
everybody	someone

The indefinite pronouns *each*, *either*, and *neither* are the ones most often misused. You can avoid a mismatch by mentally adding the word *one* after the pronoun and removing the other words between the pronoun and the verb. Look at the following examples.

Each **of the men** wants his own car.
Each **one** wants his own car.

Either **of the salesclerks** knows where the sale merchandise is located.
Either **one** knows where the sale merchandise is located.

These sentences may sound awkward because many speakers misuse these pronouns, and you are probably used to hearing them used incorrectly. Despite that, the substitution trick (*one* for the words following the pronoun) will help you avoid this mistake.

Some pronouns are always plural and require a plural verb:

both   many
few   several

Other pronouns can be either singular or plural:

all   none
any   some
most

The words or prepositional phrases following them determine whether they are singular or plural. If what follows the pronouns is plural, the verb must be plural. If what follows is singular, the verb must be singular.

All of the **work is** finished.
All of the **jobs are** finished.

Is any of the **pizza** left?
Are any of the **pieces** of pizza left?

None of the **time was** wasted.
None of the **minutes were** wasted.

Subjects Joined by *and*

If two nouns or pronouns are joined by *and*, they require a plural verb.

He and she want to buy a new house.
Jack and Jill want to buy a new house.

Subjects Joined by *or* or *nor*

If two nouns or pronouns are joined by *or* or *nor*, they require a singular verb. Think of them as two separate sentences and you'll never make a mistake in agreement.

He or she wants to buy a new house.
  He wants to buy a new house.
  She wants to buy a new house.

Neither Jack nor Jill wants to buy a new house.
  Jack wants not to buy a new house.
  Jill wants not to buy a new house.

Circle the correct verb in each of the following sentences. Answers are at the end of the chapter.

10. Every other day either Bert or Ernie (takes, take) out the trash.

11. A woman in one of my classes (works, work) at the Civic Center box office.

12. A good knowledge of the rules (helps, help) you understand the game.

13. Each of these prescriptions (causes, cause) bloating and irritability.

14. (Have, Has) either of them ever arrived on time?

VERB TENSE

The tense of a verb tells a reader when the action occurs. Present tense verbs tell the reader to imagine that action happening as it is being read, while past tense verbs tell the reader the action has already happened. Read the following two paragraphs. The first one is written in the present tense, the second in the past tense. Notice the difference in the verbs. They are highlighted to make them easier to locate.

As Horace **opens** the door, he **glances** around cautiously. He **sees** signs of danger everywhere. The centerpiece and placemats from the dining room table **are scattered** on the floor next to the table. An end table in the living room **is lying** on its side. He **sees** the curtains flapping and **notices** glass on the carpet in front of the window.

As Horace **opened** the door, he **glanced** around cautiously. He **saw** signs of danger everywhere. The centerpiece and placemats from the dining room table **were scattered** on the floor next to the table. An end table in the living room **was lying** on its side. He **saw** the curtains flapping and **noticed** glass on the carpet in front of the window.

It's easy to distinguish present tense from past tense by simply fitting the verb into a sentence.

VERB TENSE	
Present tense (Today, I ___ . . .)	**Past tense (Yesterday, I ___ . . .)**
drive	drove
think	thought
rise	rose
catch	caught

The important thing to remember about verb tense is to keep it consistent. If a passage begins in the present tense, keep it in the present tense unless there is a specific reason to change—to indicate that some action occurred in the past, for instance. If a passage begins in the past tense, it should remain in the past tense. Verb tense should never be mixed as it is in the following sentence.

Wrong: Terry **opens** the door and **saw** the crowd.
Correct: Terry **opens** the door and **sees** the crowd.
Terry **opened** the door and **saw** the crowd.

However, sometimes it is necessary to use a different verb tense in order to clarify when an action occurred. Read the following sentences and the explanations following them.

The game warden **sees** the fish that you **caught**. [The verb **sees** is in the present tense, indicating that the action is occurring in the present. However, the verb **caught** is in the past tense, indicating that the fish were caught at some earlier time.]

The house that **was built** over a century ago **sits** on top of the hill. [The verb phrase **was built** is in the past tense, indicating that the house was built in the past. However, the verb **sits** is in the present tense, indicating that the action is still occurring.]

Check yourself with these sample questions. Choose the option that uses verb tense correctly. Answers are at the end of the chapter.

15.
    a. When I cry, I always get what I want.
    b. When I cry, I always got what I want.
    c. When I cried, I always got what I want.
    d. When I cried, I always get what I wanted.

16.
    a. It all started after I came home and am in my room studying for a big test.
    b. It all started after I came home and was in my room studying for a big test.
    c. It all starts after I come home and was in my room studying for a big test.
    d. It all starts after I came home and am in my room studying for a big test.

17.
    a. The child became excited and dashes into the house and slams the door.
    b. The child becomes excited and dashed into the house and slammed the door.
    c. The child becomes excited and dashes into the house and slammed the door.
    d. The child became excited and dashed into the house and slammed the door.

PRONOUNS

PRONOUN CASE

Most of the time, a single pronoun in a sentence is easy to use correctly. In fact, most English speakers would readily identify the mistakes in the following sentences.

> **Me** went to the movie with **he**.
> My teacher gave **she** a ride to school.

Most people know that **Me** in the first sentence should be **I** and that **he** should be **him**. They would also know that **she** in the second sentence should be **her**. Such errors are easy to spot when the pronouns are used alone in a sentence. The problem occurs when a pronoun is used with a noun or another pronoun. See if you can spot the errors in the following sentences.

> The director rode with Jerry and **I**.
> Belle and **him** are going to the ice arena.

The errors in these sentences are not as easy to spot as those in the sentences with a single pronoun. The easiest way to attack this problem is to turn the sentence with two pronouns into two separate sentences. Then the error once again becomes very obvious.

> The director rode with Jerry.
> The director rode with **me** (not I).

> Belle is going to the ice arena. [Notice the singular verb *is* in place of *are*.]
> **He** (not him) is going to the ice arena.

PRONOUN AGREEMENT

Another common error in using pronouns involves singular and plural pronouns. Like subjects and verbs, pronouns must match the number of the nouns they represent. If the noun a pronoun represents is singular, the pronoun must be singular. On the other hand, if the noun a pronoun represents is plural, the pronoun must be plural. Sometimes a pronoun represents another pronoun. If so, either both pronouns must be singular or both pronouns must be plural. Consult the list of singular and plural pronouns you saw earlier in this chapter.

> The **doctor** must take a break when **she** (or **he**) is tired. [singular]
> **Doctors** must take breaks when **they** are tired. [plural]

> **One** of the girls misplaced **her** purse. [singular]
> **All** of the girls misplaced **their** purses. [Plural]

If two or more singular nouns or pronouns are joined by *and,* use a plural pronoun to represent them.

> **Buddha and Muhammad** built religions around **their** philosophies.
> If **he and she** want to know where I was, **they** should ask me.

If two or more singular nouns or pronouns are joined by *or,* use a singular pronoun. If a singular and a plural noun or pronoun are joined by *or,* the pronoun agrees with the closest noun or pronoun it represents.

> **Matthew or Jacob** will loan you **his** calculator.
> **The elephant or the moose** will furiously protect **its** young.

> Neither **the soldiers** nor **the sergeant** was sure of **his** location.
> Neither **the sergeant** nor **the soldiers** were sure of **their** location.

Circle the correct pronoun in the following sentences. Answers are at the end of the chapter.

18. Andy or Arvin will bring (his, their) camera so (he, they) can take pictures of the party.

19. One of the file folders isn't in (its, their) drawer.

20. The NAPA store sent Bob and Ray the parts (he, they) had ordered.

21. Benny and (he, him) went to the movies with Bonnie and (I, me).

22. Neither my cousins nor my uncle knows what (he, they) will do tomorrow.

EASILY CONFUSED WORD PAIRS

The following words pairs are often misused in written language. By reading the explanations and looking at the examples, you can learn to use them correctly every time.

Its/it's

Its is a possessive pronoun that means "belonging to it." *It's* is a contraction for *it is* or *it has.* The only time you will ever use *it's* is when you can also substitute the words *it is* or *it has.*

Who/that

Who refers to people. *That* refers to things.

> There is the man **who** helped me find a new pet.
> The woman **who** invented the copper-bottomed kettle died in 1995.

This is the house **that** Harold bought.

The magazine **that** I needed was no longer in print.

There/their/they're

Their is a possessive pronoun that shows ownership. *There* is an adverb that tells where an action or item is located. *They're* is a contraction for the words *they are.* Here is an easy way to remember these words.

- *Their* means "belonging to them." Of the three words, *their* can be most easily transformed into the word *them.* Extend the *r* on the right side and connect the *i* and the *r* to turn *their* into *them.* This clue will help you remember that *their* means "belonging to them."

- If you examine the word *there,* you can see from the way it's written that it contains the word *here.* Whenever you use *there,* you should be able to substitute *here.* The sentence should still make sense.

- Imagine that the apostrophe in *they're* is actually a very small letter *a.* Use *they're* in a sentence only when you can substitute *they are.*

Your/you're

Your is a possessive pronoun that means "belonging to you." *You're* is a contraction for the words *you are.* The only time you will ever use *you're* is when you can also substitute the words *you are.*

To/too/two

To is a preposition or an infinitive.

- As a preposition: to the mall, to the bottom, to my church, to our garage, to his school, to his hideout, to our disadvantage, to an open room, to a ballad, to the gymnasium

- As an infinitive (*to* followed by a verb, sometimes separated by adverbs): to walk, to leap, to see badly, to find, to advance, to read, to build, to sorely want, to badly misinterpret, to carefully peruse

Too means "also." Whenever you use the word *too,* substitute the word *also.* The sentence should still make sense.

Two is a number, as in one, two. If you give it any thought at all, you'll never misuse this form.

The key is to think consciously about these words when you see them in written language. Circle the correct form of these easily confused words in the following sentences. Answers are at the end of the chapter.

23. (Its, It's) (to, too, two) late (to, too,two) remedy the problem now.

24. This is the man (who, that) helped me find the book I needed.

25. (There, Their, They're) going (to, too, two) begin construction as soon as the plans are finished.

26. We left (there, their, they're) house after the storm subsided.

27. I think (your, you're) going (to, too, two) win at least (to, too, two) more times.

28. The corporation moved (its, it's) home office.

ANSWERING MULTIPLE-CHOICE QUESTIONS ON GRAMMAR IN SENTENCES

As you take the portion of the test that assesses your writing skills, apply what you know about the rules of grammar:
- Look for complete sentences.
- Check for endmarks, commas, and apostrophes.
- Look for subject-verb agreement and consistency in verb tense.
- Check the pronouns to make sure the correct form is used and that the number (singular or plural) is correct.
- Check those easily confused pairs of words.

CLEAR SENTENCES

Some civil service exams may ask you to read two or more written versions of the same information and to choose the one that most *clearly* presents accurate information. It may be that all the choices are more or less correct grammatically, but some of them are so poorly written that they're hard to understand. You want the *best* option, the one that's clearest and most accurate. Check for accuracy first. If the facts are wrong, the answer is wrong, no matter how well-written the answer choice is. If the facts are accurately represented in several of the answer choices, then you must evaluate the writing itself. Here are a few tips for choosing the **best** answer.

1. The **best** answer will be written in plain English in such a way that most readers can understand it the first time through. If you read through an answer choice and find you need to reread it to understand what it says, look for a better option.

2. The **best** option will present the information in logical order, usually chronological order. If the order seems questionable or is hard to follow, look for a better option.

3. The **best** option will be written with active rather than passive verbs. Answer choices written with passive verbs sound formal and stuffy. Look for an option that sounds like normal conversation. Here's an example.

Passive Voice

At 8:25 p.m., Officer Sanchez was dispatched to 18 Grand, an apartment complex, where a burglary had been reported by Milo Andrews, the manager.

Active Voice

At 8:25 p.m., Officer Sanchez responded to a burglary reported by Milo Andrews, the manager of an apartment complex at 18 Grand.

The first version uses the passive verbs "was dispatched" and "had been reported" rather than active verbs. Example 2 uses the active verb "responded."

4. The **best** answer contains clearly identified pronouns.

Unclear

Ann Dorr and the officer went to the precinct house, where she made her report.
Bob reminded his father that he had an appointment.

Clear

Ann Dorr and the officer went to the precinct house, where the officer made her report.
Bob reminded his father that Bob had an appointment.

An answer choice with clearly identified pronouns is a better choice than one with uncertain pronoun references. Sometimes the noun must be repeated to make the meaning clear.

5. The **best** option will use words clearly. Watch for unclear modifying words or phrases such as the ones in the following sentences. Misplaced and dangling modifiers can be hard to spot because your brain tries to make sense of things as it reads. In the case of misplaced or dangling modifiers, you may make a logical connection that is not present in the words.

Dangling Modifiers

Nailed to the tree, Cedric saw a "No Hunting" sign.
Waddling down the road, we saw a skunk.

Clear Modifiers

Cedric saw a "No Hunting" sign nailed to a tree.
We saw a skunk waddling down the road.

In the first version of the sentences, it sounds like *Cedric* was nailed to a tree and *we* were waddling down the road. The second version probably represents the writer's intentions: the *sign* was nailed to a tree and the *skunk* was waddling.

Misplaced Modifier

A dog followed the boy who was growling and barking.
George told us about safe sex in the kitchen.

Clear Modifiers

A dog who was growling and barking followed the boy.
In the kitchen, George told us about safe sex.

Do you think the boy was growling and barking? Did George discuss avoiding sharp knives and household poisons? The second version of each sentence represents the real situation.

6. Finally, the **best** option will use words efficiently. Avoid answer choices that are redundant (repeat unnecessarily) or wordy. Extra words take up valuable time and increase the chances that facts will be misunderstood. In the following examples, the italicized words are redundant or unnecessary. Try reading the sentences without the italicized words.

Redundant

They refunded our money *back to us.*
We can proceed *ahead* with the plan we made *ahead of time.*
The car was red *in color.*

Wordy

The reason he pursued the car *was* because it ran a stoplight.

We didn't know what *it was* we were doing.

There are many citizens *who* obey the law.

In each case, the sentence is simpler and easier to read without the italicized words. When you find an answer choice that uses unnecessary words, look for a better option.

The BEST Option:

- Is ACCURATE
- Is written in plain English
- Presents information in a logical order
- Uses active verbs
- Has clearly identified pronouns
- Uses words clearly
- Uses words efficiently

Here are four sample multiple-choice questions. By applying the principles explained in this section, choose the best version of each of the four sets of sentences. The answers and a short explanation for each question are at the end of the chapter.

29.

  a. Vanover caught the ball. This was after it had been thrown by the shortstop. Vanover was the first baseman who caught the double-play ball. The shortstop was Hennings. He caught a line drive.

  b. After the shortstop Hennings caught the line drive, he threw it to the first baseman Vanover for the double play.

  c. After the line drive was caught by Hennings, the shortstop, it was thrown to Vanover at first base for a double play.

  d. Vanover the first baseman caught the flip from shortstop Hennings.

30.

  a. This writer attended the movie *Casino* starring Robert DeNiro.

  b. The movie *Casino* starring Robert DeNiro was attended by me.

  c. The movie *Casino* starring Robert DeNiro was attended by this writer.

  d. I attended the movie *Casino* starring Robert DeNiro.

31.

  a. They gave cereal boxes with prizes inside to the children.

  b. They gave cereal boxes to children with prizes inside.

  c. Children were given boxes of cereal by them with prizes inside.

  d. Children were given boxes of cereal with prizes inside by them.

32.

a. After playing an exciting drum solo, the crowd rose to its feet and then claps and yells until the band plays another cut from their new album.

b. After playing an exciting drum solo, the crowd rose to its feet and then clapped and yelled until the band played another cut from their new album.

c. After the drummer's exciting solo, the crowd rose to its feet and then claps and yells until the band plays another cut from their new album.

d. After the drummer's exciting solo, the crowd rose to its feet and then clapped and yelled until the band played another cut from their new album.

ADDITIONAL RESOURCES

This has been a very quick review of only a few aspects of written English. For more help with these aspects and more, here are some books you can consult.

FOR NON-NATIVE SPEAKERS OF ENGLISH

- *English Made Simple* by Arthur Waldhorn and Arthur Ziegler (Made Simple Books)
- *Errors in English and How to Correct Them* by Harry Shaw (HarperCollins)
- *Living in English* by Betsy J. Blusser (National Textbook Company)

FOR EVERYONE

- *Better English by* Norman Lewis (Dell)
- *Writing Skills in 20 Minutes a Day* by Judith Olson (LearningExpress, order information at the back of this book)
- *1001 Pitfalls in English Grammar* (Barron's)

ANSWERS

1. d.		**14.** Has
2. a.		**15.** a.
3. d.		**16.** b.
4. c.		**17.** d.
5. a.		**18.** his, he
6. a.		**19.** its
7. c.		**20.** they
8. d.		**21.** he, me
9. b.		**22.** he
10. takes		**23.** It's, too, to
11. works		**24.** who
12. helps		**25.** They're, to
13. causes		**26.** their

27. you're, to, two

28. its

29. b. Answer **a** is unnecessarily wordy and the order is not logical. Answer **c** is written using passive voice verbs. Answer **d** omits a piece of important information.

30. d. Both answers **a** and **c** use the stuffy-sounding *this writer.* Answer **d** is best because it uses an active verb.

31. a. In both answers **b** and **c** the modifying phrase *with prizes inside* is misplaced. Both answers **c** and **d** are written in passive rather than active voice.

32. d. Both answers **a** and **b** contain a dangling modifier, stating that the crowd played an exciting drum solo. Both answers **b** and **c** mix past and present verb tense. Only answer **d** has clearly written modifiers and a consistent verb tense.

C·H·A·P·T·E·R 6

READING COMPREHENSION

CHAPTER SUMMARY

Because reading is such a vital skill, the Federal Clerical Exam includes a reading comprehension section that tests your ability to understand what you read. The tips and exercises in this chapter will help you improve your comprehension of written passages, so that you can increase your score in this area.

emos, policies, procedures, reports—these are all things you'll be expected to understand if you become a Federal Clerical Worker. Understanding written materials is part of almost any job. That's why the Federal Clerical Exam attempts to measure how well applicants understand what they read.

Reading comprehension tests are usually in a multiple-choice format and ask questions based on brief passages, much like the standardized tests that are offered in schools. For that matter, almost all standardized test questions test your reading skill. After all, you can't answer the question if you can't read it! Similarly, you can't study your training materials or learn new procedures once you're on the job if you can't read well. So reading comprehension is vital not only on the test but also for the rest of your career.

TYPES OF READING COMPREHENSION QUESTIONS

You have probably encountered reading comprehension questions before, where you are given a passage to read and then have to answer multiple-choice questions about it. This kind of question has two advantages for you as a test taker:

1. You don't have to know anything about the topic of the passage because
2. You're being tested only on the information the passage provides.

But the disadvantage is that you have to know where and how to find that information quickly in an unfamiliar text. This makes it easy to fall for one of the wrong answer choices, especially since they're designed to mislead you.

The best way to do well on this passage/question format is to be very familiar with the kinds of questions that are typically asked on the test. Questions most frequently ask you to:

1. identify a specific **fact or detail** in the passage
2. note the **main idea** of the passage
3. make an **inference** based on the passage
4. define a **vocabulary** word from the passage

In order for you to do well on a reading comprehension test, you need to know exactly what each of these questions is asking. **Facts and details** are the specific pieces of information that support the passage's **main idea**. The main idea is the thought, opinion, or attitude that governs the whole passage. Generally speaking, facts and details are indisputable—things that don't need to be proven, like statistics (18 million people) or descriptions (a green overcoat). Let's say, for example, you read a sentence that says *"After the department's reorganization, workers were 50% more productive."* A sentence like this, which gives you the **fact** that 50% of workers were more productive, might support a **main idea** that says, "*Every department should be reorganized.*" Notice that this main idea is not something indisputable; it is an opinion. The writer thinks all departments should be reorganized, and because this is his opinion (and not everyone shares it), he needs to support his opinion with facts and details.

An **inference**, on the other hand, is a conclusion that can be drawn based on fact or evidence. For example, you can infer—based on the fact that workers became 50% more productive after the reorganization, which is a dramatic change—that the department had not been efficiently organized. The fact sentence, *"After the department's reorganization, workers were 50% more productive,"* also implies that the reorganization of the department was the reason workers became more productive. There may, of course, have been other reasons, but we can infer only one from this sentence.

As you might expect, **vocabulary** questions ask you to determine the meaning of particular words. Often, if you've read carefully, you can determine the meaning of such words from their context—that is, how the word is used in the sentence or paragraph.

PRACTICE PASSAGE 1: USING THE FOUR QUESTION TYPES

The following is a sample test passage, followed by four questions. Read the passage carefully, and then answer the questions, based on your reading of the text, by circling your choice. Then refer to the list above and note under your answer which type of question has been asked. Correct answers appear immediately after the questions.

In the last decade, community policing has been frequently touted as the best way to reform urban law enforcement. The idea of putting more officers on foot patrol in high crime areas, where relations with police have frequently been strained, was initiated in Houston in 1983 under the leadership of then-Commissioner Lee Brown. He believed that officers should be accessible to the community at the street level. If officers were assigned to the same area over a period of time, those officers would eventually build a network of trust with neighborhood residents. That trust would mean that merchants and residents in the community would let officers know about criminal activities in the area and would support police intervention. Since then, many large cities have experimented with Community-Oriented Policing (COP) with mixed results. Some have found that police and citizens are grateful for the opportunity to work together. Others have found that unrealistic expectations by citizens and resistance from officers have combined to hinder the effectiveness of COP. It seems possible, therefore, that a good idea may need improvement before it can truly be considered a reform.

1. Community policing has been used in law enforcement since
   a. the late 1970s
   b. the early 1980s
   c. the Carter administration
   d. Lee Brown was New York City Police Commissioner

   Question type_____

2. The phrase "a network of trust" in this passage suggests that
   a. police officers can rely only on each other for support
   b. community members rely on the police to protect them
   c. police and community members rely on each other
   d. community members trust only each other

   Question type_____

3. The best title for this passage would be
   a. Community Policing: The Solution to the Drug Problem
   b. Houston Sets the Pace in Community Policing
   c. Communities and Cops: Partners for Peace
   d. Community Policing: An Uncertain Future?

   Question type_____

4. The word "touted" in the first sentence of the passage most nearly means
   a. praised
   b. denied
   c. exposed
   d. criticized

   Question type_____

ANSWERS AND EXPLANATIONS FOR PRACTICE PASSAGE 1

Don't just look at the right answers and move on. The explanations are the most important part, so read them carefully. Use these explanations to help you understand how to tackle each kind of question the next time you come across it.

1. b. Question type: 1, fact or detail. The passage says that community policing began "in the last decade." A decade is a period of ten years. In addition, the passage identifies 1983 as the first large-scale use of community policing in Houston. Don't be misled by trying to figure out when Carter was president. Also, if you happen to know that Lee Brown was New York City's police commissioner, don't let that information lead you away from the information contained in the passage alone. Brown was commissioner in Houston when he initiated community policing.

2. c. Question type: 3, inference. The "network of trust" referred to in this passage is between the community and the police, as you can see from the sentence where the phrase appears. The key phrase in the question is *in this passage.* You may think that police can rely only on each other, or one of the other answer choices may appear equally plausible to you. But your choice of answers must be limited to the one suggested *in this passage.* Another tip for questions like this: Beware of absolutes! Be suspicious of any answer containing words like *only, always,* or *never.*

3. d. Question type: 2, main idea. The title always expresses the main idea. In this passage, the main idea comes at the end. The sum of all the details in the passage suggests that community policing is not without its critics and that therefore its future is uncertain. Another key phrase is *mixed results,* which means that some communities haven't had full success with community policing.

4. a. Question type: 4, vocabulary. The word *touted* is linked in this passage with the phrase *the best way to reform.* Most people would think that a good way to reform something is praiseworthy. In addition, the next few sentences in the passage describe the benefits of community policing. Criticism or a negative response to the subject doesn't come until later in the passage.

DETAIL AND MAIN IDEA QUESTIONS

Main idea questions and fact or detail questions are both asking you for information that's right there in the passage. All you have to do is find it.

DETAIL OR FACT QUESTIONS

In detail or fact questions, you have to identify a specific item of information from the test. This is usually the simplest kind of question. You just have to be able to separate important information from less important information. However, the choices may often be very similar, so you must be careful not to get confused.

Be sure you read the passage and questions carefully. In fact, it is usually a good idea to read the questions first, *before* you even read the passage, so you'll know what details to look out for.

MAIN IDEA QUESTIONS

The main idea of a passage, like that of a paragraph or a book, is what it is *mostly* about. The main idea is like an umbrella that covers all of the ideas and details in the passage, so it is usually something general, not specific. For example, in Practice Passage 1, question 3 asked you what title would be best for the passage, and the correct answer was "Community Policing: An Uncertain Future." This is the best answer because it's the only one that includes both the positive and negative sides of community policing, both of which are discussed in the passage.

Sometimes the main idea is stated clearly, often in the first or last sentence of the passage—the main idea is expressed in the *last* sentence of Practice Passage 1, for example. The sentence that expresses the main idea is often referred to as the **topic sentence**.

At other times, the main idea is not stated in a topic sentence but is *implied* in the overall passage, and you'll need to determine the main idea by inference. Because there may be much information in the passage, the trick is to understand what all that information adds up to—the gist of what the author wants you to know. Often some of the wrong answers on main idea questions are specific facts or details from the passage. A good way to test yourself is to ask, "Can this answer serve as a *net* to hold the whole passage together?" If not, chances are you've chosen a fact or detail, not a main idea.

PRACTICE PASSAGE 2: DETAIL AND MAIN IDEA QUESTIONS

Practice answering main idea and detail questions by working on the questions that follow this passage. Circle the answers to the questions, and then check your answers against the key that appears immediately after the questions.

There are three different kinds of burns: first degree, second degree, and third degree. It is important for firefighters to be able to recognize each of these types of burns so that they can be sure burn victims are given proper medical treatment. The least serious burn is the first-degree burn, which causes the skin to turn red but does not cause blistering. A mild sunburn is a good example of a first-degree burn, and, like a mild sunburn, first-degree burns generally do not require medical treatment other than a gentle cooling of the burned skin with ice or cold tap water. Second-degree burns, on the other hand, do cause blistering of the skin and should be treated immediately. These burns should be immersed in warm water and then wrapped in a sterile dressing or bandage. (Do not apply butter or grease to these burns; despite the old wives' tale, butter does *not* help burns heal and actually increases chances of infection.) If second-degree burns cover a large part of the body, then the victim should be taken to the hospital immediately for medical care. Third-degree burns are those that char the skin and turn it black, or burn so deeply that the skin shows white. These burns usually result from direct contact with flames and have a great chance of becoming infected. All third-degree burns should receive immediate hospital care. They should not be immersed in water, and charred clothing should not be removed from the victim. If possible, a sterile dressing or bandage should be applied to burns before the victim is transported to the hospital.

1. Which of the following would be the best title for this passage?
    a. Dealing with Third-Degree Burns
    b. How to Recognize and Treat Different Burns
    c. Burn Categories
    d. Preventing Infection in Burns

2. Second-degree burns should be treated with
    a. butter
    b. nothing
    c. cold water
    d. warm water

3. First-degree burns turn the skin
   a. red
   b. blue
   c. black
   d. white

4. Which of the following best expresses the main idea of the passage?
   a. There are three different types of burns.
   b. Firefighters should always have cold compresses on hand.
   c. Different burns require different types of treatment.
   d. Butter is not good for healing burns.

ANSWERS AND EXPLANATIONS FOR PRACTICE PASSAGE 2

1. **b.** A question that asks you to choose a title for a passage is a main idea question. This main idea is expressed in the second sentence, the topic sentence: "It is important for firefighters to be able to recognize each of these types of burns so that they can be sure burn victims are given proper treatment." Answer **b** expresses this idea and is the only title that encompasses all of the ideas expressed in the passage. Answer **a** is too limited; it deals only with one of the kinds of burns discussed in the passage. Likewise, answers **c** and **d** are also too limited. Answer **c** covers types of burns but not their treatment, and **d** deals only with preventing infection, which is only a secondary part of the discussion of treatment.

2. **d.** The answer to this fact question is clearly expressed in the sentence, "These burns should be immersed in warm water and then wrapped in a sterile dressing or bandage." The hard part is keeping track of whether "These burns" refers to the kind of burns in the question, which is second-

degree burns. It's easy to choose a wrong answer here because all of the answer choices are mentioned in the passage. You need to read carefully to be sure you match the right burn to the right treatment.

3. **a.** This is another fact or detail question. The passage says that a first-degree burn "causes the skin to turn red." Again, it's important to read carefully because all of the answer choices (except **b**, which can be eliminated immediately) are listed elsewhere in the passage.

4. **c.** Clearly this is a main idea question, and **c** is the only answer that encompasses the whole passage. Answers **b** and **d** are limited to *particular* burns or treatments, and answer **a** discusses only burns and not their treatment. In addition, the second sentence tells us that "It is important for firefighters to be able to *recognize each of these types of burns so that they can be sure burn victims are given proper medical treatment.*"

INFERENCE AND VOCABULARY QUESTIONS

Questions that ask you about the meaning of vocabulary words in the passage and those that ask what the passage *suggests* or *implies* (inference questions) are different from detail or main idea questions. In vocabulary and inference questions, you usually have to pull ideas from the passage, sometimes from more than one place in the passage.

INFERENCE QUESTIONS

Inference questions can be the most difficult to answer because they require you to draw meaning from the text when that meaning is implied rather than directly stated. Inferences are conclusions that we draw based on the clues the writer has given us. When you draw inferences, you have to be something of a detective, looking for such clues as word choice, tone, and specific details that suggest a certain conclusion, attitude, or point of view. You have to read between the lines in order to make a judgment about what an author was implying in the passage.

A good way to test whether you've drawn an acceptable inference is to ask, "What evidence do I have for this inference?" If you can't find any, you probably have the wrong answer. You need to be sure that your inference is logical and that it is based on something that is suggested or implied in the passage itself—not on what you or others might think. Like a good detective, you need to base your conclusions on evidence—facts, details, and other information—not on random hunches or guesses.

VOCABULARY QUESTIONS

Questions designed to test vocabulary are really trying to measure how well you can figure out the meaning of an unfamiliar word from its context. *Context* refers to the words and ideas surrounding a vocabulary word. If the context is clear enough, you should be able to substitute a nonsense word for the one being sought and still make the right choice because you could determine meaning strictly from the sense of the sentence. For example, you should be able to determine the meaning of the italicized nonsense word below based on its context:

The speaker noted that it gave him great *terivinix* to announce the winner of the Outstanding Leadership Award.

In this sentence, *terivinix* most likely means

a. pain
b. sympathy
c. pleasure
d. anxiety

Clearly, the context of an award makes c, *pleasure*, the best choice. Awards don't usually bring pain, sympathy, or anxiety.

When confronted with an unfamiliar word, try substituting a nonsense word and see if the context gives you the clue. If you're familiar with prefixes, suffixes, and word roots, you can also use this knowledge to help you determine the meaning of an unfamiliar word.

You should be careful not to guess at the answer to vocabulary questions based on how you may have seen the word used before or what you *think* it means. Many words have more than one possible meaning, depending on the context in which they're used, and a word you've seen used one way may mean something else in a test passage. Also, if you don't look at the context carefully, you may make the mistake of confusing the vocabulary word with a similar word. For example, the vocabulary word may be *taut* (meaning *tight*), but if you read too quickly or don't check the context, you might think the word is *tout* (meaning *publicize* or *praise*) or *taunt* (meaning *tease*). Always make sure you read carefully and that what you think the word means fits into the context of the passage you're being tested on.

PRACTICE PASSAGE 3: INFERENCE AND VOCABULARY QUESTIONS

The questions that follow this passage are strictly vocabulary and inference questions. Circle the answers to the questions, and then check your answers against the key that appears immediately after the questions.

Dealing with irritable patients is a great challenge for health-care workers on every level. It is critical that you do not lose your patience when confronted by such a patient. When handling irate patients, be sure to remember that they are not angry at you; they are simply projecting their anger at something else *onto* you. Remember that if you respond to these patients as irritably as they act with you, you will only increase their hostility, making it much more difficult to give them proper treatment. The best thing to do is to remain calm and ignore any imprecations patients may hurl your way. Such patients may be irrational and may not realize what they're saying. Often these patients will purposely try to anger you just to get some reaction out of you. If you react to this behavior with anger, they win by getting your attention, but you both lose because the patient is less likely to get proper care.

1. The word "irate" as it is used in the passage most nearly means
   a. irregular, odd
   b. happy, cheerful
   c. ill-tempered, angry
   d. sloppy, lazy

2. The passage suggests that health-care workers
   a. easily lose control of their emotions
   b. are better off not talking to their patients
   c. must be careful in dealing with irate patients because the patients may sue the hospital
   d. may provide inadequate treatment if they become angry at patients

3. An "imprecation" is most likely
   a. an object
   b. a curse
   c. a joke
   d. a medication

4. Which of the following best expresses the writer's views about irate patients?
   a. Some irate patients just want attention.
   b. Irate patients are always miserable.
   c. Irate patients should be made to wait for treatment.
   d. Managing irate patients is the key to a successful career.

ANSWERS AND EXPLANATIONS FOR PRACTICE PASSAGE 3

1. **c.** This is a vocabulary question. *Irate* means *ill-tempered, angry*. It should be clear that **b**, *happy, cheerful*, is not the answer; dealing with happy patients is normally not "a great challenge." Patients that are **a**, *irregular, odd*, or **d**, *sloppy, lazy*, may be a challenge in their own way, but they aren't likely to rouse a health-care worker to anger. In addition, the passage explains that irate patients are not "*angry* at you," and *irate* is used as a synonym for *irritable*, which describes the patients under discussion in the very first sentence.

2. **d.** This is an inference question, as the phrase "the passage *suggests*" might have told you. The idea that angry health-care workers might give inadequate treatment is implied by the passage as a whole,

which seems to be an attempt to prevent angry reactions to irate patients. Furthermore, the last sentence in particular makes this inference possible: "If you react to this behavior with anger . . . you both lose because the patient is less likely to get proper care." Answer **c** is not correct, because while it may be true that some irate patients have sued the hospital in the past, there is no mention of suits anywhere in this passage. Likewise, answer **b** is incorrect; the passage does suggest ignoring patients' insults, but nowhere does it recommend not talking to patients—it simply recommends not talking angrily. And while it may be true that some health-care workers may lose control of their emotions, the passage does not provide any facts or details to support answer **a**, that they "*easily* lose control." Watch out for key works like *easily* that may distort the intent of the passage.

3. **b.** If you didn't know what an imprecation is, the context should reveal that it's something you can ignore, so neither **a**, an *object*, nor **d**, a *medication*, is a likely answer. Furthermore, **c** is not likely either, since an irate patient is not likely to be making jokes.

4. **a.** The writer seems to believe that some irate patients just want attention, as is suggested when the writer says, "Often these patients will purposely try to anger you just to get some reaction out of you. If you react to this behavior with anger, they win *by getting your attention.*" It should be clear that **b** cannot be the answer, because it includes an absolute: "Irate patients are *always* miserable." Perhaps *some* of the patients are *often* miserable, but an absolute like *always* is almost always wrong. Besides, this passage refers to patients who may be irate in the hospital, but we have no indication of what these patients are like at other times, and *miserable* and *irate* are not exactly the same thing,

either. Answer **c** is also incorrect because the purpose of the passage is to ensure that patients receive "proper treatment" and that irate patients are not discriminated against because of their behavior. Thus, "irate patients should be made to wait for treatment" is not a logical answer. Finally, **d** cannot be correct because though it may be true, there is no discussion of career advancement in the passage.

REVIEW: PUTTING IT ALL TOGETHER

A good way to solidify what you've learned about reading comprehension questions is for *you* to write the questions. Here's a passage, followed by space for you to write your own questions. Write one question of each of the four types: fact or detail, main idea, inference, and vocabulary.

The "broken window" theory was originally developed to explain how minor acts of vandalism or disrespect can quickly escalate to crimes and attitudes that break down the entire social fabric of an area. It is a theory that can easily be applied to any situation in society. The theory contends that if a broken window in an abandoned building is not replaced quickly, soon all the windows will be broken. In other words, a small violation, if condoned, leads others to commit similar or greater violations. Thus, after all the windows have been broken, the building is likely to be looted and perhaps even burned down. According to this theory, violations increase exponentially. Thus, if disrespect to a superior is tolerated, others will be tempted to be disrespectful as well. A management crisis could erupt literally overnight. For example, if one firefighter begins to disregard proper housewatch procedure by neglecting to keep

If English Isn't Your First Language

When non-native speakers of English have trouble with reading comprehension tests, it's often because they lack the cultural, linguistic, and historical frame of reference that native speakers enjoy. People who have not lived in or been educated in the U.S. often don't have the background information that comes from reading American newspapers, magazines, and textbooks.

A second problem for non-native English speakers is the difficulty in recognizing vocabulary and idioms (expressions like "chewing the fat") that assist comprehension. In order to read with good understanding, it's important to have an immediate grasp of as many words as possible in the text. Test takers need to be able to recognize vocabulary and idioms immediately so that the ideas those words express are clear.

The Long View

Read newspapers, magazines, and other periodicals that deal with current events and matters of local, state, and national importance. Pay special attention to articles related to the career you want to pursue.

Be alert to new or unfamiliar vocabulary or terms that occur frequently in the popular press. Use a highlighter pen to mark new or unfamiliar words as you read. Keep a list of those words and their definitions. Review them for 15 minutes each day. Though at first you may find yourself looking up a lot of words, don't be frustrated—you'll look up fewer and fewer as your vocabulary expands.

During the Test

When you are taking the test, make a picture in your mind of the situation being described in the passage. Ask yourself, "What did the writer mostly want me to think about this subject?"

Locate and underline the topic sentence that carries the main idea of the passage. Remember that the topic sentence—if there is one—may not always be the first sentence. If there doesn't seem to be one, try to determine what idea summarizes the whole passage.

up the housewatch administrative journal, and this firefighter is not reprimanded, others will follow suit by committing similar violations of procedure, thinking, "If he can get away with it, why can't I?" So what starts out as a small thing, a violation that may seem not to warrant disciplinary action, may actually ruin the efficiency of the entire firehouse, putting the people the firehouse serves at risk.

1. Detail question:_____
   a.
   b.
   c.
   d.

2. Main idea question:_____
   a.
   b.
   c.
   d.

3. Inference question_____
   a.
   b.
   c.
   d.

4. Vocabulary question_____
   a.
   b.
   c.
   d.

POSSIBLE QUESTIONS

Here is one question of each type based on the passage above. Your questions may be very different, but these will give you an idea of the kinds of questions that could be asked.

1. Detail question: According to the passage, which of the following could happen "overnight"?
   a. The building will be burned down.
   b. The firehouse may become unmanageable.
   c. A management crisis might erupt.
   d. The windows will all be broken.

2. Main idea question: Which of the following best expresses the main idea of the passage?
   a. Even minor infractions warrant disciplinary action.
   b. Broken windows must be repaired immediately.
   c. People shouldn't be disrespectful to their superiors.
   d. Housewatch must be taken seriously.

3. Inference question: The passage suggests that
   a. the broken window theory is inadequate
   b. managers need to know how to handle a crisis
   c. firefighters are lazy
   d. people will get away with as much as they can

4. Vocabulary question: In this passage, *condoned* most nearly means
   a. punished
   b. overlooked
   c. condemned
   d. applauded

Answers
   1. c.
   2. a.
   3. d.
   4. b.

ADDITIONAL RESOURCES

Here are some other ways you can build the vocabulary and knowledge that will help you do well on reading comprehension questions.

- Practice asking the four sample question types about passages you read for information or pleasure.
- If you belong to a computer network such as America Online or Compuserve, search out arti-

cles related to a federal clerical career. Exchange views with others on the Internet. All of these exchanges will help expand your knowledge of job-related material that may appear in a passage on the test.

- Use your library. Many public libraries have sections, sometimes called "Lifelong Learning Centers," that contain materials for adult learners. In these sections you can find books with exercises in reading and study skills. It's also a good idea to enlarge your base of information by reading related books and articles. Many libraries have computer systems that allow you to access information quickly and easily. Library personnel will show you how to use the computers and microfilm and microfiche machines.

- Begin now to build a broad knowledge of your potential profession. Get in the habit of reading articles in newspapers and magazines on job-related issues. Keep a clipping file of those articles. This will help keep you informed of trends in the profession and familiarize you with pertinent vocabulary.

- If you need more help building your reading skills and taking reading comprehension tests, consider *Reading Comprehension in 20 Minutes a Day* by Elizabeth Chesla, published by LearningExpress. Order information is in the back of this book.

WORD RELATIONS

CHAPTER SUMMARY
The Word Relations (analogy) portion of the Verbal Ability
section of the Clerical and Administrative Support Exam tests
your capacity to reason with words and to see relationships
between concepts. This chapter will describe the word relations part of the exam and give tips on how to approach it.

Some of the questions on the Verbal Ability section of the Federal Clerical Exam are Word Relations questions. These are
analogies similar to the type you may have seen on other
standardized tests. Basically these questions test your ability
to recognize what words mean and to understand the logical relationships
between words.

WHAT WORD RELATIONS QUESTIONS ARE LIKE

On this portion of the Federal Clerical Exam, you will be given a set of two
capitalized words that are related, followed by a third capitalized word and
four choices in lower case. Of the four choices, you will be asked to identify the word that best completes the second set so that it expresses the same
relationship as the first set. For each such problem, you should choose the
BEST answer. For example, you might be given the following:

1. ANTACID is related to HEARTBURN as BANDAGE is related to
   a. wound
   b. injection
   c. sprain
   d. welt

The correct answer is **a,** *wound.* This is a **use or function** analogy. (See below for a discussion of types of analogy.) *Antacid* is used to treat *heartburn;* a *bandage* is used to treat a *wound.* Note that all the other choices are loosely associated with injury or illness, but that there is only the one clearly BEST answer.

TYPES OF ANALOGIES

Below are some common types of analogies, although the list is not exhaustive.

Classification
In a **classification** analogy, one word is a type or subset of the other.

2. MOUSE is related to MAMMAL as PICKUP is related to
   a. car
   b. wheel
   c. truck
   d. driver

Choice **c** is correct. A *mouse* is a type of *mammal;* a *pickup* is a type of *truck.*

Trait or Characteristic
One word may be a **trait or characteristic** of the other.

3. MISER is related to HOARDING as TYCOON is related to
   a. luxury
   b. wealth
   c. stinginess
   d. greed

Choice **b** is correct. *Hoarding* is the main trait or characteristic of a *miser; wealth* is a main trait or characteristic of a *tycoon.*

Proportion or Degree
In another kind of analogy, one word may represent an **enlargement or diminishment,** or **increase or decrease,** of the other; there may be a difference of degree between the two words. The same difference in degree will exist between the other two words, although they may otherwise have no relation to the first set of words.

4. GALE is related to BREEZE as TERROR is related to
   a. uneasiness
   b. scream
   c. intimidation
   d. irritation

Choice **a** is correct. A *gale* is a high wind; a *breeze* is a gentle wind. *Terror* is extreme fright; *uneasiness* is mild fright.

Cause and Effect
Some analogies will rely on **cause-and-effect,** or **effect-and-cause.**

5. WEEPING is related to GRIEF as TANTRUM is related to
   a. fit

b. kicking

c. loudness

d. rage

Choice **d** is correct. *Weeping* is caused by *grief*; a *tantrum* is caused by *rage*. Always look for the relationship between the words. A *tantrum* is a **kind of** *fit*, but it is not **caused by** a fit. The two words, *tantrum* and *fit*, are not related in the same way as the words *weeping* and *grief* are related.

Use or Function

In a **use or function** analogy, one word expresses the use or function of the other.

6. GALLOWS is related to HANG as NEEDLE is related to

a. embroider

b. stitch

c. sharp

d. thread

Choice **b** is correct. A *gallows* is made expressly in order to *hang* criminals; a *needle* is made expressly to *stitch* fabric. Note that while a *needle* may be used to *embroider* (choice **a**), that is not its only, or even its main, function. A needle may be *sharp*, (choice **c**), and one may *thread* (choice **d**) a needle (that is, put thread through the eye of a needle), but neither word describes the function of a needle.

Similarity or Difference

Analogies may express a **similarity or difference**. In this type, the second word will be a synonym or antonym of the first word, and so you will have to look for an answer choice that is also a synonym or antonym.

7. LOVE is related to HATE as LIBERTINE is related to

a. lover

b. criminal

c. prude

d. minister

Love and *hate* are opposite emotions; a *libertine* and a *prude* are opposite kinds of people. Thus, the correct choice is **c**. This kind of question will test your vocabulary as well as your ability to reason about the relationships of words. If you didn't know what a *libertine* was, you might have a tough time choosing the correct answer.

Part-to-Whole or Whole-to-Part

An analogy may rely on a **part-to-whole** or **whole-to-part** relationship—that is, the second word may be a part of the thing expressed in the first word, or vice versa.

8. TEETH is related to MOUTH as BRICK is related to

a. kiln

b. wall

c. clay

d. masonry

Choice **b** is correct. *Teeth* are a part of the *mouth*; *bricks* may be part of a *wall*. One might be able to say that *clay* is a part of brick (choice **c**), but in that case the order would be reversed. Remember that if the order is part-to-whole, then the answer must be part-to-whole, not the other way around.

Association

The relationship may between the words may express a strong **association** or a connection between the meanings of the two words.

9. HALLOWEEN is related to WITCH as SHAMROCK is related to
   a. luck
   b. plant
   c. holiday
   d. health

Choice **a** is correct. There is a strong association between *witches* and *Halloween* and there is a strong association between *shamrock* and *luck*. Shamrock is a *plant* (choice **b**) and it is related to a *holiday* (choice **c**), St. Patrick's Day, but the relationship is not a strong, immediate association. Shamrock isn't associated with *health* at all (choice **d**), except that health could be thought of as luck, but that association is too distant and vague.

HOW TO PREPARE FOR ANALOGY QUESTIONS

Discern the Meaning of the Words

The first challenge is often simply to know what one or more of the words in the question mean. To learn them, you will use the skills you acquired in studying Chapter 4, Vocabulary and Spelling. Pay particular attention to word parts when you encounter an unfamiliar word. For example, suppose you had the following analogy:

10. RASH is related to SKIN as JAUNDICE is related to
    a. liver
    b. kidney
    c. lung
    d. heart

The correct answer is **a**. In order find this answer, however, you will obviously have to know what the word *jaundice* means. Remember that the best way to improve your vocabulary is to read widely.

Discern the Relationship

After discerning the meaning of the words, you must master the art of seeing relationships between concepts. Knowing the types of analogy listed above is the first step. The best way to find the relationship in a given question is to *make up a sentence to describe the relationship*, like the sentences given in the answer explanations above. For instance, examine the following analogy:

11. GROOM is related to WEDDING as LAWYER is related to
    a. crime
    b. accident
    c. trial
    d. client

This is a **part-to-whole** analogy. A sentence describing the nature of the analogy might go like this: A *groom* is a member of (or a *part* of) a *wedding*; a *lawyer* is a part of a _____. The correct answer is *trial*, as this is the only word that would logically complete the sentence.

You must *read all the choices in each question carefully*, as it is easy to mistake one kind of analogy for another and to make the wrong answer choice. Formulating a sentence that expresses the relationship is the best way to avoid this mistake. Take the following example.

12. DIRGE is related to FUNERAL as JINGLE is related to
   a. chain
   b. bell
   c. telephone
   d. commercial

Even a hasty reading will rule out *chain*; however, there is some kind of association between *jingle* and each of the other choices. But if you make up a sentence describing the kind of analogy you are dealing with, you won't choose one of the wrong answers. A *dirge* is part of a *funeral*; a *jingle* is part of a _____. Once you have established that this is a part-to-whole analogy, you will see that the answer is clearly choice **d**, *commercial*. A *jingle* is not PART of a bell or telephone in the same way that a dirge is part of a funeral, although the objects in the other choices may make a jingling sound.

Remember that a Word May Have Several Meanings

Words often have more than one meaning, or varying shades of meaning. Be careful to avoid confusion on this point. Question 12 above illustrates this point. A *jingle* may be a little song or it may be a sound. In this case, you wanted the meaning of *a little song*, because a *dirge* is a song. (You also have to have a strong enough vocabulary to know what the word *dirge* means.) Similarly, you may injure your *arm*, or you may *arm* yourself or carry *arm*s.

FOR PRACTICE

Here are some analogy questions for you practice on. Following the questions, you will find the answers and explanations. Be sure to pay close attention to the answer explanations to help you brush up on techniques for approaching the problems and to help you assess your strengths and weaknesses.

PRACTICE QUESTIONS

13. SKY is related to CLOUD as SILVER is related to
   a. tarnish
   b. luster
   c. coin
   d. metal

14. ENRAGED is related to IRRITATED as BROKEN is related to
   a. smashed
   b. damaged
   c. cracked
   d. irreparable

15. EXPLORE is related to DISCOVERY as IMBIBE is related to
   a. sobriety
   b. fermentation
   c. liquidity
   d. tipsiness

16. COMPASSION is related to KINDNESS as VALIDATE is related to
   a. keep
   b. reward
   c. confirm
   d. strengthen

17. ORGAN is related to HEART as DOG is related to
   a. canine
   b. poodle
   c. breed
   d. mammal

18. FISH is related to FIN as BIRD is related to
   a. feather
   b. wing
   c. beak
   d. song

19. HISTORY is related to ANCIENT as SCIENCE is related to
   a. natural
   b. proof
   c. biology
   d. prehistory

20. COIN is related to METAL as CLOUD is related to
   a. storm
   b. sun
   c. droplets
   d. white

TIPS FOR ANSWERING WORD RELATIONS QUESTIONS

- **Practice,** using the sample questions in this chapter.
- **Read widely** to improve your general vocabulary and your ability to analyze relationships between words
- If you are unsure of the meaning of a word, **dissect the word** to find its root and its prefix and suffix if any.
- **Discern** the meanings of the words in the analogy, and then **formulate** the relationship as a sentence.

ANSWERS

13. a. This analogy deals with a **trait or characteristic:** *Clouds* can dull the shine or color of the *sky*, just as *tarnish* can dull the luster of *silver*. Silver may have *luster* (choice **b**), but luster does not dull it. Silver may be made into a *coin* (choice **c**) and silver is a *metal* (choice **d**), but neither of these words denote a lessening of shine or color.

14. c. This analogy concerns **proportion or degree.** To be *enraged* is to be violently angry; to be *irritated* is to be mildly angry. To be *broken* is to be severely damaged; to be *cracked* is to be mildly damaged.

15. d. This is a **cause-and-effect** analogy. If you *explore*, generally this will lead you to *discovery*; if you *imbibe* (alcohol), this may lead you to *tipsiness*. Imbibing does not cause the other choices.

16. c. This is a analogy that deals with **similarities.** *Compassion* and *kindness* are similar; to *validate* and to *confirm* are the same.

17. b. This is a **classification** analogy. A *heart* is a type of *organ*. A *poodle* is a type of *dog*. Note that the order of the words in the analogy is important. In this case, the word *organ* comes first, then the subtype *heart*; similarly, the word *dog* comes first, so you want a subtype. Thus, choices **a** and **d** and are wrong; although a dog is a type of *mammal* and a type of *canine*, neither a mammal nor a canine is a type of dog. Choice **c** is wrong because a dog is of a certain *breed*, but it is not a type of breed.

18. b. This is a **use or function** analogy. A *fish* is propelled through the water by its *fins*; a *bird* is propelled through the air by its *wing*s. Choices **a** and **c**, *feather* and *beak*, are parts of a bird, and choice **d**, *song*, is something that characterizes a bird, but none of these choices aid locomotion the way a *wing* does, or the way a *fin* does. (Be careful not to confuse this with a part-to-whole analogy—if it were, there would be two correct answers, *feather* and *beak*. Again, be sure to read all the answers carefully.)

19. a. This is a **part-to-whole** analogy. *Ancient* history is a branch of *history* (that is, a category within the study of history) and *natural* science is a branch of *science* (a category within the study of science); furthermore, the words *ancient* and *natural* are commonly used as adjectives to describe these branches of *history* and *science*. Choice **b** is wrong because *proof* is neither a category nor an adjective. Choice **c** is wrong because, although *biology* is a branch of science, it is a noun and therefore not the BEST answer. Choice **d** is wrong because, although science may study *prehistory*, the word *prehistory* is a noun and it is not a word commonly used to denote a branch of science.

20. c. This is an analogy very similar to a **whole-to-part** analogy, except, in this case, an object is made up entirely of some substance. A *coin* is composed entirely of *metal*; a *cloud* is composed entirely of *droplets* of moisture. A cloud is not composed entirely of a *storm* or (obviously) of the *sun* (choices **a** and **b**). A cloud may be *white* (choice **d**), but cannot be said to be composed entirely of *white*.

C·H·A·P·T·E·R 8

NAME AND NUMBER COMPARISONS

CHAPTER SUMMARY

The Name and Number Comparison questions on the Clerical Aptitude portion of the Federal Clerical Exam are designed to test your attention to detail. All of the questions have identical answer choices, which ask you to compare a set of words or numbers and determine if they are all the same, if two of them are the same, or if they are all different. This chapter gives you some tips on the best ways to approach these questions.

The federal government, in its various departments, agencies, and bureaus, touches many, if not most, of the aspects of our daily life. It is imperative that reliable records be made and saved, logging the government's interactions with its citizens. Accuracy is crucial in federal government clerical work. That's why the Federal Clerical Exam includes a section on Clerical Aptitude.

The Clerical Aptitude portion of the Clerical and Administrative Support Exam contains four different types of questions. There is a total of 120 questions, 30 of each type. The purpose of this portion of the exam is to check your ability to work quickly as well as accurately.

Some people short themselves on their preparation time for this portion of the Federal Clerical Exam. Unlike the Verbal Abilities portion of the test, the clerical tasks seem to be things that many of us "just know"—

simple math, alphabetizing, and recognizing when words, letters, and numbers are the same or different. Nonetheless, it is as important to prepare for this part of the test as for the verbal test.

HOW TO PREPARE FOR THE TEST

TIMING

You have an average of 7.5 seconds to answer each question on the Clerical Aptitude portion of the Clerical and Administrative Support Exam, since there are a total of 120 questions that must be answered in 15 minutes. These questions appear in the test in groups of five, mixed in with groups of five of the other types of questions. So, if the test begins with five questions on Name and Number Comparisons, the next five (6 through 10) might be Alphabetizing, followed by five (11 through 15) Arithmetic questions, and finally, five (16 through 20) Number and Letter Matching questions and so on through number 120. So, you don't have time while you are taking the test to get into the rhythm of any one of the four kinds of questions. You'll be much better off if you have practiced them all many times so that you know how best to approach them and so that you can "switch gears" as you move from one kind of question to another and another and another.

THE INSTRUCTIONS

Because of the way the test is constructed, you will not have time to puzzle over each set of five questions each time they appear. To avoid this, practice each type of question until you know exactly how each of them works. However, on test day, don't neglect to listen to and read the instructions. It is unlikely that there will be any major changes on the test, but paying close attention to the instructions on test day refreshes your memory about the test.

THE ANSWER SHEET

As with any machine-scored test, it is imperative that you fill out your answer sheet correctly and that you make sure to keep your place as you work through the test. If you accidentally answer question ten, but write the answer on row nine, all of your answers from nine on will be scored as wrong. Before you enter the exam room, you should have decided on a method for marking a question as a skip. You cannot make extraneous marks on your answer sheet, but you can mark a skipped question number in your test book or jot it down on your scratch paper. Just make sure if you skip a question, you skip that row on your answer sheet!

GUESSING

In the Clerical Aptitude portion of the Federal Clerical Exam, you should **not** guess the answer to a question unless you are fairly certain about your guess. There is a penalty on this test for wrong answers. The test is scored by adding up the number of correct answers, and then subtracting one-fourth of the total of the wrong answers. However, there is no penalty for skipping a question. So, if you answer a total of 87 questions (meaning that you skip or don't have time for 33 questions), and you get 79 questions correct (meaning that you get 8 questions incorrect), your score will be 77—that is, 79 (the number correct) minus 2 (one-quarter of the number wrong) equals 77. Since your time is limited and there is a penalty for wrong answers, when you come across a question that you just can't seem to figure out, your best bet is to skip it. Mark it as a skip and, if you have time, you can come back and try to figure it out; however, remember that it is better to leave it blank than to get it wrong.

WHAT NAME AND NUMBER COMPARISON QUESTIONS ARE LIKE

Thirty of the questions on the Clerical Aptitude portion of the Federal Clerical Exam are Name and Number Comparison questions. For these questions, all of the answer choices are the same for each set:

- choice **a** is always "if ALL THREE names or numbers are exactly ALIKE"
- choice **b** is always "if only the FIRST and SECOND names or numbers are exactly ALIKE"
- choice **c** is always "if only the FIRST and THIRD names or numbers are exactly ALIKE"
- choice **d** is always "if only the SECOND and THIRD names or numbers are exactly ALIKE"
- choice **e** is always "if ALL THREE names or numbers are DIFFERENT"

These answer choices are repeated with each set of five Name and Number Comparison questions; you don't have to memorize them or flip back and forth between pages. Nevertheless, you should become very familiar with these choices so that you don't have to waste time during the exam looking up to see what each answer letter means.

The questions in the Name and Number Comparison portion consist of three names or numbers. The numbers are usually seven digits; the names are usually people's names. For each of the questions, you must decide if all three numbers or names are the same, if only two are the same, or if they are all different. The best thing you can do to prepare for these questions is to practice Name and Number Comparisons before you take your Federal Clerical Exam.

Remember: The more you practice these questions, the more familiar you will be with the format. Here is what these questions look like:

In questions 1 through 5, compare the three names or numbers and mark the answer:

    a. if ALL THREE names or numbers are exactly ALIKE
    b. if only the FIRST and SECOND names or numbers are exactly ALIKE
    c. if only the FIRST and THIRD names or numbers are exactly ALIKE
    d. if only the SECOND and THIRD names or numbers are exactly ALIKE
    e. if ALL THREE names or numbers are DIFFERENT

1.	Larry W. Cramden	Larry M. Cramden	Larry W. Cramden
2.	8380215	8380215	8830215
3.	Jessica Street	Jessica Sheet	Jessica Streit
4.	3947120	3947120	3947120
5.	Michael Seyler, Jr.	Michael Sayler, Jr.	Michael Sayler, Jr.

How to Approach Name and Number Comparison Questions

Look again at the five answer choices (**a, b, c, d,** and **e**) in the sample questions. Remember that the answer choices are always the same for each of the Name and Number Comparison questions. Remember, too, that they are repeated with each set of five questions, so *you don't need to memorize the answer choices.* If you have practiced these questions, however, you will note that you don't have to read the "small print" in the answer—that is, the important information is capitalized. So, what you need to know is, **a** is ALL THREE, ALIKE; **b** is FIRST, SECOND ALIKE, and so on. As you look at each question and determine the relationship among the names and numbers, a mere glance at the answer choices will tell which is the correct one.

ATTENDING TO DETAIL

Now look at the five sample questions above. You will notice that the names and numbers are very similar. Chances are you won't encounter questions in which the numbers all have a different number of digits or the names all begin with different letters. The purpose of this portion of the exam is to test how well you attend to detail.

Can you quickly see the difference, for example, between the letter *W* and the letter *M*, as in question 1? Note that, in positions one and three, the name is Larry **W.** Cramden, while in position two, the name is Larry **M.** Cramden. So the answer is **c**, because only the first and third names are alike.

Similarly, can you quickly see the difference between *838* and *883*, as in question 2? Note that, in positions one and two, the number is **838**0215, while in position three it is **883**0215. The correct answer here is **b**, "FIRST, SECOND ALIKE."

The most important thing to keep in mind is that *you have to read what is actually on the page, not what you think you see.* These tests are written so that the differences between name and numbers are difficult to detect. When you are in a hurry, a *3* looks a great deal like an *8*, and an *M* and a *W* are very similar.

Now see if you can do questions 3, 4, and 5.

The correct answer to question 3 is **e**—that is, all three of the names are different. If you missed that, look again. All of the first names are the same—Jessica—but there are slight variations in the last names: Street, Sheet, and Streit. When you read quickly, your eyes may skip over things or "fill in the blanks." Sometimes, this results in incorrect information. If your eyes skim over these three names, the *h* in Sheet may look like *tr*; the *i* in Streit may look like an *e*. The result is that the names appear to be Jessica Street, Jessica Street, and Jessica Street—all the same—when in fact they are all different. With practice, you will learn to read more attentively, without sacrificing speed.

The correct answer to question 4 is **a**; all three of the numbers are exactly alike. For some people, reading numbers is more difficult than reading words. It will help you if you learn to say them silently to yourself. (Don't say them out loud, or you won't be very popular on test day!) It also seems to be easier to remember a series of digits if you think of them as a set of two or three digit numbers. In other words, when reading question 4 to yourself, read the choices as "thirty-nine, forty-seven, one twenty," rather than "three, nine, four, seven, one, two, zero." In the first case, you only have to "remember" three numbers; in the second, you are dealing with seven.

The correct answer to question 5 is **d**, the second and third names are the same; the first is different. As with question 3, if you missed this one, you may have been reading too quickly and your eyes may have changed the *e* in the first name (Seyler) to an *a* (Sayler), making them all the same. Another distracting thing in this question is the use of "Jr." Because this is the only question of the five in which a name has any kind of designation after it, your subconscious tends to assume that is where the difference lies—and it just might be, though it isn't in this question. In this case, once you notice that all of the names include a "Jr.", you might assume they are all the same, but you would be wrong.

Other kinds of distracters include academic degrees like "M.D." or titles like "Dr." In addition, middle initials (as in question 1) can serve to distract you. If you read in too much of a hurry and do not attend to detail, you might assume that, if each choice has an initial and if each initial is the same, all three names are the same, but that may not be the case. Remember, in tests like these, there is roughly the same number of **a** answers as there are of **b**, **c**, **d**, and **e** answers. So, statistically, it will be unusual for all of the choices in a question to be exactly the same.

PRACTICE, PRACTICE, PRACTICE!

On the Clerical Aptitude portion of the test, the Name and Number Comparison questions will appear in groups of five, with a total of thirty. To get used to answering these questions, though, you need to get used to their rhythm. Here are 30 Name and Number Comparison test questions—as many as would be on one exam. See if you can answer these questions.

Then check your answers against the correct answers that follow. For each question that you get wrong, go back and see if you can spot your mistake. You may want to write your answers on a separate piece of paper, rather than marking in this book. That way, when you take the practice exams in this book, if you are having trouble with Name and Number Comparison, you can come back and do this practice set again.

PRACTICE QUESTIONS

In the questions below, compare the names or numbers, and mark the answer:
  a. if ALL THREE names or numbers are exactly ALIKE
  b. if only the FIRST and SECOND names or numbers are exactly ALIKE
  c. if only the FIRST and THIRD names or numbers are exactly ALIKE
  d. if only the SECOND and THIRD names or numbers are exactly ALIKE
  e. if ALL THREE names or numbers are DIFFERENT

1.	Ralph H. Grant	Ralph N. Grant	Ralph H. Grant
2.	3875092	3857092	3785092
3.	Rachel Martinelli	Rachel Martinelli	Rachel Martinelli
4.	9409284	9490284	9490284
5.	Martin Hogan	Martin Hogan	Martin Hogen
6.	0934877	0934877	0934877
7.	3985712	3895712	3987512
8.	Helen P. Richard	Helen P. Rickard	Helen P. Richard
9.	Margaret Joiner	Margaret Joiner	Margarite Joiner
10.	Susan Gregory	Suzan Gregory	Suzan Gregory
11.	Mallary Jolley	Mallary Jolley	Mallary Jolley
12.	3482812	3482812	3482812
13.	7490384	7490834	7490384
14.	Juanita Pfeffer	Juanita Pfeffer	Juanita Pepper
15.	Colin Walsh III	Colin Walch III	Colin Walsh II
16.	1278450	1278430	1278430
17.	Michael Coleman	Michelle Coleman	Michael Coleman
18.	Ellis Peabody	Ellis Peabody	Ellis Peabody
19.	3240957	3420957	3420957
20.	Clay Astin	Clay Austin	Clay Austin

In the questions below, compare the names or numbers, and mark the answer:

a. if ALL THREE names or numbers are exactly ALIKE
b. if only the FIRST and SECOND names or numbers are exactly ALIKE
c. if only the FIRST and THIRD names or numbers are exactly ALIKE
d. if only the SECOND and THIRD names or numbers are exactly ALIKE
e. if ALL THREE names or numbers are DIFFERENT

21.	8935743	8953743	8935743
22.	Darlene Marr	Darlene Marr	Darlene Mark
23.	Phoebe Olson	Phoebe Olsson	Phoebe Olsen
24.	2345876	2345876	2345879
25.	9457238	9457238	9457238
26.	4952089	4953089	4852089
27.	Philip Albert	Philip Alberts	Philip Alberts
28.	8429572	8492572	8429572
29.	Lon Nguyen	Lon Nguyen	Lom Nguyen
30.	Alexander Gusev	Aleksander Gusev	Alexander Gusav

ANSWERS

1. c.	**11.** a.	**21.** c.
2. e.	**12.** a.	**22.** b.
3. a.	**13.** c.	**23.** e.
4. d.	**14.** b.	**24.** b.
5. b.	**15.** e.	**25.** a.
6. a.	**16.** d.	**26.** e.
7. e.	**17.** c.	**27.** d.
8. c.	**18.** a.	**28.** c.
9. b.	**19.** d.	**29.** b.
10. d.	**20.** d.	**30.** e.

C·H·A·P·T·E·R
ALPHABETIZING

CHAPTER SUMMARY
The Alphabetizing questions on the Clerical Aptitude portion of the Clerical and Administrative Support Exam are designed to test your ability to file documents quickly and accurately. These questions ask you to place a name in the proper order among five other names. This chapter gives you some tips on the best ways to approach these questions.

It is very unusual to find an office these days in which clerks do not do any filing. It may not be the most exciting task you will do as a federal government clerk, but it is an important one. The government produces a great deal of paperwork, and if there is no accurate system for keeping track of those papers, they won't do anyone any good. Chances are that the office you go to work in will already have a filing system in place, and you will just have to learn to use it. Most of the time, the filing system that you will work with will be an alphabetical one. The Alphabetizing questions on the Clerical Aptitude portion of the Federal Clerical Exam test your skill at alphabetizing.

All of the general tips in Chapter 8 about the Clerical Aptitude portion of the test apply to the Alphabetizing portion of the test as well. As with the other types of questions, the Alphabetizing questions are in groups of five, interspersed among the other types of questions, and you will have an average of 7.5 seconds to answer each question. Practice the Alphabetizing questions until you are sure you understand them, and then listen carefully to the instructions on test day.

WHAT ALPHABETIZING QUESTIONS ARE LIKE

Thirty of the 120 questions on the Clerical Aptitude portion of the Federal Clerical Exam are Alphabetizing questions, presented in six groups of five. Each question consists of one name in the left column, enclosed in a box, and four names in the right column. These four names are in alphabetical order. In the spaces before, after, and between the four names on the right are the letters **a, b, c, d,** and **e.** Here is an example of an alphabetizing question:

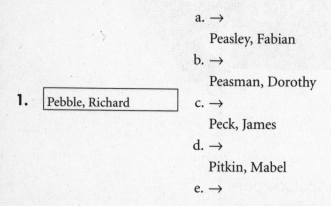

a. →

Peasley, Fabian

b. →

Peasman, Dorothy

1. | Pebble, Richard | c. →

Peck, James

d. →

Pitkin, Mabel

e. →

You are to decide where the name in the box—Pebble, Richard—would fit among the names on the right. The letter choices on the right relate to the spaces between the names, not to the names themselves. Therefore, you would have to decide whether Pebble, Richard goes before Peasley, Fabian (choice **a**); between Peasley and Peasman, Dorothy (choice **b**); between Peasman and Peck, James (choice **c**); between Peck and Pitkin, Mabel (choice **d**); or after Pitkin (choice **e**). It is as though you have a file drawer that looks like this:

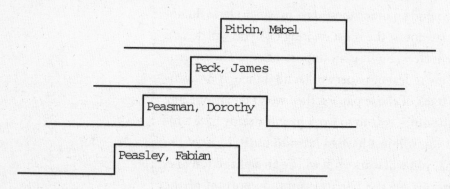

You need to decide where you will file:

Pebble, Richard

You wouldn't file Pebble in the same place as any of the other files; you would file it before them all, between two of them, or after them all. That is the real-life situation that the Alphabetizing test is replicating on paper. In an office, you would file Pebble, Richard between Peasman, Dorothy and Peck, James. Look again at the sample question. The correct answer is **c**, because **c** represents the space between Peasman and Peck. Remember that the letter answer choices represent *the spaces between (and before and after)* the list of alphabetical names on the right. All you need to do is find the correct space for the name on the right and mark its corresponding letter on your answer sheet.

HOW TO APPROACH ALPHABETIZING QUESTIONS

You learned the alphabet years ago. Still, the rules pertaining to alphabetizing are a bit more complicated than simply knowing your ABCs. When alphabetizing a group of names, the first rule to remember is that names are alphabetized by surname—that is, by last name. So, Betty Adams comes before Alan Brickman because the *A* in Adams comes before the *B* in Brickman. You ignore the fact that Alan would come before Betty. On the Clerical Aptitude portion of the Clerical and Administrative Support Exam, the names are written "Last Name, First Name," so it should be easy to remember that you want to put the names in order by surname.

When arranging a series of names alphabetically, start by looking at the first letters of the last names—the *A* in Adams and the *B* in Brickman in the above example. If the first letters are all different, you simply put them in order and you are done. Often, however, the first letters will not all be different, as with these names:

Adams, Betty
Allen, Leonard
Bates, Jessie
Brickman, Alan.

In these cases, you first group all the like first letters together and put them in order—all the *A*'s, followed by all the *B*'s, followed by all the *C*'s, and so on. Then, you have to put the names within each group in order. Do this by looking at the second letter of the last name. If these letters are not the same—as is the case with the *d* in Adams and the *l* in Allen, as well as the *a* in Bates and the *r* in Brickman—you put these letters in order. So, Adams comes before Allen and Bates comes before Brickman. If the second letters of the last name are the same, as, for example, in Brickman and Brock, you go to the third letters (*i* and *o*) and so on. See if you can put these five names in order:

Smith, Marjorie
Schneider, Louise
Snyder, Douglas
Schmidt, Harold

The correct order is:

Schmidt, Harold
Schneider, Louise
Smith, Marjorie
Snyder, Douglas

With Schmidt and Schneider, you have to go to the fourth letter—*m* and *n*—before you find different letters you can use to put the names in order.

What if all the last names contain the same letters in the same order, that is, are all the same name? Then you go to the first names to put the list in order, so Rawlings, James comes before Rawlings, Karen. If necessary, you go to the second letter (and so on) in the first name. Therefore, Rawlings, James comes before Rawlings, John. See if you can put these names in order:

Garcia, Rachel
Garcia, Katrina
Garcia, Tony
Garcia, Katherine

The correct order is:

Garcia, Katherine
Garcia, Katrina
Garcia, Rachel
Garcia, Tony

In the case of Katherine and Katrina, you have to go to the fourth letters of the first names before you find one that is different.

SPECIAL RULES FOR ALPHABETIZING

Following are some special rules to keep in mind when presented with an alphabetizing task:

1. If you are presented with a name that contains only a first initial—for example, Garcia, K.—it is filed before any other names beginning with the letter *K*. In other words, K. standing on its own comes before Karen or Kyle, or even just "Ka." In the list above, Garcia, K. would be filed before Garcia, Katherine and Garcia, Katrina.

2. If two names are spelled the same except for an additional letter at the end of one word, the shorter word comes first alphabetically. An example of this is the names Forman and Formann. In alphabetizing, a "blank" comes before even *a*. In the case of Hanna and Hannah, the "blank" that follows the second *a* in Hanna comes before the *h* that follows the second *a* in Hannah.

3. If you are given names in which the surname and the first name are exactly alike, as in Shaw, Thomas L. and Shaw, Thomas P., use the middle initial to put the names in order—in this case, *L*" before *P*.

4. If you are presented with a name that contains an abbreviation, such as St. Peter, Fred, alphabetize the name as though the abbreviation were spelled out—that is, Saint Peter, Fred would come before Sergeant, Margaret.

5. If you are given names with "Mac" and "Mc," treat them as though there was no capitalization and then order them like any other name. So, if your choices are MacDonald, Gretchen; McDonald, Gregory; and McDonald, Greta; simply read them without the capital letters and order them like this:

Macdonald, Gretchen
Mcdonald, Gregory
Mcdonald, Greta

PRACTICE, PRACTICE, PRACTICE

On the Clerical Aptitude test, the Alphabetizing questions will appear in groups of five, with a total of thirty. To get used to answering these questions, though, you need to get used to their rhythm. Here are 30 Alphabetizing test questions—as many as would be on one exam. See if you can answer these questions.

Then check your answers against the correct answers that follow. For each question that you get wrong, go back and see if you can spot your mistake. (You may want to write your answers on a separate piece of paper, rather than marking in this book. That way, when you take the practice exams in the back of this book, if you are having trouble with Alphabetizing, you can come back and do this practice set again.)

PRACTICE QUESTIONS

In the questions below, find the correct place for the name in the box.

a. →

  Ballenger, Rachel

b. →

  Edgeton, Mary

1. | Gordon, Donald P. | c. →

  Jones, Michael

d. →

  Lawson, Rachel

e. →

a. →

  Davis, Vincent

b. →

  Destry, Blanche

2. | Darnell, Melvin | c. →

  Deter, Charles Q.

d. →

  Dickens, Evelyn

e. →

a. →

  Stansfield, Gloria

b. →

  Stanton, Glenn

3. | Sterling, M. B. | c. →

  Stellton, Carol

d. →

  Sterlin, Gary

e. →

a. →

Beladen, Lionel

b. →

Bennington, A. L.

4. Belanger, Edith   c. →

Berry, John

d. →

Best, Peter

e. →

a. →

Hache, Marilyn

b. →

Hadley, Paula

5. Haight, P. D.   c. →

Hagen, Roger

d. →

Hall, Sandra

e. →

a. →

Mooar, J. L.

b. →

Moody, Mitch

6. Mooers, Shelley   c. →

Moon, Shawn

d. →

Moor, Terrence

e. →

a. →

Devine, Terry

b. →

Devine, Vickie

7. Devinney, Alice   c. →

Deviner, Matthew

d. →

Devinney, Caitlin

e. →

a. →

Winder, Brian

b. →

Windham, Denise

8. | Winde, Timothy | c. →

Windrush, Kristen

d. →

Windsor, Leland

e. →

a. →

Higgins, Barbara

b. →

Higgins, Craig

9. | Higgins, Patricia | c. →

Higgins, James

d. →

Higgins, Michael

e. →

a. →

Lehman, Arthur

b. →

Lehmann, Brad O.

10. | Lehman, Cynthia S. | c. →

Lehmann, Dennis

d. →

Lehmann, Edgar

e. →

a. →

Norris, Damon

b. →

Norris, Howard

11. | Norris, C. | c. →

Norstrand, Dolly

d. →

Norstrand, Helen

e. →

a. →

   Singer, Richard

b. →

   Singer, Walter

12. | Singer, Roberta | c. →

   Singh, Indira

d. →

   Singh, L. L.

e. →

a. →

   Connolly, Eugene

b. →

   Connolly, Louis

13. | Connolly, Melissa | c. →

   Connor, Nancy

d. →

   Connors, Angela

e. →

a. →

   Laskey, Wendy

b. →

   Laskoff, Mervin

14. | Lasselle, Antonio | c. →

   Laslie, Mark

d. →

   Lasson, Carla

e. →

a. →

   Roberson, Edgar

b. →

   Roberson, Felicity

15. | Robertson, Bud | c. →

   Roberson, Ingrid

d. →

   Roberson, Kevin

e. →

16. Bagley, Elizabeth

a. →
Bagley, Debra
b. →
Bagley, Fiona
c. →
Bagley, Isabel
d. →
Bagley, Janice
e. →

17. Malloy, Warren

a. →
Mallot, Webster
b. →
Malloy, Thomas
c. →
Malloy, Vincent
d. →
Malloy, Wentworth
e. →

18. Udomsay, P. T.

a. →
Udomsay, F. T.
b. →
Udomsay, K. M.
c. →
Udomsay, N. S.
d. →
Udomsay, N. T.
e. →

19. Juris, Alan

a. →
Juris, Aaron
b. →
Juris, Adam
c. →
Juris, Andre
d. →
Juris, Astin
e. →

a. →

Perla, Bethany

b. →

Perla, Hannah

20. | Perla, Mabel | c. →

Perla, Ophelia

d. →

Perla, Samantha

e. →

a. →

Chesker, Uri

b. →

Chesler, Tomas

21. | Chesker, Ramon | c. →

Chesler, Victoria

d. →

Chesler, Wanda

e. →

a. →

Morris, Chad

b. →

Morris, Felicia

22. | Morris, Owen | c. →

Morris, Lance

d. →

Norris, Leonard

e. →

a. →

Wahl, Candace

b. →

Wahl, Constance

23. | Wahl, Catherine | c. →

Wahl, Dennis

d. →

Wahl, Devon

e. →

a. →

Fiedler, Alvin

b. →

Fiedler, Charles

24. Fidler, Mary   c. →

Fiedler, Ethel

d. →

Fiedler, Gavin

e. →

a. →

Lamond, Lynn

b. →

Lamond, Paula

25. Lamont, Chuck   c. →

Lamone, Michael

d. →

Lamone, Pablo

e. →

a. →

Pouliot, Basil

b. →

Pouliot, Grace

26. Pouliot, Eva   c. →

Pouliot, Ishmael

d. →

Pouliot, Jason

e. →

a. →

Zabot, Maurice

b. →

Zabot, Nancy

27. Zabot, Quentin   c. →

Zabot, Olive

d. →

Zabot, Peter

e. →

a. →

Xu, Ho

b. →

Xu, Lon

28. Xu, Fan

c. →

Xu, Mong

d. →

Xu, Ng

e. →

a. →

Dorr, Alphonse

b. →

Dorr, Carmen

29. Dorr, Rose

c. →

Dorr, Hamish

d. →

Dorr, Sammy

e. →

a. →

Newman, L. S.

b. →

Newman, Leland

30. Newman, Monroe S.

c. →

Newman, N. P.

d. →

Newman, Nathan

e. →

ANSWERS

1. c.	**11.** a.	**21.** a.
2. a.	**12.** b.	**22.** d.
3. e.	**13.** c.	**23.** b.
4. b.	**14.** d.	**24.** a.
5. d.	**15.** e.	**25.** e.
6. c.	**16.** b.	**26.** b.
7. d.	**17.** d.	**27.** e.
8. a.	**18.** e.	**28.** a.
9. e.	**19.** c.	**29.** d.
10. b.	**20.** c.	**30.** c.

C · H · A · P · T · E · R

ARITHMETIC

10

CHAPTER SUMMARY

The arithmetic portion of the Clerical Aptitude section of the Clerical and Administrative Support Exam is designed to test your ability to perform simple arithmetic calculations. This chapter gives you some tips on the best ways to approach these questions.

t is a rare office in which clerks can get by with doing no arithmetic at all. If your boss tells you to finish a project in two hours and it's 9:00, you need to know what time the task should be done. If you are handed 1,347 pages that need to be proofread and told to divide them up among the five clerks in the office, you need to know how many pages to give to each clerk. The arithmetic questions on the Clerical Aptitude part of the Federal Clerical Exam are intended to test your ability to do simple math. The questions consist of addition, subtraction, multiplication, and division problems. Each question includes five answer choices— four numbers and a "none of these" choice. The problems all use whole numbers; there are no fractions, no decimals, and no word problems. The questions contain numbers of no more than three digits.

All of the general tips in Chapter 8 about the Clerical Aptitude portion of the Federal Clerical Exam apply to the arithmetic problems. As with the other types of questions, the arithmetic questions are in groups of five, interspersed among the other types of questions, and you will have an average of 7.5 seconds to answer each question. Practice the arithmetic questions in this book, until you are sure you understand them; try to pick up as much speed as you can while still maintaining accuracy; and then listen carefully to the instructions on test day.

WHAT ARITHMETIC QUESTIONS ARE LIKE

Thirty of the 120 questions on the Clerical Aptitude section of the exam are arithmetic questions. They are presented in six groups of five. Each question begins by telling you what arithmetic operation you will be performing: add, subtract, multiply, or divide. To the right of that is the problem itself and, at the far right of the page, the answer choices. Here are some examples of arithmetic questions:

1. Add:

    93
    +18

  a. 100
  b. 111
  c. 113
  d. 118
  e. none of these

2. Subtract:

    142
    −17

  a. 125
  b. 130
  c. 135
  d. 140
  e. none of these

3. Multiply:

    34
    ×7

  a. 223
  b. 228
  c. 231
  d. 233
  e. none of these

4. Divide:

$5\,\overline{|80}$

  a. 13
  b. 14
  c. 16
  d. 19
  e. none of these

All you need to do is complete the arithmetic operations. The correct answers are:

1. b.
2. a.
3. e.
4. c.

HOW TO APPROACH ARITHMETIC QUESTIONS

If you have forgotten all the math you learned in school (or, like many of us, are trying to forget), keep these tips in mind:

- Use your scratch paper to make your calculations. Even with simple problems, you increase your chance of making a mistake if you try to work in your head.

- If a problem stumps you, mark it and skip it. You can come back if there is time. Remember that you lose one-quarter of a point for wrong answers.
- Check your work **only** if you have time. Otherwise, just:
- Trust yourself.
- The Arithmetic answer choices include a choice of "none of these" answers. If you've done the problem and checked your work and the answer you got is not **a**, **b**, **c**, or **d**, it is probably **e**, none of these. Mark **e** on your answer sheet and move on.

As you can see, these are basic arithmetic calculations, but don't let that make you over-confident. Make sure you review all the arithmetic basics, so you don't forget them when you are in a hurry. This is a part of the test that can really boost your score, but not if you make careless errors. Remember, the operation is spelled out for you in words (add, subtract, multiply, and divide), and the arithmetic symbols ($+$, $-$, $\times$, $\overline{}$) are also used. These don't help you any, however, if you work so recklessly that your eye slips from one question to another. Make sure, for example, if the question says "Add" the symbol in the problem you're working on is "$+$." That may sound simple, but when you're in a hurry it's easy to lose your place. Use your finger to trace across the questions and keep your place on the page.

If you are moving quickly through the test and have plenty of time, you can check your answers, as discussed below, and be absolutely sure of your answer. This is an especially good idea if you are choosing **e**, "none of these."

If, on the other hand, you are having trouble keeping up with the strict time limits on this section of the test, don't be afraid to "fudge" your answers a little. If you're short of time and you're confronted with question 1 above, you don't actually have to work out the

whole problem. Just add the numbers in the ones column, 3 and 8. You get 11. The last digit of the answer has to be 1. That leaves you only with choice **b**, 111, and choice **e**, none of these. Pick one and move on. Yes, there's a one-quarter point penalty for wrong answers, but you have a one in two chance of being right. Do this four times and you should get two right, and only one-half point will be subtracted, for your two wrong answers; you'll get one and a half points. It's better than no points for those four problems because you didn't have time to do them! Naturally it's better to add the whole problem, but try this trick out as you work the sample problems in this book, to see how you can save yourself time if you need to for some other kind of question in the Clerical Aptitude section.

One of the most important things to keep in mind while doing arithmetic questions is that it is possible that the answer you get when you work a problem will not be one of the choices. This does **not** mean you are wrong. Remember, in tests of this kind, there are approximately equal numbers of **a**, **b**, **c**, **d**, and **e** answers. (That's not a rule that tells you where each answer falls, by the way, so don't check your work by counting how many of each you got.) This means that roughly one-fifth of the correct answers will be **e**, none of these. So, if you get an answer that is not one of the choices, mark space **e** on your answer sheet and move confidently on to the next question.

SOME TIPS ON CHECKING YOUR WORK

Work each problem on your scratch paper. After you arrive at an answer, if you still have time, check your work. The best way to check your work is to perform the opposite operation—addition and subtraction are opposites and multiplication and division are opposites.

You check an addition problem by performing a subtraction calculation; you check a multiplication problem by doing a division calculation. Here are some examples.

5. Add:

    46
    +37

a. 81
b. 83
c. 85
d. 87
e. none of these

When you do the calculation *46 plus 37* on your scratch paper, you get the answer *83*. To check this, you take your answer—83—and subtract 37 from it. If you have done the problem correctly, the answer to this subtraction problem should be 46. Another way to think of it is to "work backwards" or read from bottom to top. So, on your scratch paper you write the original calculation as

    46
    +37
    83

Now simply read it backwards and subtract instead of add, as follows:

    46
    −37
    83

In other words, working from bottom to top, read this as *83 minus 37 equals 46*. When this subtraction

problem is correct, it means your original addition calculation is also correct.

Here's another example:

6. Subtract:

    78
    −56

a. 12
b. 22
c. 32
d. 42
e. none of these

When you do the calculation *78 minus 56* on your scratch paper, you get the answer *22*. To check this, you take your answer—22—and add 56 to it. If you have done the problem correctly, the answer to this addition problem should be 78. Your original calculation looks like this:

    78
    −56
    22

Now read the problem from bottom to top, adding instead of subtracting:

    78
    +56
    22

That is, *22 plus 56 equals 78*. When this addition problem is correct, it means your original subtraction calculation is also correct.

Here's an example of a multiplication problem you could check using division:

7. Multiply:

```
   48
  ×8
```

a. 384
b. 394
c. 404
d. 414
e. none of these

When you do the calculation *48 times 8* on your scratch paper, you get the answer *384*. To check this, you take your answer—384—and divide it by 8. If you have done the problem correctly, the answer to this division problem should be 48. That is, your original calculation looks like this:

```
   48
  ×8
  384
```

Now read from bottom to top, dividing instead of multiplying:

```
   48
    8
    ÷
  384
```

Reading from bottom to top, *384 divided by 8 equals 48*. When this division problem is correct, it means your original multiplication calculation is also correct.

8. Divide:

17 |952

a. 36
b. 46
c. 56
d. 66
e. none of these

When you do the calculation *952 divided by 17* on your scratch paper, you get the answer *56*. To check this, you take your answer—56—and multiply it by 17. If you have done the problem correctly, the answer to this multiplication problem should be 952. On your scratch paper, write the original calculation like this:

```
  952
   ÷
   17
   56
```

Now read from bottom to top, multiplying instead of dividing.

```
  952
  ×17
   56
```

When this multiplication problem is correct, it means your original division calculation is also correct.

PRACTICE, PRACTICE, PRACTICE

On the Clerical Aptitude portion of the Federal Clerical Exam, the arithmetic questions will appear in groups of five, for a total of thirty. To get used to answering these questions, though, you need to get used to their rhythm. Here are 30 arithmetic test questions—as many as would be on one exam. See if you can answer these questions; the correct answers follow. For each question that you get wrong, go back and see if you can spot your mistake. (You may want to write your answers on a separate piece of paper, rather than marking in this book. That way, when you take the practice exams in the back of this book, if you are having trouble with Arithmetic, you can come back and do this practice set again.)

1. Multiply:

    17
    $\times$12

a. 200
b. 202
c. 204
d. 206
e. none of these

2. Add:

    89
    +34

a. 123
b. 125
c. 133
d. 135
e. none of these

3. Divide:

23 $\overline{)138}$

a. 3
b. 4
c. 5
d. 6
e. none of these

4. Add:

    41
    +70

a. 101
b. 111
c. 121
d. 131
e. none of these

5. Subtract:

    67
    −39

a. 27
b. 28
c. 29
d. 31
e. none of these

6. Multiply:

    18
    $\times$15

a. 265
b. 266
c. 267
d. 268
e. none of these

7. Divide:

23 | 391

a. 17

b. 18

c. 19

d. 20

e. none of these

8. Subtract:

98

−49

a. 46

b. 47

c. 48

d. 49

e. none of these

9. Add:

56

+34

a. 70

b. 80

c. 90

d. 100

e. none of these

10. Divide:

54 | 486

a. 5

b. 6

c. 7

d. 8

e. none of these

11. Multiply:

32

×7

a. 222

b. 224

c. 226

d. 228

e. none of these

12. Subtract:

561

−44

a. 507

b. 511

c. 515

d. 517

e. none of these

13. Add:

26

+19

a. 45

b. 47

c. 49

d. 55

e. none of these

14. Multiply:

91

×3

a. 263

b. 267

c. 273

d. 277

e. none of these

15. Subtract:

   75
   −46

   a. 28
   b. 30
   c. 32
   d. 34
   e. none of these

16. Divide:

   26⟌312

   a. 12
   b. 13
   c. 14
   d. 15
   e. none of these

17. Add:

   78
   +6

   a. 80
   b. 81
   c. 82
   d. 83
   e. none of these

18. Multiply:

   49
   ×3

   a. 137
   b. 147
   c. 157
   d. 167
   e. none of these

19. Multiply:

   34
   ×17

   a. 576
   b. 577
   c. 578
   d. 579
   e. none of these

20. Divide:

   83⟌415

   a. 3
   b. 4
   c. 5
   d. 6
   e. none of these

21. Subtract:

   645
   −86

   a. 556
   b. 557
   c. 558
   d. 559
   e. none of these

22. Add:

   256
   +37

   a. 293
   b. 295
   c. 297
   d. 299
   e. none of these

23. Divide:

33)‾759

a. 25

b. 27

c. 31

d. 33

e. none of these

24. Divide:

17)‾153

a. 8

b. 9

c. 11

d. 12

e. none of these

25. Subtract:

70
−34

a. 33

b. 34

c. 35

d. 36

e. none of these

26. Add:

76
+34

a. 100

b. 102

c. 104

d. 106

e. none of these

27. Subtract:

92
−13

a. 77

b. 78

c. 79

d. 80

e. none of these

28. Multiply:

49
×5

a. 245

b. 247

c. 249

d. 251

e. none of these

29. Subtract:

23
−15

a. 6

b. 7

c. 8

d. 9

e. none of these

30. Divide:

14)‾224

a. 15

b. 16

c. 17

d. 18

e. none of these

ANSWERS

1. c.
2. a.
3. d.
4. b.
5. b.
6. e.
7. a.
8. d.
9. c.
10. e.
11. b.
12. d.
13. a.
14. c.
15. e.

16. a.
17. e.
18. b.
19. c.
20. c.
21. d.
22. a.
23. e.
24. b.
25. d.
26. e.
27. c.
28. a.
29. c.
30. b.

C·H·A·P·T·E·R 11

NUMBER AND LETTER MATCHING

CHAPTER SUMMARY

The Number and Letter Matching questions on the Clerical Aptitude portion of the Federal Clerical Exam are designed to test your speed and accuracy, as well as your attention to detail. This chapter gives you some tips on the best ways to approach number and letter matching questions.

The work performed by clerks in federal government offices is detailed and demanding. You must be able to perform your tasks quickly, but also accurately. If you are, for example, sorting mail, you need to recognize that the zip code 04101 goes in a different stack from the zip code 40101. If your boss wants a copy of 37 Code of Federal Regulations section 201.13, a copy of section 201.23 is not an acceptable substitute. When you consider the extensive use of Social Security Numbers, you can imagine the mess that can result when a careless clerk jots down the wrong one.

On the other hand, government clerks must be able to work rapidly. While you certainly may have slow times in a federal government office, they will be rare. Most often, you will need to sort that mail, copy that CFR section, or record that Social Security Number quickly, as well as correctly. The Number and Letter Matching questions on the Federal Clerical Exam are designed to test the skills needed for these kinds of jobs.

All of the general tips in Chapter 8 about the Clerical Aptitude section of the Clerical and Administrative Support Exam apply to the Number and Letter Matching portion of the test as well. As with the other types of questions, the Number and Letter Matching questions are in groups of five, interspersed among the other types of questions, and you will have an average of 7.5 seconds to answer each question. Practice the Number and Letter Matching questions until you are sure you understand them, and then listen carefully to the instructions on test day.

WHAT NUMBER AND LETTER MATCHING QUESTIONS LOOK LIKE

Each Number and Letter Matching question consists of four letters and four numbers in random order. There will be five of these questions in a group. Each question will look something like this:

1. 6 J 7 4 P K 2 W

The numbers and letters are in no particular order, nor do they necessarily alternate—that is, you may find two or more numbers or letters in a row, like 7, 4 and P, K above. Each group of five questions will be followed by five options called *Suggested Answers*, each option containing two letters and two numbers. You must determine which of four suggested answers (**a**, **b**, **c**, or **d**) contains letters and numbers that are also in the question. If none of the suggested answers is correct, you will choose the fifth option, "none of these" (**e**). Suggested answers **a**, **b**, **c**, and **d** contain four characters— two numbers followed by two letters. Here the letters

and numbers are in order, so the lower number is first and the letters are alphabetical. Suggested answer **e** is always *none of these*. Here is an example of suggested answers that might appear with question 1 above.

Suggested Answers
- a. = 4, 6, J, W
- b. = 2, 9, D, G
- c. = 5, 8, V, X
- d. = 3, 6, L, T
- e. = none of these

In order to correctly answer the Number and Letter Matching questions, you must find the suggested answer—**a**, **b**, **c**, or **d**—that contains letters and numbers that are also in the question, or you must choose option **e**, *none of these*. While the letters and numbers are not necessarily in the same order in the question and in the suggested answer, all of the numbers and letters in a suggested answer must appear in a given question in order for that answer to be correct. So, for sample question 1 above, the correct answer is **a**, because 4, 6, J, and W all appear in question 1.

1. 6 J 7 4 P K 2 W

The answer cannot be **d**, for example, because, while there is a 6 in the question, there is no 3, L, or T. In the case of **b** and **c**, none of the letters and numbers match (except the 2 in **b**), and the answer cannot be **e** because there is a correct choice.

Note that all the letters in the question will not be in the answer, nor will the numbers and letters necessarily be in the same order. However, for an answer to be correct, both of the two numbers and both of the two letters must appear in the row of letters and numbers in the question. Each set of five on the Clerical

Aptitude portion of the exam will contain five questions and along with a set of suggested answers **a**, **b**, **c**, **d**, and **e**, like this:

1. 4 7 K W 5 9 D L

2. L 8 2 E T 3 J 5

3. R 9 6 G M S 2 5

4. 9 H P 3 1 V A 2

5. F S 7 1 8 K 4 R

Suggested
Answers
{
a. = 1, 9, P, V
b. = 5, 8, E, J
c. = 7, 9, K, W
d. = 2, 5, M, R
e. = none of these

The answers to this set of questions appear in the next section.

TWO APPROACHES TO NUMBER AND LETTER MATCHING QUESTIONS

METHOD 1

The best way to approach these questions is to work backwards, from the suggested answers (each of which contains only four characters) to the questions (each of which contains eight characters). However, it is imperative that you devise a system for keeping track that will allow you to be certain that you fill in the correct answer circle for the correct number on your answer sheet. You may want to write your answer in your test booklet (if allowed) next to the appropriate question, and then transfer the answers to the answer sheet when you have finished all five questions in a given set. Or, you may choose to write the question numbers on your scratch paper, jotting down the correct answer and then transferring all five at once. You may, of course, choose to mark your answers directly on the answer sheet without one of these intermediate steps. Be aware that, while this is the fastest and most accurate method for answering these questions, it is easy to make an error marking your answer sheet, because you will not be answering the questions in numerical order. Let's examine this method more closely.

Look at the five sample questions above. On most types of test questions, you answer question 1 first, then move on to question 2, and so forth. However, in this case it is easier to look first, not at the question, but at the answers, beginning with suggested answer **a**, 1, 9, P, V. This is because all you have to do is locate those four letters and numbers in the eight letters and numbers in each of the questions. After looking at suggested answer **a**, look at question 1. We can eliminate it as a match for suggested answer **a** immediately, because question 1 does not contain the number 1. It is not necessary to look further at question 1 now, but if you do, you will see that the only common character between 1 and **a** is the number 9, as there is no P or V in question 1. Similarly, questions 2 and 3 contain no number 1, so they are not a match for **a**. Both questions 4 and 5 contain the number 1, so either of them *could* be correct as far as the number 1 is concerned. Continuing to look at question 4, we find it contains a 9, as well as a P and a V and is, therefore, a match for **a**. So, the answer to question 4 is **a**, and you need to make a note of this. You may want to mark it this way in your test booklet:

4. 9 H P 3 1 V A 2 [a]

Or, you may have made a list of the numbers of these five questions on your scratch paper, and you will write down **a** next to the number 4, like this:

1.

2.

3.

4. a

5.

After you have completed all five questions in this group, you can then fill in the answer circles on your answer sheet with the correct answers for questions 1 through 5. You may have decided to record the answers directly on your answer sheet. If you do this, be sure to remember that you have just answered question number 4 and mark your sheet accordingly, like this:

IMPORTANT: As you're working, after you have determined that suggested answer **a** is a match for question number 4, remember that this does not mean it is time to move on to suggested answer **b**. Keep in mind that an answer may repeat in any given set. Therefore, you must also check question 5 (questions 1, 2, and 3 have been eliminated already) to see if question 5 is a match for suggested answer **a**. As you can see, while there is a 1 in question 5, it is the only character that suggested answer **a** and question 5 have in common, so the answer to question 5 cannot be **a**. As you move on to check suggested answer **b**, remember that you will not have to check question 4 again, since every

question can only have one answer. You may want to cross out 4 now that you are done with it. However, you will have to check answer **b** against **all** of the remaining questions; you cannot stop when you find a match. See if you can answer the remaining questions, 2 through 5 above, using this method.

The answers are:

1. c.

2. b.

3. d.

4. a.

5. e.

This method of working backwards from the answer to the question is confusing—it goes against everything you are used to doing in tests like this. Don't worry at this point if you stumbled, maybe marking an answer on the wrong line. Go ahead and try the practice questions at the end of this chapter. With a little practice, this method will start to seem more natural.

METHOD 2

If you cannot seem to adjust, however, don't despair. You can still approach these questions in a more traditional fashion. It may take a little longer, but you certainly can still complete the exam in the given time. Here are five more questions and suggested answers:

6. 8 R 4 T 5 G B 3

7. W 7 6 P R 3 D 5

8. 9 2 F H 8 E 4 S

9. 3 L D 9 Q 8 5 Y

10. 4 1 C 3 M 6 U S

Suggested Answers
{
a. = 2, 9, E, F
b. = 3, 7, P, W
c. = 5, 8, D, Y
d. = 4, 5, B, G
e. = none of these
}

Look at question 6. Note that the first character is an 8. Now look at the suggested answers for any that contain an 8 and you will see that only **c** does. Option **c**, then, may possibly be the answer to question 6. But, look at the second character in question 6, which is an R. Suggested answer **c** does not contain an R. Of course, the answer cannot contain all of the characters in the question, so don't give up on **c** yet. The third character in question 6 is a 4. There is no 4 in answer **c**. Continuing to check suggested answer **c**, note that, while there is a 5 in both **c** and question 6, the letters in **c** do not appear in question 6. So **c** is not the correct answer. If you continue to check in this fashion, you will see that **d** is the correct answer for question 6. Both question 6 and answer **d** contain the characters 4, 5, B, and G:

6.   8 R **4** T **5** **G** **B** 3

Now see if you can answer questions 7 through 10.

The answers are:

6. d.

7. b.

8. a.

9. c.

10. e.

PRACTICE, PRACTICE, PRACTICE

On the Clerical Aptitude portion of the Federal Clerical Exam, the Number and Letter Matching questions will appear in groups of five, with a total of thirty. To get used to answering these questions, though, you need to get used to their rhythm. Here are 30 Number and Letter Matching test questions—as many as there would be on one exam. See if you can answer these questions; then check your answers against the key that follows the questions. Try the first method discussed above first, as it is faster. If you just cannot get comfortable with that method, try the second.

For each question that you get wrong, go back and see if you can spot your mistake. You may want to write your answers on a separate piece of paper, rather than marking in this book. That way, after you take the practice exams in the back of this book, if you are having trouble with Number and Letter Matching questions you can come back and do this practice set again.

PRACTICE QUESTIONS

For questions 1–5, choose the suggested answer that contains numbers and letters all of which appear in that question.

1. 9 S 3 K 5 4 D W

2. E 7 N Y 2 8 P 6

3. R 3 L 8 T 5 1 F

4. 2 U 9 Q B 7 H 1

5. C 2 K 6 T 3 M 9

Suggested Answers
$\begin{cases} a. &=& 3, 8, L, R \\ b. &=& 4, 5, D, K \\ c. &=& 2, 6, M, T \\ d. &=& 7, 8, P, Y \\ e. &=& \text{none of these} \end{cases}$

For questions 6–10, choose the suggested answer that contains numbers and letters all of which appear in that question.

6. L 2 6 E 9 J 3 P

7. 5 3 F D 8 7 M S

8. 2 T 5 1 K W 4 R

9. R 4 6 A 7 Y Q 2

10. 8 Z C 9 1 J R 5

Suggested Answers
$\begin{cases} a. &=& 2, 3, J, P \\ b. &=& 2, 5, K, R \\ c. &=& 1, 9, C, Z \\ d. &=& 4, 6, Q, Y \\ e. &=& \text{none of these} \end{cases}$

For questions 11–15, choose the suggested answer that contains numbers and letters all of which appear in that question.

11. P 5 9 W D 6 F 1

12. 3 M K 2 7 E 4 S

13. J 5 2 R Y T 8 3

14. B P 4 5 W S 3 9

15. Q 9 L V 8 7 4 G

Suggested Answers
$\begin{cases} a. &=& 4, 7, E, M \\ b. &=& 5, 9, P, W \\ c. &=& 7, 8, G, L \\ d. &=& 2, 5, J, R \\ e. &=& \text{none of these} \end{cases}$

For questions 16–20, choose the suggested answer that contains numbers and letters all of which appear in that question.

16. 9 D M 3 2 W G 5

17. S 8 X C 4 1 7 A

18. E 3 7 6 R L 5 Y

19. 3 A Q 8 N J 4 5

20. T 2 U H 4 6 E 1

Suggested Answers
$\begin{cases} a. &=& 1, 6, H, T \\ b. &=& 3, 7, E, Y \\ c. &=& 5, 9, D, G \\ d. &=& 7, 8, A, C \\ e. &=& \text{none of these} \end{cases}$

For questions 21–25, choose the suggested answer that contains numbers and letters all of which appear in that question.

21. K 7 3 F 2 P C 9

22. 6 S 4 L N 1 8 Z

23. 4 2 E U W 5 1 D

24. H W 6 7 3 Q R 4

25. J 9 A 8 B 5 V 1

Suggested Answers
$\left\{\begin{array}{l}\text{a.} = 2, 7, F, K \\ \text{b.} = 4, 6, L, N \\ \text{c.} = 1, 5, E, U \\ \text{d.} = 3, 6, Q, R \\ \text{e.} = \text{none of these}\end{array}\right.$

For questions 26–30, choose the suggested answer that contains numbers and letters all of which appear in that question.

26. R T 7 3 W M 1 2

27. C 8 3 R 6 7 L T

28. 4 N P 6 D Y 9 2

29. 6 3 V K 2 S A 9

30. 1 E 4 F 6 J 8 Q

Suggested Answers
$\left\{\begin{array}{l}\text{a.} = 4, 6, D, P \\ \text{b.} = 3, 7, R, T \\ \text{c.} = 1, 8, D, S \\ \text{d.} = 4, 5, B, 6, 8, F, JG \\ \text{e.} = \text{none of these}\end{array}\right.$

ANSWERS

1. b.
2. d.
3. a.
4. e.
5. c.
6. a.
7. e.
8. b.
9. d.
10. c.
11. b.
12. a.
13. d.
14. b.
15. c.

16. c.
17. d.
18. b.
19. e.
20. a.
21. a.
22. b.
23. c.
24. d.
25. e.
26. b.
27. b.
28. a.
29. e.
30. d.

FEDERAL CLERICAL PRACTICE EXAM 1

CHAPTER SUMMARY

This is the second of the three practice tests in this book based on the Federal Clerical Exam. After analyzing your score on the diagnostic exam in Chapter 3 and working through the instructional material in the previous chapters, take this test to see how much your score has improved.

L
ike the exam in Chapter 3, this one is of the same type as the real Clerical and Administrative Support Exam you will be taking. The exam is divided into two parts: the Verbal Abilities section, which consists of multiple-choice questions based on vocabulary, grammar, spelling, word relations (analogies), and reading comprehension; and the Clerical Aptitude section, which consists of multiple-choice questions based on number-and-letter matching, name-and-number comparison, alphabetization, and general math—addition, subtraction, multiplication, and division.

For this exam, you should simulate the actual test-taking experience as closely as you can. Find a quiet place to work where you won't be disturbed. Tear out the answer sheet on the next page and find some number 2 pencils to fill in the circles with. Allow yourself 50 minutes for the exam: 35 minutes for the Verbal Abilities section and 15 minutes for the Clerical Aptitude section. Set a timer or stopwatch, but do not worry too much if you go over the allotted time on this practice exam. You still have the third practice exam to go (Chapter 13), and when you take that exam you can work more on timing.

After the exam, use the answer key that follows it to see how you did and to find out why the correct answers are correct. The answer key is followed by a section on how to score your exam.

VERBAL ABILITIES

1.	ⓐ ⓑ ⓒ ⓓ		31.	ⓐ ⓑ ⓒ ⓓ		61.	ⓐ ⓑ ⓒ ⓓ
2.	ⓐ ⓑ ⓒ ⓓ		32.	ⓐ ⓑ ⓒ ⓓ		62.	ⓐ ⓑ ⓒ ⓓ
3.	ⓐ ⓑ ⓒ ⓓ		33.	ⓐ ⓑ ⓒ ⓓ		63.	ⓐ ⓑ ⓒ ⓓ
4.	ⓐ ⓑ ⓒ ⓓ		34.	ⓐ ⓑ ⓒ ⓓ		64.	ⓐ ⓑ ⓒ ⓓ
5.	ⓐ ⓑ ⓒ ⓓ		35.	ⓐ ⓑ ⓒ ⓓ		65.	ⓐ ⓑ ⓒ ⓓ
6.	ⓐ ⓑ ⓒ ⓓ		36.	ⓐ ⓑ ⓒ ⓓ		66.	ⓐ ⓑ ⓒ ⓓ
7.	ⓐ ⓑ ⓒ ⓓ		37.	ⓐ ⓑ ⓒ ⓓ		67.	ⓐ ⓑ ⓒ ⓓ
8.	ⓐ ⓑ ⓒ ⓓ		38.	ⓐ ⓑ ⓒ ⓓ		68.	ⓐ ⓑ ⓒ ⓓ
9.	ⓐ ⓑ ⓒ ⓓ		39.	ⓐ ⓑ ⓒ ⓓ		69.	ⓐ ⓑ ⓒ ⓓ
10.	ⓐ ⓑ ⓒ ⓓ		40.	ⓐ ⓑ ⓒ ⓓ		70.	ⓐ ⓑ ⓒ ⓓ
11.	ⓐ ⓑ ⓒ ⓓ		41.	ⓐ ⓑ ⓒ ⓓ		71.	ⓐ ⓑ ⓒ ⓓ
12.	ⓐ ⓑ ⓒ ⓓ		42.	ⓐ ⓑ ⓒ ⓓ		72.	ⓐ ⓑ ⓒ ⓓ
13.	ⓐ ⓑ ⓒ ⓓ		43.	ⓐ ⓑ ⓒ ⓓ		73.	ⓐ ⓑ ⓒ ⓓ
14.	ⓐ ⓑ ⓒ ⓓ		44.	ⓐ ⓑ ⓒ ⓓ		74.	ⓐ ⓑ ⓒ ⓓ
15.	ⓐ ⓑ ⓒ ⓓ		45.	ⓐ ⓑ ⓒ ⓓ		75.	ⓐ ⓑ ⓒ ⓓ
16.	ⓐ ⓑ ⓒ ⓓ		46.	ⓐ ⓑ ⓒ ⓓ		76.	ⓐ ⓑ ⓒ ⓓ
17.	ⓐ ⓑ ⓒ ⓓ		47.	ⓐ ⓑ ⓒ ⓓ		77.	ⓐ ⓑ ⓒ ⓓ
18.	ⓐ ⓑ ⓒ ⓓ		48.	ⓐ ⓑ ⓒ ⓓ		78.	ⓐ ⓑ ⓒ ⓓ
19.	ⓐ ⓑ ⓒ ⓓ		49.	ⓐ ⓑ ⓒ ⓓ		79.	ⓐ ⓑ ⓒ ⓓ
20.	ⓐ ⓑ ⓒ ⓓ		50.	ⓐ ⓑ ⓒ ⓓ		80.	ⓐ ⓑ ⓒ ⓓ
21.	ⓐ ⓑ ⓒ ⓓ		51.	ⓐ ⓑ ⓒ ⓓ		81.	ⓐ ⓑ ⓒ ⓓ
22.	ⓐ ⓑ ⓒ ⓓ		52.	ⓐ ⓑ ⓒ ⓓ		82.	ⓐ ⓑ ⓒ ⓓ
23.	ⓐ ⓑ ⓒ ⓓ		53.	ⓐ ⓑ ⓒ ⓓ		83.	ⓐ ⓑ ⓒ ⓓ
24.	ⓐ ⓑ ⓒ ⓓ		54.	ⓐ ⓑ ⓒ ⓓ		84.	ⓐ ⓑ ⓒ ⓓ
25.	ⓐ ⓑ ⓒ ⓓ		55.	ⓐ ⓑ ⓒ ⓓ		85.	ⓐ ⓑ ⓒ ⓓ
26.	ⓐ ⓑ ⓒ ⓓ		56.	ⓐ ⓑ ⓒ ⓓ			
27.	ⓐ ⓑ ⓒ ⓓ		57.	ⓐ ⓑ ⓒ ⓓ			
28.	ⓐ ⓑ ⓒ ⓓ		58.	ⓐ ⓑ ⓒ ⓓ			
29.	ⓐ ⓑ ⓒ ⓓ		59.	ⓐ ⓑ ⓒ ⓓ			
30.	ⓐ ⓑ ⓒ ⓓ		60.	ⓐ ⓑ ⓒ ⓓ			

CLERICAL APTITUDE

1. ⓐ ⓑ ⓒ ⓓ ⓔ	41. ⓐ ⓑ ⓒ ⓓ ⓔ	81. ⓐ ⓑ ⓒ ⓓ ⓔ
2. ⓐ ⓑ ⓒ ⓓ ⓔ	42. ⓐ ⓑ ⓒ ⓓ ⓔ	82. ⓐ ⓑ ⓒ ⓓ ⓔ
3. ⓐ ⓑ ⓒ ⓓ ⓔ	43. ⓐ ⓑ ⓒ ⓓ ⓔ	83. ⓐ ⓑ ⓒ ⓓ ⓔ
4. ⓐ ⓑ ⓒ ⓓ ⓔ	44. ⓐ ⓑ ⓒ ⓓ ⓔ	84. ⓐ ⓑ ⓒ ⓓ ⓔ
5. ⓐ ⓑ ⓒ ⓓ ⓔ	45. ⓐ ⓑ ⓒ ⓓ ⓔ	85. ⓐ ⓑ ⓒ ⓓ ⓔ
6. ⓐ ⓑ ⓒ ⓓ ⓔ	46. ⓐ ⓑ ⓒ ⓓ ⓔ	86. ⓐ ⓑ ⓒ ⓓ ⓔ
7. ⓐ ⓑ ⓒ ⓓ ⓔ	47. ⓐ ⓑ ⓒ ⓓ ⓔ	87. ⓐ ⓑ ⓒ ⓓ ⓔ
8. ⓐ ⓑ ⓒ ⓓ ⓔ	48. ⓐ ⓑ ⓒ ⓓ ⓔ	88. ⓐ ⓑ ⓒ ⓓ ⓔ
9. ⓐ ⓑ ⓒ ⓓ ⓔ	49. ⓐ ⓑ ⓒ ⓓ ⓔ	89. ⓐ ⓑ ⓒ ⓓ ⓔ
10. ⓐ ⓑ ⓒ ⓓ ⓔ	50. ⓐ ⓑ ⓒ ⓓ ⓔ	90. ⓐ ⓑ ⓒ ⓓ ⓔ
11. ⓐ ⓑ ⓒ ⓓ ⓔ	51. ⓐ ⓑ ⓒ ⓓ ⓔ	91. ⓐ ⓑ ⓒ ⓓ ⓔ
12. ⓐ ⓑ ⓒ ⓓ ⓔ	52. ⓐ ⓑ ⓒ ⓓ ⓔ	92. ⓐ ⓑ ⓒ ⓓ ⓔ
13. ⓐ ⓑ ⓒ ⓓ ⓔ	53. ⓐ ⓑ ⓒ ⓓ ⓔ	93. ⓐ ⓑ ⓒ ⓓ ⓔ
14. ⓐ ⓑ ⓒ ⓓ ⓔ	54. ⓐ ⓑ ⓒ ⓓ ⓔ	94. ⓐ ⓑ ⓒ ⓓ ⓔ
15. ⓐ ⓑ ⓒ ⓓ ⓔ	55. ⓐ ⓑ ⓒ ⓓ ⓔ	95. ⓐ ⓑ ⓒ ⓓ ⓔ
16. ⓐ ⓑ ⓒ ⓓ ⓔ	56. ⓐ ⓑ ⓒ ⓓ ⓔ	96. ⓐ ⓑ ⓒ ⓓ ⓔ
17. ⓐ ⓑ ⓒ ⓓ ⓔ	57. ⓐ ⓑ ⓒ ⓓ ⓔ	97. ⓐ ⓑ ⓒ ⓓ ⓔ
18. ⓐ ⓑ ⓒ ⓓ ⓔ	58. ⓐ ⓑ ⓒ ⓓ ⓔ	98. ⓐ ⓑ ⓒ ⓓ ⓔ
19. ⓐ ⓑ ⓒ ⓓ ⓔ	59. ⓐ ⓑ ⓒ ⓓ ⓔ	99. ⓐ ⓑ ⓒ ⓓ ⓔ
20. ⓐ ⓑ ⓒ ⓓ ⓔ	60. ⓐ ⓑ ⓒ ⓓ ⓔ	100. ⓐ ⓑ ⓒ ⓓ ⓔ
21. ⓐ ⓑ ⓒ ⓓ ⓔ	61. ⓐ ⓑ ⓒ ⓓ ⓔ	101. ⓐ ⓑ ⓒ ⓓ ⓔ
22. ⓐ ⓑ ⓒ ⓓ ⓔ	62. ⓐ ⓑ ⓒ ⓓ ⓔ	102. ⓐ ⓑ ⓒ ⓓ ⓔ
23. ⓐ ⓑ ⓒ ⓓ ⓔ	63. ⓐ ⓑ ⓒ ⓓ ⓔ	103. ⓐ ⓑ ⓒ ⓓ ⓔ
24. ⓐ ⓑ ⓒ ⓓ ⓔ	64. ⓐ ⓑ ⓒ ⓓ ⓔ	104. ⓐ ⓑ ⓒ ⓓ ⓔ
25. ⓐ ⓑ ⓒ ⓓ ⓔ	65. ⓐ ⓑ ⓒ ⓓ ⓔ	105. ⓐ ⓑ ⓒ ⓓ ⓔ
26. ⓐ ⓑ ⓒ ⓓ ⓔ	66. ⓐ ⓑ ⓒ ⓓ ⓔ	106. ⓐ ⓑ ⓒ ⓓ ⓔ
27. ⓐ ⓑ ⓒ ⓓ ⓔ	67. ⓐ ⓑ ⓒ ⓓ ⓔ	107. ⓐ ⓑ ⓒ ⓓ ⓔ
28. ⓐ ⓑ ⓒ ⓓ ⓔ	68. ⓐ ⓑ ⓒ ⓓ ⓔ	108. ⓐ ⓑ ⓒ ⓓ ⓔ
29. ⓐ ⓑ ⓒ ⓓ ⓔ	69. ⓐ ⓑ ⓒ ⓓ ⓔ	109. ⓐ ⓑ ⓒ ⓓ ⓔ
30. ⓐ ⓑ ⓒ ⓓ ⓔ	70. ⓐ ⓑ ⓒ ⓓ ⓔ	110. ⓐ ⓑ ⓒ ⓓ ⓔ
31. ⓐ ⓑ ⓒ ⓓ ⓔ	71. ⓐ ⓑ ⓒ ⓓ ⓔ	111. ⓐ ⓑ ⓒ ⓓ ⓔ
32. ⓐ ⓑ ⓒ ⓓ ⓔ	72. ⓐ ⓑ ⓒ ⓓ ⓔ	112. ⓐ ⓑ ⓒ ⓓ ⓔ
33. ⓐ ⓑ ⓒ ⓓ ⓔ	73. ⓐ ⓑ ⓒ ⓓ ⓔ	113. ⓐ ⓑ ⓒ ⓓ ⓔ
34. ⓐ ⓑ ⓒ ⓓ ⓔ	74. ⓐ ⓑ ⓒ ⓓ ⓔ	114. ⓐ ⓑ ⓒ ⓓ ⓔ
35. ⓐ ⓑ ⓒ ⓓ ⓔ	75. ⓐ ⓑ ⓒ ⓓ ⓔ	115. ⓐ ⓑ ⓒ ⓓ ⓔ
36. ⓐ ⓑ ⓒ ⓓ ⓔ	76. ⓐ ⓑ ⓒ ⓓ ⓔ	116. ⓐ ⓑ ⓒ ⓓ ⓔ
37. ⓐ ⓑ ⓒ ⓓ ⓔ	77. ⓐ ⓑ ⓒ ⓓ ⓔ	117. ⓐ ⓑ ⓒ ⓓ ⓔ
38. ⓐ ⓑ ⓒ ⓓ ⓔ	78. ⓐ ⓑ ⓒ ⓓ ⓔ	118. ⓐ ⓑ ⓒ ⓓ ⓔ
39. ⓐ ⓑ ⓒ ⓓ ⓔ	79. ⓐ ⓑ ⓒ ⓓ ⓔ	119. ⓐ ⓑ ⓒ ⓓ ⓔ
40. ⓐ ⓑ ⓒ ⓓ ⓔ	80. ⓐ ⓑ ⓒ ⓓ ⓔ	120. ⓐ ⓑ ⓒ ⓓ ⓔ

VERBAL ABILITIES

Read the directions carefully, and then choose the best answer from the four choices. You have 35 minutes to complete this section.

For questions 1–3, choose the correctly spelled word.

1. a. shrivel
b. shrivvel
c. shrivell
d. shrival

2. a. sittuation
b. situation
c. situachun
d. sitiation

3. a. clamby
b. clamy
c. clammy
d. clammby

4. BICYCLE is related to PEDAL as CANOE is related to
a. water
b. kayak
c. oar
d. fleet

5. PROPOSE is related to SUGGESTION as TERMINATE is related to
a. ending
b. duration
c. initiation
d. rule

6. PEN is related to POET as NEEDLE is related to
a. thread
b. button
c. sewing
d. tailor

For questions 7–11, choose the answer that is most clearly and correctly expressed.

7. a. Ramona tends to be poor at spelling while she is an intelligent woman.
b. Ramona tends to be poor at spelling and is an intelligent woman.
c. Although Ramona tends to be poor at spelling, she is an intelligent woman.
d. Tending to be poor at spelling, Romana is an intelligent woman.

8. a. Of all the dogs in the K-9 Corps, Zelda is the most bravest.
b. Of all the dogs in the K-9 Corps, Zelda is the bravest.
c. Of all the dogs in the K-9 Corps, Zelda is the braver.
d. Of all the dogs in the K-9 Corps, Zelda is the more brave.

9. a. When his workday is over, billing clerk Bob Bigby likes to watch TV, preferring police dramas to situation comedies.
b. When his workday is over. Billing clerk Bob Bigby likes to watch TV, preferring police dramas to situation comedies.
c. When his workday is over, billing clerk Bob Bigby likes to watch TV. Preferring police dramas to situation comedies.
d. When his workday is over, billing clerk Bob Bigby likes to watch TV, preferring police dramas. To situation comedies.

10. a. All day the exhausted volunteers had struggled through snake-ridden underbrush. In search of the missing hikers, who still had not been found.
   b. All day the exhausted volunteers had struggled through snake-ridden underbrush in search of the missing hikers, who still had not been found.
   c. All day the exhausted volunteers had struggled through snake-ridden underbrush in search of the missing hikers. Who still had not been found.
   d. All day the exhausted volunteers had struggled through snake-ridden underbrush. In search of the missing hikers. Who still had not been found.

11. a. My office mate Rosie and I, we did not like each other at first, but now we get along fine.
   b. My office mate Rosie and I did not like each other at first, but now her and I get along fine.
   c. My office mate Rosie and me did not like each other at first, but now she and I get along fine.
   d. My office mate Rosie and I did not like each other at first, but now we get along fine.

12. *Mesa* means most nearly
   a. forest
   b. plateau
   c. wagon
   d. dwelling

13. *Ado* means most nearly
   a. idiom
   b. punishment
   c. cost
   d. fuss

14. *Intimate* means most nearly
   a. frightening
   b. curious
   c. private
   d. characteristic

15. *Obscure* means most nearly
   a. hidden
   b. obvious
   c. reckless
   d. subjective

Electronic mail (E-mail) has been in widespread use for more than a decade. E-mail simplifies the flow of ideas, connects people from distant offices, eliminates the need for meetings, and often boosts productivity. But E-mail should be carefully managed to avoid unclear and inappropriate communication. E-mail messages should be concise and limited to one topic. When complex issues need to be addressed, phone calls are still best.

16. The paragraph best supports the statement that E-mail
   a. is not always the easiest way to connect people from distant offices
   b. has changed considerably since it first began a decade ago
   c. causes people to be unproductive when it is used incorrectly
   d. is most effective when it is wisely managed

Starting a new secretarial job can often be stressful. Secretaries should realize that they are not perfect and that they will sometimes make mistakes. If you are beginning a new position, don't be afraid to ask questions. Be patient and use company-sponsored training as one way to learn. But most of all, don't give up. Your new experience will help you grow as a person and in your career.

17. The paragraph best supports the statement that when starting a new job, secretaries should
    a. understand the need for patience
    b. make mistakes so they can learn from them
    c. see training as a means of job promotion
    d. ask questions to avoid making mistakes

Administrative office positions hold greater prestige than they did just two decades ago. This advance in reputation is due in part to the advanced skills and technical abilities needed to perform the required tasks.

18. The paragraph best supports the statement that
    a. administrative office positions require technical skills
    b. greater prestige results in better work performance
    c. the reputation of administrative office workers is holding steady
    d. two decades ago, there were fewer administrative office positions

19. CAMERA is related to PHOTOGRAPH as OVEN is related to
    a. dinner
    b. stove
    c. cake
    d. bakery

20. CACTUS is related to DESERT as TROUT is related to
    a. fish
    b. river
    c. bass
    d. lizard

For questions 21 and 22, choose the answer that is most clearly and correctly expressed.

21.
    a. A sharpshooter for many years, Miles Johnson could shoot a pea off a person's shoulder from 70 yards away.
    b. Miles Johnson could shoot a pea off a person's shoulder from 70 yards away, a sharpshooter for many years.
    c. A sharpshooter for many years, a pea could be shot off a person's shoulder by Miles Johnson from 70 yards away.
    d. From 70 yards away, a sharpshooter for many years, Miles Johnson could shoot a pea off a person's shoulder.

22.
    a. Betty Cooper was the most toughest supervisor we had ever had, yet she was also the fairest.
    b. Betty Cooper was the toughest supervisor we had ever had, yet she was also the most fair.
    c. Betty Cooper was the toughest supervisor we had ever had, yet she was also the most fairer.
    d. Betty Cooper was the tough supervisor we had ever had, yet she was also the most fair.

More and more office workers telecommute from offices in their own homes. The upside of telecommuting is both greater productivity and greater flexibility. Telecommuters produce, on average, 20 percent more than if they were to work in an office, and their flexible schedule allows them to balance both their family and work responsibilities.

23. The paragraph best supports the statement that telecommuters

   a. have more family responsibilities than workers who travel to the office

   b. get more work done in a given time period than workers who travel to the office

   c. produce a better quality work product than workers who travel to the office

   d. are more flexible in their personal lives than workers who travel to the office

Fax machines have made it possible for information to be transmitted to distant locations within minutes, but what about confidential information? Are faxes always secure? To avoid having faxes misdirected, arrange for authorized persons to receive and transmit confidential messages. Always phone the recipient about an incoming confidential fax, and make contact a second time to make sure the fax was received.

24. The paragraph best supports the statement that

   a. the majority of faxes contain confidential information

   b. faxes should not be sent if the information is confidential

   c. fax machines should be locked up in secure offices

   d. precautions should be taken before a confidential fax message is sent

Keeping busy at important tasks is much more motivating than having too little to do. Today's office employees are not afraid of responsibility. Most people are willing to take on extra responsibility in order to have more variety on their jobs. Along with more responsibility should come the authority to carry out newly assigned tasks.

25. The paragraph best supports the statement that

   a. variety on the job helps increase employee motivation

   b. office employees like responsibility more than authority

   c. most people do a lot more work than their jobs require of them

   d. today's office employees are fearful of having too many extra tasks

26. To *consider* means most nearly to

   a. promote

   b. require

   c. adjust

   d. deem

27. *Opportunity* means most nearly

   a. sensitivity

   b. arrogance

   c. chance

   d. reference

For questions 28–30, choose the correctly spelled word.

28. a. ruff

   b. rouff

   c. ruf

   d. rough

29. a. rodant

   b. rodent

   c. rodint

   d. roddent

30. a. humor

   b. hummor

   c. humorr

   d. humer

31. MEANINGFUL is related to INSIGNIFICANT as ESSENTIAL is related to
   a. unnecessary
   b. important
   c. unremarkable
   d. basic

32. SCALE is related to WEIGHT as THERMOME-TER is related to
   a. illness
   b. pounds
   c. temperature
   d. degrees

33. PYRAMID is related to TRIANGLE as CUBE is related to
   a. ice
   b. shape
   c. circle
   d. square

34. SIMPLE is related to COMPLEX as TRIVIAL is related to
   a. inconspicuous
   b. significant
   c. permanent
   d. irrelevant

As more and more offices use desktop publishing to enhance the appearance of their printed information, the use of graphics will continue to increase. Color printers will continue to gain in popularity, and workers as well as customers will become accustomed to very sophisticated visual messages.

35. The paragraph best supports the statement that in offices today
   a. desktop publishing will soon be obsolete
   b. color printers are being replaced by new technology
   c. the use of desktop publishing is increasing
   d. customers demand color-printed messages

Nothing is more valuable today than learning to reinvent a job according to a company's changing needs. To do this, secretaries need to take a new look at the company's existing programs and then assume responsibilities that go beyond the basic job description.

36. The paragraph best supports the statement that secretaries
   a. must change jobs frequently to maintain their positions in the company
   b. who recognize changing needs are valuable to their companies
   c. should take time to revise the company's existing programs
   d. who assume the most responsibility will be promoted

Learning to use your copy machine efficiently can save time and increase your productivity. New copiers have lots of features, but they are also easy to use. Familiarize yourself with every option on your copier and learn how to program the machine. The best features will save you time. You should be able to use your copier as if it were an administrative assistant. Your copier should sort, duplex, and staple.

37. The paragraph best supports the statement that
   a. in the future, copiers will replace many administrative assistants
   b. learning how to program and use a copier could result in saving time
   c. copiers that sort and duplex are difficult to learn but save money
   d. the use of older copiers results in a decrease in productivity

Managing job and family is not simple. Both commitments make strong demands on people and are sometimes in direct opposition to each other. Saying yes to one means saying no to the other, and stress can often result. Being realistic and creating a balance in life can help set priorities.

38. The paragraph best supports the statement that
   a. most family responsibilities cause stress at home and at work
   b. it is important to avoid making commitments to other people
   c. because it pays the bills, a job must take priority over other commitments
   d. it is important to have a balance between job and family responsibilities

39. *Obsolete* means most nearly
   a. current
   b. dedicated
   c. unnecessary
   d. outmoded

40. *Malicious* means most nearly
   a. spiteful
   b. changeable
   c. murderous
   d. dangerous

For questions 41–44, choose the correctly spelled word.

41. a. superb
   b. supperb
   c. supurb
   d. sepurb

42. a. jellous
   b. jealous
   c. jealuse
   d. jeolous

43. a. teriffic
   b. terrific
   c. terriffic
   d. terific

44. a. sherrif
   b. sherriff
   c. sherif
   d. sheriff

45. EXACTLY is related to PRECISELY as EVIDENTLY is related to
   a. positively
   b. apparently
   c. narrowly
   d. unquestionably

46. OPTIMIST is related to CHEERFUL as PESSIMIST is related to
   a. gloomy
   b. malicious
   c. petty
   d. benevolent

47. PSYCHOLOGIST is related to NEUROSIS as OPHTHALMOLOGIST is related to
   a. cataract
   b. eyes
   c. vision
   d. glasses

For questions 48–51, choose the answer that is most clearly and correctly expressed.

48. a. Mr. Chen thought they should hire temporary help; moreover, his supervisor disagreed.
    b. Mr. Chen thought they should hire temporary help; meanwhile, his supervisor disagreed.
    c. Mr. Chen thought they should hire temporary help; however, his supervisor disagreed.
    d. Mr. Chen thought they should hire temporary help; furthermore, his supervisor disagreed.

49. a. The TV show *Colombo* is said to have been inspired in part of the classic Russian novel, *Crime and Punishment*.
    b. The TV show *Colombo* is said to have been inspired in part by the classic Russian novel, *Crime and Punishment*.
    c. The TV show *Colombo* is said to have been inspired in part off of the classic Russian novel, *Crime and Punishment*.
    d. The TV show *Colombo* is said to have been inspired in part from the classic Russian novel, *Crime and Punishment*.

50. a. My sister and I, respected members of the Girl Scouts, has roasted marshmallows for the troop.
    b. My sister and I, respected members of the Girl Scouts, roasts marshmallows for the whole troop.
    c. My sister and I, respected members of the Girl Scouts, roasting marshmallows for the whole troop.
    d. My sister and I, respected members of the Girl Scouts, roasted marshmallows for the whole troop.

51. a. When offered a bonus to be working overtime and skipping supper, not a single employee refused.
    b. When offered a bonus to have worked overtime and to have skipped supper, not a single employee refused.
    c. When offered a bonus to work overtime and skip supper, not a single employee refused.
    d. When offered a bonus to work overtime and be skipping supper, not a single employee refused.

52. *Impartial* means most nearly
    a. complete
    b. prejudiced
    c. unbiased
    d. erudite

53. To *articulate* means most nearly to
    a. trust
    b. refine
    c. verify
    d. express

54. *Expansive* means most nearly
    a. obsolete
    b. meager
    c. spacious
    d. costly

55. *Detrimental* means most nearly
    a. decisive
    b. harmful
    c. worthless
    d. advantageous

Today's secretaries often spend long hours in front of a visual display terminal (VDT). Surveys show that many of these computer users complain of eyestrain (tired or watery eyes, blurred vision, or headaches). To avoid eyestrain, several professional groups have suggested that users wear the right glasses; adjust their monitors so that the screen is at, or slightly below, eye level; and take a fifteen-minute break from the computer every hour or two.

56. The paragraph best supports the statement that eyestrain

a. may be caused by spending too much time in front of a computer screen

b. may be caused by headaches, blurred vision, and watery eyes

c. can be cured by taking a two-hour break from the computer screen

d. is a serious, though infrequent, complaint in some offices

Secretaries should have a desk reference guide, or "road map," in case they have to be away and a substitute must fill in. A desk reference should have a company-wide organizational chart, a list of standards and procedures, a documentation process such as a calendar for meetings, an organized work space, and a glossary of terms used by the company.

57. The paragraph best supports the statement that

a. secretaries should be responsible for drawing up company-wide organizational charts

b. if a secretary must leave the office, a substitute should be appointed to fill in

c. desk reference guides are helpful tools for workers who must fill in for an absent secretary

d. the term "road map" is another way of saying "company-wide organizational chart"

For questions 58–60, choose the correctly spelled word.

58. a. obssession

b. obsessian

c. obsession

d. obsessiun

59. a. jeoperdy

b. jepardy

c. jeapardy

d. jeopardy

60. a. magniffisent

b. magnifisent

c. magnificent

d. magnifficent

For questions 61–63, choose the answer that is most clearly and correctly expressed.

61. a. Recession, as well as budget cuts, is hard on us all.

b. Recession and budget cuts is hard on hard on us all.

c. Recession, as well as budget cuts, are hard on us all.

d. Budget cuts, as well as the recession, is hard on us all.

62. a. Jury members become impatient with both prosecution and defense when they were sequestered for months.

b. When jury members are sequestered for months, they are becoming impatient with both prosecution and defense.

c. Jury members became impatient with both prosecution and defense when they are sequestered for months.

d. When jury members are sequestered for months, they become impatient with both prosecution and defense.

63.
a. Doctor Falkenrath believes that neither immorality nor amorality is a spiritual defect.
b. Doctor Falkenrath believes that neither immorality nor amorality are a spiritual defect.
c. Doctor Falkenrath believes that immorality and amorality are not a spiritual defect.
d. Doctor Falkenrath believes that both immorality and amorality is not spiritual defects.

64. To *harass* means most nearly to
a. trick
b. confuse
c. betray
d. humiliate

65. *Fortified* means most nearly
a. reinforced
b. altered
c. disputed
d. developed

66. To *delegate* means most nearly to
a. analyze
b. respect
c. criticize
d. assign

As more businesses are being restructured, the role of the office professional is changing. Due to downsizing, the workload is increasing. The outlook for the future is that responsibilities will continue to grow. Office professionals should also expect an increase in networking and collaborations.

67. The paragraph best supports the statement that
a. in the future there will be fewer jobs for office professionals
b. when workers begin to network, their responsibilities increase
c. most business today are going through restructuring
d. when businesses downsize, office professionals have more work to do

In order to be successful, secretaries need to determine which characteristics help them perform their jobs better. Secretaries should be serious and independent; that is, they should understand the seriousness of their work and show an independence of judgment about when to use critical skills. But they should also be compliant and helpful; that is, they should be willing to do routine work and be courteous and sensitive to others.

68. The paragraph best supports the statement that secretaries perform their jobs better when they
a. understand which specific qualities contribute to success
b. take on more routine jobs than creative jobs
c. combine seriousness with dependence and compliance
d. develop characteristics that other secretaries do not have

Some secretaries who complain of boredom on the job blame the job when they are really to blame. They have allowed themselves to become too familiar with the duties of the job. A solution to the problem of boredom can be as simple as enrolling in an adult education course to improve verbal and mental skills.

69. The paragraph best supports the statement that
   a. routine jobs quickly become boring
   b. education can relieve boredom
   c. boredom is usually a myth
   d. improving mental skills will improve verbal skills

70. AERIE is related to EAGLE as HOUSE is related to
   a. government
   b. building
   c. unit
   d. person

71. ELEPHANT is related to PACHYDERM as KANGAROO is related to
   a. pouch
   b. plains
   c. marsupial
   d. jump

72. SKEIN is related to YARN as REAM is related to
   a. hundreds
   b. tangle
   c. paper
   d. quantity

For questions 73–75, choose the answer that is most clearly and correctly expressed.

73. a. An IRS official can expect to put in extra hours when you work on April 15.
   b. An IRS official can expect to put in extra hours when one works on April 15.
   c. An IRS official can expect to put in extra hours when working on April 15.
   d. An IRS official can expect to put in extra hours when we work on April 15.

74. a. Jennifer phoned her roommate every day when she was in the hospital.
   b. When her roommate was in the hospital, Jennifer phoned her every day.
   c. When in the hospital, a phone call was made every day by Jennifer to her roommate.
   d. Her roommate received a phone call from Jennifer every day while she was in the hospital.

75. a. Some of the reports I have to type are very long, but that doesn't bother one if they are interesting.
   b. Some of the reports I have to type are very long, but that doesn't bother you if they are interesting.
   c. Some of the reports I have to type are very long, but that doesn't bother a person if they are interesting.
   d. Some of the reports I have to type are very long, but that doesn't bother me if they are interesting.

A recent survey suggests that administrative assistants today support an average of four professionals. The most useful skill an administrative assistant should have, therefore, is the ability to juggle multiple assignments from several supervisors.

76. The paragraph supports the statement that administrative assistants
   a. are overworked and treated unfairly
   b. are often the subject of office surveys
   c. should be skilled at working for several people
   d. try to do too many assignments at once

If you aren't sure what your priorities are, take a professional inventory. In other words, take a few minutes to think about your job. What is the most important thing you need to accomplish today? Next, what is the most important task you need to do during the next hour? What about the next ten minutes? In order to accomplish your goals, you must make a work plan for the day.

77. The paragraph best supports the statement that
   a. setting priorities will help you accomplish your goals
   b. planning your day is one way to increase motivation
   c. accomplishing your goals is not always possible
   d. taking a professional inventory is a simple task

78. To *arouse* means most nearly to
   a. inform
   b. abuse
   c. waken
   d. deceive

79. *Accountable* means most nearly
   a. laudable
   b. compensatory
   c. responsible
   d. approachable

For questions 80–83, choose the answer that is correctly spelled.

80. a. paralel
   b. paralell
   c. parallal
   d. parallel

81. a. stablize
   b. stableize
   c. stableise
   d. stabilize

82. a. irelevent
   b. irelevant
   c. irrelevant
   d. irrelevent

83. a. peculior
   b. peculiar
   c. peculliar
   d. puculior

84. EXPLORE is related to DISCOVER as RESEARCH is related to
   a. read
   b. learn
   c. write
   d. think

85. TYPE is related to CLASSIFY as ALPHABETIZE is related to
   a. revise
   b. autograph
   c. count
   d. file

CLERICAL APTITUDE

Choose the correct answer to each problem. You have 15 minutes to complete this section.

1. Divide:

3 ⟌ 36

 a. 13
 b. 12
 c. 9
 d. 8
 e. none of these

2. Add:

19
+12

 a. 31
 b. 25
 c. 27
 d. 17
 e. none of these

3. Multiply:

17
×4

 a. 57
 b. 59
 c. 65
 d. 68
 e. none of these

4. Add:

12
+18

 a. 17
 b. 30
 c. 27
 d. 19
 e. none of these

5. Add:

14
+15

 a. 30
 b. 21
 c. 23
 d. 20
 e. none of these

For questions 6–10, choose the suggested answer that contains numbers and letters all of which appear in that question.

6. S J 9 6 T 8 4 L

7. 7 8 K R G H 6 4

8. 8 K 6 R 3 J 9 L

9. J 7 R 9 8 K 6 T

10. 3 J 7 6 K R G 9

Suggested Answers
{
 a. = 3, 6, G, J
 b. = 4, 7, H, K
 c. = 3, 8, L, R
 d. = 4, 9, S, T
 e. = none of these
}

For questions 11–15, compare the three names and numbers, and select the answer from the five choices below:

a. if ALL THREE names or numbers are exactly ALIKE

b. if only the FIRST and SECOND names or numbers are exactly ALIKE

c. if only the FIRST and THIRD names or numbers are exactly ALIKE

d. if only the SECOND and THIRD names or numbers are exactly ALIKE

e. if ALL THREE names or numbers are DIFFERENT

11. 2071836   2071836   2071386

12. Melissa Toolan   Melissa Toolan   Melissa Toolan

13. 6557255   6657255   6557725

14. 8629481   8629841   8629481

15. 2894814   2894914   2894914

For questions 16–20, choose the correct place for the name in the box.

16. Howe, Susan

    a. →

      Howe, Rachel

    b. →

      Howe, Theresa

    c. →

      Hower, Elaine

    d. →

      Howes, Bridget

    e. →

17. Norman, Owen

    a. →

      Norman, Brett

    b. →

      Norman, Eileen

    c. →

      Norman, O. W.

    d. →

      Norman, Patricia

    e. →

18. Roman, Gwen

    a. →

      Roma, Darrin

    b. →

      Roma, Kevin

    c. →

      Roman, Callie

    d. →

      Roman, Inez

    e. →

19. Simond, Marie

    a. →

      Simon, Edward

    b. →

      Simon, Michael

    c. →

      Simone, Robert

    d. →

      Simoni, Dennis

    e. →

20. | Hugger, Tammy |

    a. →

       Huggin, Sharon

    b. →

       Huggins, Rebecca

    c. →

       Hughen, Russell

    d. →

       Hughes, Randy

    e. →

For questions 21–25, choose the suggested answer that contains numbers and letters all of which appear in that question.

21. F 5 6 P 7 Y W 8

22. 3 E 7 Y 5 P 6 S

23. 8 T R F 6 7 W 4

24. R 6 7 F 5 4 P T

25. T 5 3 8 R F S 4

Suggested Answers
- a. = 4, 8, F, T
- b. = 3, 5, R, W
- c. = 4, 6, E, Y
- d. = 5, 7, P, S
- e. = none of these

26. Subtract:

    59
   −15

    a. 54
    b. 49
    c. 44
    d. 40
    e. none of these

27. Divide:

  3) 69

    a. 21
    b. 23
    c. 33
    d. 36
    e. none of these

28. Multiply:

    15
   ×6

    a. 70
    b. 75
    c. 80
    d. 86
    e. none of these

29. Subtract:

    37
   −13

    a. 16
    b. 20
    c. 21
    d. 24
    e. none of these

30. Divide:

  9) 72

    a. 8
    b. 9
    c. 7
    d. 6
    e. none of these

For questions 31–35, choose the correct place for the name in the box.

31. | Lansbury, Nathaniel |

   a. →

   Lansbury, Cecil

   b. →

   Lansbury, Paul

   c. →

   Lansbury, Ross

   d. →

   Lansbury, Vernon

   e. →

32. | Montero, M. K. |

   a. →

   Monterio, A. K.

   b. →

   Monterio, G. D.

   c. →

   Montero, D. P.

   d. →

   Montero, J. L.

   e. →

33. | Payne, Anthony |

   a. →

   Payne, Andrew

   b. →

   Payne, Arthur

   c. →

   Payne, Aston

   d. →

   Payne, Ava

   e. →

34. | Sargeant, Marilyn |

   a. →

   Sargeant, Alice

   b. →

   Sargeant, Dennis

   c. →

   Sargent, Faith

   d. →

   Sargent, Janice

   e. →

35. | Wallace, Peggy |

   a. →

   Wallace, Baxter

   b. →

   Wallace, Gregory

   c. →

   Wallace, Lauren

   d. →

   Wallace, Sarah

   e. →

For questions 36–40, compare the three names and numbers, and select the answer from the five choices below.

a. if ALL THREE names or numbers are exactly ALIKE
b. if only the FIRST and SECOND names or numbers are exactly ALIKE
c. if only the FIRST and THIRD names or numbers are exactly ALIKE
d. if only the SECOND and THIRD names or numbers are exactly ALIKE
e. if ALL THREE names or numbers are DIFFERENT

36. Alan Rickmar   Alan Rickmar   Alan Richmar

37. Emma Parrott   Emma Parrot   Emma Parrott

38. 2809874   2809874   2809874

39. Thomas L. Jones   Thomas I. Jones   Thomas L. Jones

40. 3419686   3416986   3419668

41. Multiply:
    12
    ×6
    a. 84
    b. 76
    c. 72
    d. 81
    e. none of these

42. Add:
    42
    +11
    a. 55
    b. 53
    c. 51
    d. 47
    e. none of these

43. Divide:
    9 | 54
    a. 6
    b. 5
    c. 4
    d. 3
    e. none of these

44. Multiply:
    13
    ×8
    a. 92
    b. 96
    c. 98
    d. 104
    e. none of these

45. Add:
    17
    +13
    a. 27
    b. 30
    c. 32
    d. 28
    e. none of these

For questions 46–50, choose the suggested answer that contains numbers and letters all of which appear in that question.

46. S D 6 7 R K 5 2

47. 6 R K 4 P 7 3 D

48. S 6 2 D R P 7 4

49. B K 6 P 4 2 D 5

50. 2 5 K 6 7 S D R

Suggested Answers
$\begin{cases} \text{a.} = 2, 5, \text{B}, \text{P} \\ \text{b.} = 3, 4, \text{D}, \text{R} \\ \text{c.} = 2, 6, \text{K}, \text{S} \\ \text{d.} = 4, 7, \text{D}, \text{S} \\ \text{e.} = \text{none of these} \end{cases}$

For questions 51–55, choose the correct place for the name in the box.

51. | Murray, Daniel |

   a. →

     Murray, Dean

   b. →

     Murray, Donald

   c. →

     Murray, Erin

   d. →

     Murray, Fran

   e. →

52. | Renger, Deborah |

   a. →

     Rendall, Joseph

   b. →

     Rende, Bruce

   c. →

     Renell, Pauline

   d. →

     Renfrew, George

   e. →

53. | Winters, Helen |

   a. →

     Winterberg, Ingrid

   b. →

     Winterhalder, Mary

   c. →

     Wintersteen, Caleb

   d. →

     Winthrop, Avis

   e. →

54. | Marston, Kenneth |

   a. →

     Marston, K. P.

   b. →

     Marston, Kevin

   c. →

     Marston, Kimberly

   d. →

     Marston, Kurt

   e. →

55. | Perkins, Herbert |

  a. →

     Perham, Leslie

  b. →

     Perillo, Carlos

  c. →

     Perin, Meredith

  d. →

     Perley, Dana

  e. →

For questions 56–60, compare the three names and numbers, and select the answer from the five choices below:

  a. if ALL THREE names or numbers are exactly ALIKE

  b. if only the FIRST and SECOND names or numbers are exactly ALIKE

  c. if only the FIRST and THIRD names or numbers are exactly ALIKE

  d. if only the SECOND and THIRD names or numbers are exactly ALIKE

  e. if ALL THREE names or numbers are DIFFERENT

56. 9362071   9632071   9632071

57. W. Richard   W. Richard   W. Richard
     Walpole   Walpole   Walpole

58. Rita Cassese   Rita Cassese   Rita Cassesse

59. 5055216   5055216   5055215

60. Rachel Gervais   Rachel Gervas   Rachel Gervas

61. Subtract:

    47
   −13

  a. 30

  b. 26

  c. 34

  d. 38

  e. none of these

62. Multiply:

    7
   ×8

  a. 45

  b. 49

  c. 53

  d. 56

  e. none of these

63. Add:

    32
  +54

  a. 85

  b. 82

  c. 78

  d. 74

  e. none of these

64. Subtract:

    34
   −8

  a. 20

  b. 23

  c. 26

  d. 25

  e. none of these

65. Divide:

$8\,\overline{)32}$

a. 6
b. 4
c. 8
d. 7
e. none of these

For questions 66–70, choose the suggested answer that contains numbers and letters all of which appear in that question.

66. Q H 5 9 8 V D 7

67. 5 Q 3 G H 9 8 D

68. 8 G Q P R 5 7 3

69. 8 9 G R 5 7 V H

70. V 5 D 3 Q P 7 9

Suggested Answers
$\left\{\begin{array}{l}\text{a.} = 7, 9, G, H \\ \text{b.} = 7, 8, Q, R \\ \text{c.} = 5, 9, P, V \\ \text{d.} = 3, 5, D, H \\ \text{e.} = \text{none of these}\end{array}\right.$

For questions 71–75, choose the correct place for the name in the box.

71. | Savary, Karen |

a. →
Savage, Mabel
b. →
Savard, Janice
c. →
Savast, Pierre
d. →
Savery, Barney
e. →

72. | Whitling, Marlan |

a. →
Whitlock, Mark
b. →
Whitlow, Scott
c. →
Whitman, Faye
d. →
Whitmore, Carrie
e. →

73. | Hood, William |

a. →
Hood, Diane
b. →
Hood, Jessica
c. →
Hood, Lynn
d. →
Hood, Viola
e. →

74. | Lauder, Amy |

a. →
Lauber, Robin
b. →
Laubner, Brad
c. →
Laubner, Eugene
d. →
Lauder, Francis
e. →

75. | Riley, Ernest |

   a. →

      Riley, Abbie

   b. →

      Riley, Ronald

   c. →

      Riley, Susan

   d. →

      Riley, Wanda

   e. →

For questions 76–80, compare the three names and numbers, and select the answer from the five choices below:

   a. if ALL THREE names or numbers are exactly ALIKE

   b. if only the FIRST and SECOND names or numbers are exactly ALIKE

   c. if only the FIRST and THIRD names or numbers are exactly ALIKE

   d. if only the SECOND and THIRD names or numbers are exactly ALIKE

   e. if ALL THREE names or numbers are DIFFERENT

76. 6448156   6648156   6468156

77. Nanci   Nancy   Nanci
     Lamattina   Lamattina   Lamattina

78. Gaston   Gaston   Gaston
     Robichaud   Robicheau   Robicheau

79. 5871796   5871796   5871796

80. 4811436   4811436   4814436

81. Add:

$$\begin{array}{r} 7 \\ +5 \\ \hline \end{array}$$

   a. 15

   b. 17

   c. 14

   d. 11

   e. none of these

82. Subtract:

$$\begin{array}{r} 17 \\ -8 \\ \hline \end{array}$$

   a. 11

   b. 10

   c. 9

   d. 7

   e. none of these

83. Divide:

$2\,\overline{)\,36}$

   a. 18

   b. 16

   c. 14

   d. 13

   e. none of these

84. Multiply:

$$\begin{array}{r} 14 \\ \times 8 \\ \hline \end{array}$$

   a. 114

   b. 112

   c. 108

   d. 103

   e. none of these

85. Subtract:

34

−20

a. 12

b. 13

c. 14

d. 16

e. none of these

For questions 86–90, choose the suggested answer that contains numbers and letters all of which appear in that question.

86. S 6 2 K J 5 W 4

87. 3 2 W C T K 6 4

88. Y 2 4 S 6 5 C W

89. W J 3 4 S C 6 5

90. 3 K 4 S 5 Y W 6

Suggested Answers
{
a. = 2, 5, J, S
b. = 3, 5, S, W
c. = 2, 4, K, T
d. = 4, 6, C, Y
e. = none of these
}

For questions 91–95, choose the correct place for the name in the box.

91. | Snell, Barbara |

a. →

Snelder, Patricia

b. →

Snell, Axel

c. →

Snell, Beth

d. →

Snell, Carl

e. →

92. | Alston, Leon |

a. →

Alson, Michael

b. →

Alson, Philip

c. →

Alston, Hazel

d. →

Alston, Norris

e. →

93. | Goss, John |

a. →

Goss, Lillian

b. →

Goss, Peter

c. →

Gosse, Henry

d. →

Gosse, Karen

e. →

94. Jones, Herschel

  a. →

    Jones, Emily

  b. →

    Jones, Gloria

  c. →

    Jones, Gordon

  d. →

    Jones, Harold

  e. →

95. McKelvey, T. T.

  a. →

    McKellar, R. Q.

  b. →

    McKelway, O. S.

  c. →

    McKendry, D.A.

  d. →

    McKenna, M.J.

  e. →

For questions 96–100, compare the three names and numbers, and select the answer from the five choices below:

  a. if ALL THREE names or numbers are exactly ALIKE

  b. if only the FIRST and SECOND names or numbers are exactly ALIKE

  c. if only the FIRST and THIRD names or numbers are exactly ALIKE

  d. if only the SECOND and THIRD names or numbers are exactly ALIKE

  e. if ALL THREE names or numbers are DIFFERENT

96.

| Cynthia Wormwood | Cynthia Wormword | Cynthia Warmwood |

97.

| 9248137 | 9284137 | 9248137 |

98.

| Henry L. Conohan | Henry L. Conohan | Henry L. Conohan |

99. Victoria Erickson   Victoria Ericson   Victoria Ericson

100. Hillary Mayol   Hillary Mayor   Hilary Mayol

101. Divide:

$7\,\overline{)\,35}$

  a. 6

  b. 5

  c. 7

  d. 8

  e. none of these

102. Multiply:

$$\begin{array}{r} 7 \\ \times 9 \\ \hline \end{array}$$

  a. 63

  b. 59

  c. 68

  d. 55

  e. none of these

103. Add:

$$\begin{array}{r} 23 \\ +45 \\ \hline \end{array}$$

  a. 44

  b. 45

  c. 52

  d. 68

  e. none of these

104. Divide:

$12\overline{)72}$

a. 7

b. 8

c. 5

d. 6

e. none of these

105. Multiply:

8

×3

a. 27

b. 26

c. 24

d. 25

e. none of these

For questions 106–110, choose the correct place for the name in the box.

106. Rathbone, Rachel

a. →

Rathbone, Gayle

b. →

Rathbun, Penny

c. →

Rathbun, Rose

d. →

Rathburn, Mavis

e. →

107. Sutton, Lindsay

a. →

Sutter, Vera

b. →

Thomas, Jason

c. →

Veetch, Luke

d. →

Waters, David

e. →

108. Rice, Dana

a. →

Rice, Edith

b. →

Rice, Ethel

c. →

Rice, Frank

d. →

Rice, Gary

e. →

109. Peternek, Alice

a. →

Peterlin, Eric

b. →

Peterlin, Jesse

c. →

Peternel, Jeralyn

d. →

Peternel, Roger

e. →

110. Sims, Linda

   a. →

      Simms, Mathew

   b. →

      Simms, Peter

   c. →

      Sims, Debora

   d. →

      Sims, Pamela

   e. →

For questions 111–115, compare the three names and numbers, and select the answer from the five choices below:

a. if ALL THREE names or numbers are exactly ALIKE

b. if only the FIRST and SECOND names or numbers are exactly ALIKE

c. if only the FIRST and THIRD names or numbers are exactly ALIKE

d. if only the SECOND and THIRD names or numbers are exactly ALIKE

e. if ALL THREE names or numbers are DIFFERENT

111. 2569692   2569692   2566992

112. 7145659   7145659   7145659

113. 8747146   8477146   8747146

114. Angela Paradis   Angela Paredis   Angela Paradia

115. A. Louis   A. Louise   A. Louise
     Schiller   Schiller   Schiller

For questions 116–120, choose the suggested answer that contains numbers and letters all of which appear in that question.

116. L 3 9 F 8 7 H R

117. F 4 N L 9 3 8 P

118. 7 F R 9 N 4 P 3

119. 3 L 7 R 8 F Q 9

120. L 3 Q 4 9 P 7 M

Suggested Answers
- a. = 8, 9, H, L
- b. = 3, 4, M, P
- c. = 3, 7, N, R
- d. = 7, 9, F, Q
- e. = none of these

ANSWERS

VERBAL ABILITIES

Answer explanations are given for all questions except spelling. If you are not sure why the designated answer is correct for a spelling question, consult a dictionary.

1. a.

2. b.

3. c.

4. c. A bicycle is put in motion by means of a pedal. A canoe is put into motion by means of an oar. The answer is not **a** because the substance water does not necessarily put the canoe into motion. Kayak (choice **b**) is incorrect because it is a type of boat similar to a canoe. Choice **d** is incorrect because a fleet is a group of boats.

5. a. To propose something is to make a suggestion. To terminate something is to make an ending. Choice **b** is incorrect because terminating something does not cause a duration. Choice **c** is incorrect because an initiation is the beginning of something, not an ending. In this analogy, choice **d** has no relationship to terminate.

6. d. A pen is a tool used by a poet. A needle is a tool used by a tailor. The answer is not **a**, **b**, or **c** because none are people and therefore cannot complete the analogy.

7. c. The transitional word *although* correctly establishes a contrast.

8. b. *Bravest* is the correct form of the adjective.

9. a. The other choices contain sentence fragments.

10. b. The other choices contain sentence fragments.

11. d. The correct pronoun case forms are used. Choice **a** contains a redundant subject (*My part-*

ner Rosie and I, we . . .). Choices **b** and **c** contain incorrect pronoun case forms.

12. b. A *mesa* and a *plateau* are both hills with flat tops.

13. d. To make much *ado* and to *fuss* both mean to bustle about.

14. c. *Intimate* and *private* both mean personal.

15. a. *Obscure* and *hidden* both mean concealed.

16. d. The correct answer is implied by the statement in the third sentence that carefully managed E-mail results in effective communication. Choice **a** is wrong because the opposite is true. Choice **b** is wrong because even though E-mail is more widespread, it has not necessarily changed *considerably*. Choice **c** is not indicated in the paragraph.

17. a. The fourth sentence points to the need for patience in a new job. Choice **b** is wrong because the paragraph does not say that mistakes should be made on purpose. Choice **c** is not mentioned in the paragraph. Choice **d** is incorrect because even though it is true that asking questions may avoid mistakes, the paragraph does not mention this relationship.

18. a. The second sentence indicates that technical skills are needed to perform the required tasks of the job. Although choice **b** may indeed be true, the paragraph does not state this. Choice **c** is not mentioned. Choice **d** is incorrect because even though administrative office positions have greater prestige, there is no way of knowing if there are more positions available.

19. c. A camera is used to make a photograph. An oven is used to make a cake. Choice **a** is incorrect because even though an oven may be involved in the making of a dinner, the word is too general.

Choices **b** and **d** are incorrect because a stove and a bakery are not created in an oven.

20. b. A cactus lives in the desert, and a trout lives in a river. The answer is not **a** because a trout is a type of fish; a fish is not a place where a trout lives. Choice **c** is incorrect because bass is another type of fish. Lizard (choice **d**) is incorrect because it, too, is not a trout habitat.

21. a. The modifier *a sharpshooter for many years* is clearly and correctly placed only in this choice.

22. b. This choice is the only one that contains the correct forms of the adjectives *tough* and *fair*.

23. b. This choice is correct because the third sentence states that telecommuters produce 20 percent more than their on-location counterparts. Choice **a** is not mentioned in the paragraph. Choice **c** is wrong because more productivity does not necessarily mean better quality. Choice **d** is not mentioned.

24. d. The last two sentences point to the need for precautions when sending a fax. There is no indication in the paragraph that choice **a** is true. Choice **b** is incorrect because the paragraph indicates that, with caution, confidential faxes can be sent. Choice **c** is not mentioned.

25. a. The answer is stated in the first sentence. Choices **b** and **d** are not mentioned in the paragraph. Choice **c** is attractive, but it is incorrect because the paragraph is talking about more responsibility, not necessarily a lot more work.

26. d. To *consider* and to *deem* both mean to regard as or to judge.

27. c. An *opportunity* to do something is the same as a *chance* to do it.

28. d.

29. b.

30. a.

31. a. *Meaningful* is the opposite of *insignificant*. *Essential* is the opposite of *unnecessary*. Choice **b** is incorrect because the word *important* has a similar meaning to *essential*. The answer is not **c** or **d** because neither is the opposite of *essential*.

32. c. A scale is an instrument used to measure weight. A thermometer is an instrument used to measure temperature. The answer is not **a** because a thermometer might be used when someone is ill, but it does not measure illness. Choices **b** and **d** are incorrect because a thermometer is not used to measure either of these.

33. d. The sides of a pyramid are triangles. The sides of a cube are squares. The answer is not **a** because ice is the same shape as a cube. Choices **b** and **c** are incorrect because neither represents the side of a cube.

34. b. *Simple* is the opposite of *complex*. *Trivial* is the opposite of *significant*. The answer is not **a** or **c** because neither of these is the opposite of *trivial*. Choice **d** is incorrect because *irrelevant* means about the same as *trivial*.

35. c. The paragraph points to the increased use of graphics and color printing, both part of desktop publishing. Choices **a** and **b** are wrong because the opposite is true. Choice **d** is incorrect because the paragraph says that customers will be accustomed to these features, but it does not say that they demand them.

36. b. The first sentence indicates that adapting to changing needs is important to a company. Choices **a**, **c**, and **d** are not mentioned in the paragraph.

37. b. The first sentence points to the need to learn how to use a copier, and the third sentence indicates that learning to program a copier is the way to learn to use it. Choice **a** is wrong because even though the paragraph says that copiers may be used like administrative assistants, it does not indicate that these machines will replace people. Choice **c** is incorrect because the paragraph doesn't say that copiers are difficult to learn. Choice **d** is not mentioned.

38. d. The last sentence points to the need for balancing responsibilities. Choices **a, b,** and **c** are not mentioned in the paragraph.

39. d. *Obsolete* and *outmoded* both mean no longer in use.

40. a. A *malicious* action and a *spiteful* action are both intended to harm.

41. a.

42. b.

43. b.

44. d.

45. b. *Exactly* and *precisely* are synonyms, and *evidently* and *apparently* are synonyms. Choices **a, c,** and **d** are incorrect because none mean the same as *apparently*.

46. a. An optimist is a person whose outlook is cheerful. A pessimist is a person whose outlook is gloomy. The answer is not **b** because a pessimist does not have to be malicious. Choices **c** and **d** are incorrect because neither of these adjectives describes the outlook of a pessimist.

47. a. A psychologist treats a neurosis, which is a disorder. An ophthalmologist treats a cataract, which is a disorder. Choices **b, c,** and **d** are incorrect because they are not disorders.

48. c. *However* is the clearest and most logical transitional word.

49. b. The correct preposition is *by*; choices **a, c,** and **d** contain incorrect prepositions: *of, off of,* and *from*.

50. d. This is the only choice in which the subject and verb agree and there are no shifts in tense.

51. c. *To work* and *to skip* are the logical forms of these verbs.

52. c. *Impartial* and *unbiased* both mean unprejudiced.

53. d. To *articulate* and to *express* both mean to set forth in words.

54. c. *Expansive* and *spacious* both mean vast.

55. b. *Detrimental* and *harmful* both mean injurious.

56. a. The answer is implied in the first two sentences. Choice **b** is incorrect because these are symptoms of eyestrain, not causes. Choice **c** is incorrect because there is no mention of a *cure* for eyestrain. Choice **d** is not mentioned.

57. c. The first sentence points to the need for desk reference guides. Choice **a** is incorrect because although a desk reference guide may include an organizational chart, the paragraph does not say that secretaries are responsible for drawing them up. Choice **b** is wrong because even though the paragraph indicates that a substitute may fill in, it does not say that this *should* happen. Choice **d** is wrong because an organization chart is just one part of the "road map."

58. c.

59. d.

60. c.

61. a. The noun *recession* agrees in number with its verb *is*; in choices **b, c,** and **d** the subjects and verbs do not agree. (The phrase introduced by *as well as* is a parenthetical phrase, and should not be considered in finding the answer.)

62. d. The verbs *are sequestered* and *become* are consistently in the present tense; in choices **a, b,** and **c** there are unnecessary shifts in tense.

63. a. The verb *is* agrees with its noun *neither*.

64. d. To *harass* and to *humiliate* both mean to torment.

65. a. *Fortified* and *reinforced* both mean strengthened.

66. d. To *delegate* and to *assign* both mean to authorize or to appoint.

67. d. This answer is clearly stated in the second sentence. Choice **a** is incorrect because even though the paragraph mentions downsizing, it does not say that there will be fewer office professionals. Choice **b** is not mentioned. Choice **c** is incorrect because the passage does not say that most businesses are downsizing.

68. a. The first sentence points to the relationship between success and an understanding of the attributes that contribute to successful secretaries. Choice **b** is incorrect because even though secretaries should take on routine jobs, the paragraph does not indicate that there should be more routine jobs than any other types of jobs. Choice **c** is wrong because secretaries should be independent, not dependent. Choice **d** is not mentioned.

69. b. The third sentence points to the relationship between taking a course and relieving boredom. Choices **a** and **c** are not mentioned in the paragraph. Choice **d** is incorrect because the paragraph does not indicate that improving one skill will necessarily improve the other.

70. d. An aerie is where an eagle lives; a house is where a person lives. Choices **a**, **b**, and **c** are incorrect because they are not living things.

71. c. An elephant is a type of pachyderm. A kangaroo is a type of marsupial. The other choices are incorrect because they are not classifications of animals.

72. c. A skein is a unit of measure for yarn. A ream is a unit of measure for paper. Choice **a** is a quantity or amount but not a unit of measure. Choice **b** is not a unit of measure but a condition of material. Choice **d** is not a unit of measure but a synonym for amount.

73. c. Choices **a**, **b**, and **d** contain unnecessary shifts in person from *IRS official* (he or she) to *you*, *one*, and *we*.

74. b. In the other choices, the pronoun reference is ambiguous. The reader cannot tell who is in the hospital. Choice **c** also contains a misplaced modifier, *When in the hospital*, which seems to refer to *a phone call*.

75. d. The other answers contain unnecessary shifts in person from *I* to *one*, *you*, and *a person*.

76. c. The second sentence clearly states the answer. Choices **a**, **b**, and **d** are not indicated in the paragraph.

77. a. The last sentence points to the need for a work plan, which is the same as setting priorities. Choice **b** is wrong because even though the paragraph indicates that planning helps accomplish goals, it does not indicate that planning helps motivation. Choices **c** and **d** are not mentioned.

78. c. To *arouse* and to *waken* both mean to stir or to cause to become alert.

79. c. To be held *accountable* and to be held *responsible* both mean to be held answerable for something.

80. d.

81. d.

82. c.

83. b.

84. b. One explores in order to discover; one researches in order to learn. Choices **a**, **c**, and **d** are incorrect because reading, writing, and thinking are not the goals of research, although each is the means to reach that goal.

85. d. One types an item (that is, puts it in a category) in order to classify it; one alphabetizes an item (that is, puts it in a category) in order to file it. To revise something, autograph it, or count it does not in itself put that thing into a category, so choices **a**, **b**, and **c** are incorrect.

CLERICAL APTITUDE

No answer explanations are given in this section. Once you know the correct answer, you should be able to go back to the question and see why it is right. Most mistakes in this section are the result of having to work quickly.

1. b.	33. b.
2. a.	34. c.
3. d.	35. d.
4. b.	36. b.
5. e.	37. c.
6. d.	38. a.
7. b.	39. c.
8. c.	40. e.
9. e.	41. c.
10. a.	42. b.
11. b.	43. a.
12. a.	44. d.
13. e.	45. b.
14. c.	46. c.
15. d.	47. b.
16. b.	48. d.
17. d.	49. a.
18. d.	50. c.
19. c.	51. a.
20. a.	52. e.
21. e.	53. c.
22. d.	54. b.
23. a.	55. d.
24. e.	56. d.
25. a.	57. a.
26. c.	58. b.
27. b.	59. b.
28. e.	60. d.
29. d.	61. c.
30. a.	62. d.
31. b.	63. e.
32. e.	64. c.

65. b.		93. a.	
66. e.		94. e.	
67. d.		95. b.	
68. b.		96. e.	
69. a.		97. c.	
70. c.		98. a.	
71. c.		99. d.	
72. a.		100. e.	
73. e.		101. b.	
74. d.		102. a.	
75. b.		103. d.	
76. e.		104. d.	
77. c.		105. c.	
78. d.		106. b.	
79. a.		107. b.	
80. b.		108. a.	
81. e.		109. c.	
82. c.		110. d.	
83. a.		111. b.	
84. b.		112. a.	
85. c.		113. c.	
86. a.		114. e.	
87. c.		115. d.	
88. d.		116. a.	
89. b.		117. e.	
90. b.		118. c.	
91. c.		119. d.	
92. d.		120. b.	

SCORING

In order to figure your total score on this exam, you'll need to figure your score for the Verbal Abilities and Clerical Aptitude sections separately. For the Verbal Abilities section, simply count up the number you got right. Questions you didn't answer or got wrong don't count.

1. Number of questions right: _____

For the Clerical Aptitude section, the scoring is a little more complicated. First, count up your right answers. Then count your wrong answers separately. Do not count questions you skipped. In order to figure the penalty for your wrong answers, divide your number of wrong answers by four, and then subtract the result from your total number of right answers.

2. Number of questions right: _____

3. Number of questions wrong: _____

4. Divide number **3** by 4: _____

5. Subtract number **4** from number **2**: _____

Now you have your total raw score for both the Verbal Abilities and Clerical Aptitude sections. Add them together, and then divide by 205 to determine your total percentage score.

6. Add numbers **1** and **5** together: _____

7. Divide number **6** by 205: _____

The table on this page will help you check your math by giving you percentage equivalents for some possible scores. Use this percentage score to compare your score on this exam to your scores on the other exams in this book. This percentage score may not be equivalent to the kind of score that will be reported to you on your Notification of Results when you take the real Clerical and Administrative Support Exam.

Number of questions right	Approximate percentage
205	100%
190	93%
176	86%
161	79%
145	71%
131	64%
116	57%
102	50%

As previously stated, you will need a score of at least 80 to pass; however, you should strive for the best score you can achieve in order to have a better chance at a wider range of good jobs. You have probably seen improvement between your first practice exam score and this one; however, if you didn't improve as much as you would like, following are some options:

- **If you scored below 60 percent,** you should seriously consider whether you're ready for the Federal Clerical Exam at this time. A good idea would be to take an adult education course in reading comprehension at a high school or community college. If you don't have time for a course, you might try to get some private tutoring.

- **If your score is in the 60 to 80 percent range,** you need to work as hard as you can to improve your skills. The LearningExpress book *Reading Comprehension in 20 Minutes a Day* (order information at the back of this book) or other books from your public library will undoubtedly help. Also, re-read and pay close attention to all the advice in Chapters 4–11 of this book in order to improve your score. Again, it will be helpful to ask friends and family to make up mock test questions and quiz you on them.

- **If your score is between 80 and 90 percent,** you could still benefit from additional work by going back to Chapters 4–11 and by brushing up your reading comprehension and general math skills before the exam.

- **If you scored above 90 percent,** that's great! This kind of score should make you a good candidate in the eyes of the federal government. Don't lose your edge, though; keep studying right up to the day before the exam.

If you didn't score as well as you would like, be sure to try to figure out the reasons why. Ask yourself the following questions: Did I run out of time before I could answer all the questions? Did I go back and change my answers from right to wrong? Did I get flus-

tered and sit staring at a hard question for what seemed like hours? If you had any of these problems, be sure to go over the EasySmart Test Preparation System in Chapter 2 again to learn how to avoid them.

Finally, again examine how you did on each kind of question on the test, in order to spot where your strengths and weaknesses lie. That way you'll know which areas require special effort in the time you have left before the exam. The table on this page identifies which questions on the second practice exam fall into which categories and lets you know which chapters to review if you had trouble with a particular type.

After you've spent some time brushing up on your weakest areas, try the third practice exam in Chapter 13.

VERBAL ABILITIES

Question Type	Question Numbers	Chapter
Vocabulary	12–15, 26, 27, 39, 40, 52–55, 64–66, 78, 79	Chapter 4, Vocabulary and Spelling
Spelling	1–3, 28–30, 41–44, 58–60, 80–83	Chapter 4, Vocabulary and Spelling
Grammar	7–11, 21, 22, 48–51, 61–63, 73–75	Chapter 5, Grammar
Reading Comprehension	16–18, 23–25, 35–38, 56, 57, 67–69, 76, 77	Chapter 6, Reading Comprehension
Word Relations (Analogies)	4–6, 19, 20, 31–34, 45–47, 70–72, 84, 85	Chapter 7, Word Relations

CLERICAL APTITUDE

Question Type	Question Numbers	Chapter
Name and Number Comparisons	11–15, 36–40, 56–60, 76–80, 96–100, 111–115	Chapter 8, Name and Number Comparisons
Alphabetizing	16–20, 31–35, 51–55, 71–75, 91–95, 106–110	Chapter 9, Alphabetizing
Arithmetic	1–5, 26–30, 41–45, 61–65, 81–85, 101–105	Chapter 10, Arithmetic
Number & Letter Matching	6–10, 21–25, 46–50, 66–70, 86–90, 116–120	Chapter 11, Number and Letter Matching

C·H·A·P·T·E·R

FEDERAL CLERICAL PRACTICE EXAM 2

13

CHAPTER SUMMARY

This is the third of three practice tests in this book based on the Federal Clerical Exam. This test will give you more practice and an opportunity to build on your strengths and correct your weaknesses.

L
ike the previous practice exams, this one is divided into two parts, Verbal Abilities and Clerical Aptitude. Verbal Abilities includes questions on vocabulary, grammar, spelling, word relations (analogies), and reading comprehension. Clerical Aptitude includes questions on number-and-letter matching, name-and-number comparison, alphabetization, and general math—addition, subtraction, multiplication, and division.

For this exam, you should simulate the actual test-taking experience very closely, trying to do the whole test in the time you will be allotted on the actual exam—about 50 minutes in all, 35 minutes for the Verbal Abilities section and 15 minutes for the Clerical Aptitude section. Use a kitchen timer or stopwatch to time yourself accurately. There will probably be no breaks during the actual exam, so don't take one when you do this practice exam, either. Again, find a quiet place to work. Tear out the answer sheet on the next page and fill in the circles with your number 2 pencil.

After the exam, use the answer key that follows it to see how you did and to find out why the correct answers are correct. The answer key is again followed by a section on how to score your exam.

VERBAL ABILITIES

1.	ⓐ	ⓑ	ⓒ	ⓓ	31.	ⓐ	ⓑ	ⓒ	ⓓ	61.	ⓐ	ⓑ	ⓒ	ⓓ
2.	ⓐ	ⓑ	ⓒ	ⓓ	32.	ⓐ	ⓑ	ⓒ	ⓓ	62.	ⓐ	ⓑ	ⓒ	ⓓ
3.	ⓐ	ⓑ	ⓒ	ⓓ	33.	ⓐ	ⓑ	ⓒ	ⓓ	63.	ⓐ	ⓑ	ⓒ	ⓓ
4.	ⓐ	ⓑ	ⓒ	ⓓ	34.	ⓐ	ⓑ	ⓒ	ⓓ	64.	ⓐ	ⓑ	ⓒ	ⓓ
5.	ⓐ	ⓑ	ⓒ	ⓓ	35.	ⓐ	ⓑ	ⓒ	ⓓ	65.	ⓐ	ⓑ	ⓒ	ⓓ
6.	ⓐ	ⓑ	ⓒ	ⓓ	36.	ⓐ	ⓑ	ⓒ	ⓓ	66.	ⓐ	ⓑ	ⓒ	ⓓ
7.	ⓐ	ⓑ	ⓒ	ⓓ	37.	ⓐ	ⓑ	ⓒ	ⓓ	67.	ⓐ	ⓑ	ⓒ	ⓓ
8.	ⓐ	ⓑ	ⓒ	ⓓ	38.	ⓐ	ⓑ	ⓒ	ⓓ	68.	ⓐ	ⓑ	ⓒ	ⓓ
9.	ⓐ	ⓑ	ⓒ	ⓓ	39.	ⓐ	ⓑ	ⓒ	ⓓ	69.	ⓐ	ⓑ	ⓒ	ⓓ
10.	ⓐ	ⓑ	ⓒ	ⓓ	40.	ⓐ	ⓑ	ⓒ	ⓓ	70.	ⓐ	ⓑ	ⓒ	ⓓ
11.	ⓐ	ⓑ	ⓒ	ⓓ	41.	ⓐ	ⓑ	ⓒ	ⓓ	71.	ⓐ	ⓑ	ⓒ	ⓓ
12.	ⓐ	ⓑ	ⓒ	ⓓ	42.	ⓐ	ⓑ	ⓒ	ⓓ	72.	ⓐ	ⓑ	ⓒ	ⓓ
13.	ⓐ	ⓑ	ⓒ	ⓓ	43.	ⓐ	ⓑ	ⓒ	ⓓ	73.	ⓐ	ⓑ	ⓒ	ⓓ
14.	ⓐ	ⓑ	ⓒ	ⓓ	44.	ⓐ	ⓑ	ⓒ	ⓓ	74.	ⓐ	ⓑ	ⓒ	ⓓ
15.	ⓐ	ⓑ	ⓒ	ⓓ	45.	ⓐ	ⓑ	ⓒ	ⓓ	75.	ⓐ	ⓑ	ⓒ	ⓓ
16.	ⓐ	ⓑ	ⓒ	ⓓ	46.	ⓐ	ⓑ	ⓒ	ⓓ	76.	ⓐ	ⓑ	ⓒ	ⓓ
17.	ⓐ	ⓑ	ⓒ	ⓓ	47.	ⓐ	ⓑ	ⓒ	ⓓ	77.	ⓐ	ⓑ	ⓒ	ⓓ
18.	ⓐ	ⓑ	ⓒ	ⓓ	48.	ⓐ	ⓑ	ⓒ	ⓓ	78.	ⓐ	ⓑ	ⓒ	ⓓ
19.	ⓐ	ⓑ	ⓒ	ⓓ	49.	ⓐ	ⓑ	ⓒ	ⓓ	79.	ⓐ	ⓑ	ⓒ	ⓓ
20.	ⓐ	ⓑ	ⓒ	ⓓ	50.	ⓐ	ⓑ	ⓒ	ⓓ	80.	ⓐ	ⓑ	ⓒ	ⓓ
21.	ⓐ	ⓑ	ⓒ	ⓓ	51.	ⓐ	ⓑ	ⓒ	ⓓ	81.	ⓐ	ⓑ	ⓒ	ⓓ
22.	ⓐ	ⓑ	ⓒ	ⓓ	52.	ⓐ	ⓑ	ⓒ	ⓓ	82.	ⓐ	ⓑ	ⓒ	ⓓ
23.	ⓐ	ⓑ	ⓒ	ⓓ	53.	ⓐ	ⓑ	ⓒ	ⓓ	83.	ⓐ	ⓑ	ⓒ	ⓓ
24.	ⓐ	ⓑ	ⓒ	ⓓ	54.	ⓐ	ⓑ	ⓒ	ⓓ	84.	ⓐ	ⓑ	ⓒ	ⓓ
25.	ⓐ	ⓑ	ⓒ	ⓓ	55.	ⓐ	ⓑ	ⓒ	ⓓ	85.	ⓐ	ⓑ	ⓒ	ⓓ
26.	ⓐ	ⓑ	ⓒ	ⓓ	56.	ⓐ	ⓑ	ⓒ	ⓓ					
27.	ⓐ	ⓑ	ⓒ	ⓓ	57.	ⓐ	ⓑ	ⓒ	ⓓ					
28.	ⓐ	ⓑ	ⓒ	ⓓ	58.	ⓐ	ⓑ	ⓒ	ⓓ					
29.	ⓐ	ⓑ	ⓒ	ⓓ	59.	ⓐ	ⓑ	ⓒ	ⓓ					
30.	ⓐ	ⓑ	ⓒ	ⓓ	60.	ⓐ	ⓑ	ⓒ	ⓓ					

CLERICAL APTITUDE

1. ⓐ ⓑ ⓒ ⓓ ⓔ	41. ⓐ ⓑ ⓒ ⓓ ⓔ	81. ⓐ ⓑ ⓒ ⓓ ⓔ
2. ⓐ ⓑ ⓒ ⓓ ⓔ	42. ⓐ ⓑ ⓒ ⓓ ⓔ	82. ⓐ ⓑ ⓒ ⓓ ⓔ
3. ⓐ ⓑ ⓒ ⓓ ⓔ	43. ⓐ ⓑ ⓒ ⓓ ⓔ	83. ⓐ ⓑ ⓒ ⓓ ⓔ
4. ⓐ ⓑ ⓒ ⓓ ⓔ	44. ⓐ ⓑ ⓒ ⓓ ⓔ	84. ⓐ ⓑ ⓒ ⓓ ⓔ
5. ⓐ ⓑ ⓒ ⓓ ⓔ	45. ⓐ ⓑ ⓒ ⓓ ⓔ	85. ⓐ ⓑ ⓒ ⓓ ⓔ
6. ⓐ ⓑ ⓒ ⓓ ⓔ	46. ⓐ ⓑ ⓒ ⓓ ⓔ	86. ⓐ ⓑ ⓒ ⓓ ⓔ
7. ⓐ ⓑ ⓒ ⓓ ⓔ	47. ⓐ ⓑ ⓒ ⓓ ⓔ	87. ⓐ ⓑ ⓒ ⓓ ⓔ
8. ⓐ ⓑ ⓒ ⓓ ⓔ	48. ⓐ ⓑ ⓒ ⓓ ⓔ	88. ⓐ ⓑ ⓒ ⓓ ⓔ
9. ⓐ ⓑ ⓒ ⓓ ⓔ	49. ⓐ ⓑ ⓒ ⓓ ⓔ	89. ⓐ ⓑ ⓒ ⓓ ⓔ
10. ⓐ ⓑ ⓒ ⓓ ⓔ	50. ⓐ ⓑ ⓒ ⓓ ⓔ	90. ⓐ ⓑ ⓒ ⓓ ⓔ
11. ⓐ ⓑ ⓒ ⓓ ⓔ	51. ⓐ ⓑ ⓒ ⓓ ⓔ	91. ⓐ ⓑ ⓒ ⓓ ⓔ
12. ⓐ ⓑ ⓒ ⓓ ⓔ	52. ⓐ ⓑ ⓒ ⓓ ⓔ	92. ⓐ ⓑ ⓒ ⓓ ⓔ
13. ⓐ ⓑ ⓒ ⓓ ⓔ	53. ⓐ ⓑ ⓒ ⓓ ⓔ	93. ⓐ ⓑ ⓒ ⓓ ⓔ
14. ⓐ ⓑ ⓒ ⓓ ⓔ	54. ⓐ ⓑ ⓒ ⓓ ⓔ	94. ⓐ ⓑ ⓒ ⓓ ⓔ
15. ⓐ ⓑ ⓒ ⓓ ⓔ	55. ⓐ ⓑ ⓒ ⓓ ⓔ	95. ⓐ ⓑ ⓒ ⓓ ⓔ
16. ⓐ ⓑ ⓒ ⓓ ⓔ	56. ⓐ ⓑ ⓒ ⓓ ⓔ	96. ⓐ ⓑ ⓒ ⓓ ⓔ
17. ⓐ ⓑ ⓒ ⓓ ⓔ	57. ⓐ ⓑ ⓒ ⓓ ⓔ	97. ⓐ ⓑ ⓒ ⓓ ⓔ
18. ⓐ ⓑ ⓒ ⓓ ⓔ	58. ⓐ ⓑ ⓒ ⓓ ⓔ	98. ⓐ ⓑ ⓒ ⓓ ⓔ
19. ⓐ ⓑ ⓒ ⓓ ⓔ	59. ⓐ ⓑ ⓒ ⓓ ⓔ	99. ⓐ ⓑ ⓒ ⓓ ⓔ
20. ⓐ ⓑ ⓒ ⓓ ⓔ	60. ⓐ ⓑ ⓒ ⓓ ⓔ	100. ⓐ ⓑ ⓒ ⓓ ⓔ
21. ⓐ ⓑ ⓒ ⓓ ⓔ	61. ⓐ ⓑ ⓒ ⓓ ⓔ	101. ⓐ ⓑ ⓒ ⓓ ⓔ
22. ⓐ ⓑ ⓒ ⓓ ⓔ	62. ⓐ ⓑ ⓒ ⓓ ⓔ	102. ⓐ ⓑ ⓒ ⓓ ⓔ
23. ⓐ ⓑ ⓒ ⓓ ⓔ	63. ⓐ ⓑ ⓒ ⓓ ⓔ	103. ⓐ ⓑ ⓒ ⓓ ⓔ
24. ⓐ ⓑ ⓒ ⓓ ⓔ	64. ⓐ ⓑ ⓒ ⓓ ⓔ	104. ⓐ ⓑ ⓒ ⓓ ⓔ
25. ⓐ ⓑ ⓒ ⓓ ⓔ	65. ⓐ ⓑ ⓒ ⓓ ⓔ	105. ⓐ ⓑ ⓒ ⓓ ⓔ
26. ⓐ ⓑ ⓒ ⓓ ⓔ	66. ⓐ ⓑ ⓒ ⓓ ⓔ	106. ⓐ ⓑ ⓒ ⓓ ⓔ
27. ⓐ ⓑ ⓒ ⓓ ⓔ	67. ⓐ ⓑ ⓒ ⓓ ⓔ	107. ⓐ ⓑ ⓒ ⓓ ⓔ
28. ⓐ ⓑ ⓒ ⓓ ⓔ	68. ⓐ ⓑ ⓒ ⓓ ⓔ	108. ⓐ ⓑ ⓒ ⓓ ⓔ
29. ⓐ ⓑ ⓒ ⓓ ⓔ	69. ⓐ ⓑ ⓒ ⓓ ⓔ	109. ⓐ ⓑ ⓒ ⓓ ⓔ
30. ⓐ ⓑ ⓒ ⓓ ⓔ	70. ⓐ ⓑ ⓒ ⓓ ⓔ	110. ⓐ ⓑ ⓒ ⓓ ⓔ
31. ⓐ ⓑ ⓒ ⓓ ⓔ	71. ⓐ ⓑ ⓒ ⓓ ⓔ	111. ⓐ ⓑ ⓒ ⓓ ⓔ
32. ⓐ ⓑ ⓒ ⓓ ⓔ	72. ⓐ ⓑ ⓒ ⓓ ⓔ	112. ⓐ ⓑ ⓒ ⓓ ⓔ
33. ⓐ ⓑ ⓒ ⓓ ⓔ	73. ⓐ ⓑ ⓒ ⓓ ⓔ	113. ⓐ ⓑ ⓒ ⓓ ⓔ
34. ⓐ ⓑ ⓒ ⓓ ⓔ	74. ⓐ ⓑ ⓒ ⓓ ⓔ	114. ⓐ ⓑ ⓒ ⓓ ⓔ
35. ⓐ ⓑ ⓒ ⓓ ⓔ	75. ⓐ ⓑ ⓒ ⓓ ⓔ	115. ⓐ ⓑ ⓒ ⓓ ⓔ
36. ⓐ ⓑ ⓒ ⓓ ⓔ	76. ⓐ ⓑ ⓒ ⓓ ⓔ	116. ⓐ ⓑ ⓒ ⓓ ⓔ
37. ⓐ ⓑ ⓒ ⓓ ⓔ	77. ⓐ ⓑ ⓒ ⓓ ⓔ	117. ⓐ ⓑ ⓒ ⓓ ⓔ
38. ⓐ ⓑ ⓒ ⓓ ⓔ	78. ⓐ ⓑ ⓒ ⓓ ⓔ	118. ⓐ ⓑ ⓒ ⓓ ⓔ
39. ⓐ ⓑ ⓒ ⓓ ⓔ	79. ⓐ ⓑ ⓒ ⓓ ⓔ	119. ⓐ ⓑ ⓒ ⓓ ⓔ
40. ⓐ ⓑ ⓒ ⓓ ⓔ	80. ⓐ ⓑ ⓒ ⓓ ⓔ	120. ⓐ ⓑ ⓒ ⓓ ⓔ

VERBAL ABILITIES

Read the directions carefully, and then choose the best answer from the four choices. You have 35 minutes to complete this section.

All secretaries need a good reminder system, sometimes known as a "tickler" system because it tickles the memory. One type of tickler system is the index-card file with 12 large dividers, one for each month, and 31 small dividers, one for each day. Whenever secretaries need to schedule a reminder, they jot it down on a card and place it behind the appropriate divider. Each morning, they review the reminders for that particular day.

1. The paragraph best supports the statement that
   a. most secretaries have poor memories
   b. an index-card system is a good way to schedule reminders
   c. secretaries should file their reminders early in the morning
   d. filing is the most important job a secretary does each day

Learning to standardize routine jobs is one way secretaries can boost their efficiency and begin to work smarter rather than harder. Smart secretaries look for patterns in their work. For example, if much of their correspondence concerns the same few issues, they draw up a form letter to cover these points. If they are constantly responding to the same questions over and over again, they develop a small brochure. Smart secretaries also learn to consolidate their movements and efforts by making phone calls or doing filing in batches rather than one at a time.

2. The paragraph best supports the statement that smart secretaries
   a. work harder than other secretaries
   b. make very few phone calls each day
   c. develop ways to save time on the job
   d. treat all customers as if they were the same person

3. CUP is related to COFFEE as BOWL is related to
   a. dish
   b. soup
   c. spoon
   d. food

4. RODENT is related to MOUSE as TREE is related to
   a. leaf
   b. trunk
   c. elm
   d. squirrel

5. MARATHON is related to RACE as HIBERNATION is related to
   a. sleep
   b. bear
   c. nap
   d. winter

6. ELATED is related to DESPONDENT as ENLIGHTENED is related to
   a. aware
   b. ignorant
   c. miserable
   d. tolerant

For questions 7 and 8, choose the correctly spelled word.

7. a. beleif
b. bilief
c. belief
d. bilief

8. a. insite
b. encite
c. ensight
d. insight

For questions 9–11, choose the answer that is most clearly and correctly expressed.

9. a. He did not come home from the office until 6:00 a.m.; however, we were all concerned.
b. While we were all concerned, he did not come home from the office until 6:00 a.m.
c. He did not come home from the office until 6:00 a.m., whether we were all concerned.
d. Because he did not come home from the office until 6:00 a.m., we were all concerned.

10. a. Most of us believed the bank teller's story, and Officer Rinehart thought he was lying.
b. Most of us believed the bank teller's story, whereas Officer Rinehart thought he was lying.
c. Most of us believed the bank teller's story, when Officer Rinehart thought he was lying.
d. Most of us believed the bank teller's story, or Officer Rinehart thought he was lying.

11. a. The auditor ordered me to produce all my records, including receipts, with a sneer.
b. The auditor ordered me to produce all my records, with a sneer, including receipts.
c. The auditor ordered me with a sneer. To produce all my records including receipts.
d. With a sneer, the auditor ordered me to produce all my records including receipts.

12. To *croon* means most nearly to
a. swim
b. vocalize
c. stroke
d. yell

13. To *humidify* means most nearly to
a. moisten
b. warm
c. gather
d. spray

14. *Philosophy* means most nearly
a. bias
b. principle
c. evidence
d. process

For questions 15 and 16, choose the correctly spelled word.

15. a. sinsitive
b. sensitive
c. sensative
d. sinsative

16. a. magizine
b. magazene
c. magezine
d. magazine

Today's secretaries are often the connection between the customer and the company, so their verbal skills are an important part of the job. Since office professionals often feel overworked, vocabulary building is not something they feel they have time for. But acquiring verbal skills can be a painless process. Listening carefully and reading carefully are two ways to expand vocabulary skills. Some secretaries keep notebooks to jot down unfamiliar words and then spend just a few minutes each day finding the definitions in the dictionary.

17. The paragraph best supports the statement that secretaries
   a. have above-average verbal and communication skills
   b. should carry dictionaries with them at all times
   c. can learn new verbal skills in short periods of time
   d. teach others to listen and read carefully

Before you begin to compose a business letter, sit down and think about your purpose (why you are writing your letter). Do you want to request information, order a product, register a complaint, or apply for something? Do some brainstorming and gather information before you begin writing. Always keep your objective in mind.

18. The paragraph best supports the statement that
   a. planning is an important part of writing a business letter
   b. business letters are frequently complaint letters
   c. the purpose of a business letter is often difficult to determine
   d. brainstorming and writing take equal amounts of time

19. *Sphere* means most nearly
   a. air
   b. spread
   c. globe
   d. enclosure

For question 20, choose the answer that is most clearly and correctly expressed.

20. a. All the clerks got out their pencils and sharpened them.
   b. All the clerks have gotten out their pencils and sharpen them.
   c. All the clerks got out their pencils and have sharpened them.
   d. All the clerks gotten out their pencils and sharpened them.

For questions 21–23, choose the correctly spelled word.

21. a. magic
   b. magick
   c. magek
   d. maggic

22. a. acces
   b. acess
   c. access
   d. exess

23. a. prominent
   b. promanent
   c. prominant
   d. promenent

For questions 24–27, choose the answer that is most clearly and correctly expressed.

24. a. At first I was liking the shouts of the traders on the stock exchange floor, but later they got on my nerves.
    b. At first I liked the shouts of the traders on the stock exchange floor, but later they have gotten on my nerves.
    c. At first I like the shouts of the traders on the stock exchange floor, but later they got on my nerves.
    d. At first I liked the shouts of the traders on the stock exchange floor, but later they got on my nerves.

25. a. The owl parrot looks like a bird of prey; however, it feeds on vegetable matter.
    b. Feeding on vegetable matter, the owl parrot looks like a bird of prey.
    c. Looking like a bird of prey, the owl parrot feeds on vegetable matter.
    d. The owl parrot feeds on vegetable matter, and it looks like a bird of prey.

26. a. I do not like my job, although the work I do is boring.
    b. I do not like my job, whereas the work I do is boring.
    c. While the work I do is boring, I do not like my job.
    d. Because the work I do is boring, I do not like my job.

27. a. Increased efficiency, caused by owning a good computer system.
    b. Owning a good computer system, for one to have increased efficiency.
    c. To have increased efficiency by one's owning a good computer system.
    d. Owning a good computer system can help one have increased efficiency.

28. To *refine* means most nearly to
    a. condone
    b. provide
    c. change
    d. purify

29. To *muse* means most nearly to
    a. tune
    b. ponder
    c. encourage
    d. read

30. *Gangly* means most nearly
    a. illegally
    b. closely
    c. ugly
    d. lanky

Rotating employees to several different positions within an organization is a good way to increase job satisfaction. Most employees enjoy learning new jobs and improving their technical skills. Job rotation also reduces boredom, increases motivation, and strengthens commitment to the organization.

31. The paragraph best supports the statement that
    a. most organizations rotate their employees to different jobs
    b. boredom on the job increases when job satisfaction increases
    c. employees with few technical skills cannot learn new jobs
    d. employees who have the chance to learn new jobs are less bored

Occasionally, secretaries have to fight negative stereotypes in the workplace. One of the easiest ways to improve a professional image is to dress appropriately. A secretary's clothes should be clean, neat, and professional. Even in offices where casual dress is acceptable, tailored clothing and jackets can add a professional touch.

32. The paragraph best supports the statement that
    a. secretaries must continually fight stereotypes at work
    b. casual dress is acceptable is most business offices
    c. tailored clothing is one way secretaries can show their professionalism
    d. what is appropriate dress in one office may be inappropriate in another

During the past decade, technology has brought many changes to traditional secretarial roles. It has simplified many routine secretarial tasks such as letter writing and has allowed many managers to perform their own administrative tasks. Secretaries are now becoming presenters, meeting planners, trainers, and graphic designers. But new technologies like electronic mail and voice mail have made the workplace much less personal. Secretaries might communicate with someone on an important matter for several days without actually ever speaking to them.

33. The paragraph best supports the statement that new technologies have
    a. given secretaries new challenges and responsibilities
    b. allowed secretaries to work fewer hours
    c. made office managers less communicative
    d. simplified the traditional office meeting

34. COMMUNICATION is related to TELEPHONE as TRANSPORTATION is related to
    a. aviation
    b. travel
    c. information
    d. bus

35. TACTFUL is related to DIPLOMATIC as BASHFUL is related to
    a. timid
    b. confident
    c. uncomfortable
    d. bold

36. WINDOW is related to PANE as BOOK is related to
    a. novel
    b. glass
    c. reader
    d. page

37. YARD is related to INCH as QUART is related to
    a. gallon
    b. ounce
    c. milk
    d. liquid

For questions 38–40, choose the correctly spelled word.

38. a. annonimous
    b. anonimous
    c. anounymous
    d. anonymous

39. a. extraordinery
    b. extrordinary
    c. extraordinary
    d. ecstraordinary

40. a. asurrance
b. assurance
c. assurence
d. assureance

For questions 41 and 42, choose the answer that is most clearly and correctly expressed.

41. a. One of the first modern detectives in literature were created by Edgar Allen Poe.
b. One of the first modern detectives in literature was created by Edgar Allen Poe.
c. Edgar Allen Poe having created one of the first modern detectives in literature.
d. In literature, one of the first modern detectives, created by Edgar Allen Poe.

42. a. The audit took place without incident. Except for a brief argument between the two accountants.
b. The audit took place. Without incident except for a brief argument between the two accountants.
c. The audit, took place without incident, except for a brief argument between the two accountants.
d. The audit took place without incident, except for a brief argument between the two accountants.

43. *Sage* means most nearly
a. obnoxious
b. conceited
c. wise
d. heartless

44. To *navigate* means most nearly to
a. search
b. decide
c. steer
d. assist

45. *Dormant* means most nearly
a. hidden
b. slumbering
c. rigid
d. misplaced

46. SCARCELY is related to MOSTLY as QUIETLY is related to
a. secretly
b. rudely
c. loudly
d. silently

47. BAKER is related to BREAD as CONGRESSMAN is related to
a. senator
b. law
c. state
d. politician

The process of composing business memos is very similar to the process of composing letters. The difference is that memos communicate information within a business organization. Business memos generally have one of two functions: to convey information or to persuade the reader.

48. The paragraph best supports the statement that business memos
a. have the same function as business letters
b. are more informational than persuasive
c. generally communicate two pieces of information
d. are written for people inside an organization

One reason people have difficulty solving problems on the job is that they look for complex solutions. Often it is much easier and more productive to look for a simpler answer to a problem. Looking for a simpler answer first will frequently lead you toward a more comprehensive and lasting solution.

49. The paragraph best supports the statement that
    a. it is difficult to solve complex problems on the job
    b. if a problem is complex, the answer will be complex
    c. it is easier to solve a complex problem than a simple one
    d. one good way to solve problems is to look for simple answers

As today's office professionals find themselves involved in many more aspects of a business, they may also find themselves attending business dinners. A business career can be stalled because the person did not follow simple rules of etiquette. Although everyone may make a little mistake, the serious errors can be costly. Here are some mistakes to avoid: Don't order a messy meal. Don't hold up an order because you can't decide what you want. Place your napkin on your lap, not inside your shirt. Don't fight over the check; the host should pay.

50. The paragraph best supports the statement that
    a. ordering is the longest part of a business dinner
    b. business dinners are stressful for most participants
    c. improper etiquette at dinner can hurt a business career
    d. placing a napkin inside a shirt is a simple mistake everyone makes

51. EMBARRASSED is related to HUMILIATED as FRIGHTENED is related to
    a. terrified
    b. agitated
    c. courageous
    d. reckless

52. ODOMETER is related to MILEAGE as COMPASS is related to
    a. speed
    b. hiking
    c. needle
    d. direction

53. CONTROL is related to DOMINATE as MAGNIFY is related to
    a. enlarge
    b. preserve
    c. decrease
    d. divide

54. To *banish* means most nearly to
    a. exile
    b. decorate
    c. succumb
    d. encourage

55. To *tailor* means most nearly to
    a. measure
    b. construct
    c. launder
    d. alter

56. To *yield* means most nearly to
    a. merge
    b. relinquish
    c. destroy
    d. hinder

57. *Journal* means most nearly
    a. trip
    b. receipt
    c. diary
    d. list

For questions 58–60, choose the answer that is most clearly and correctly expressed.

58. a. They finished their inventory, left the warehouse, and return to the main office.
b. They finished their inventory, left the warehouse, and returns to the main office.
c. They finished their inventory, left the warehouse, and returned to the main office.
d. They finished their inventory, left the warehouse, and returning to the main office.

59. a. Searching for evidence, police officers, must be mindful of the Fourth Amendment.
b. Searching for evidence. Police officers must be mindful of the Fourth Amendment.
c. When searching for evidence. Police officers, must be mindful of the Fourth Amendment.
d. When searching for evidence, police officers must be mindful of the Fourth Amendment.

60. a. The report had been improperly typed, the account was lost.
b. Because the report had been improperly typed, the account was lost.
c. Because the report had been improperly typed. The account was lost.
d. The report had been improperly typed the account lost.

For questions 61–64, choose the correctly spelled word.

61. a. frequently
b. frequintly
c. frequentlly
d. frequentley

62. a. enphasis
b. emphisis
c. emphasis
d. emfasis

63. a. encouredging
b. encouraging
c. incurraging
d. incouraging

64. a. commitment
b. committment
c. comittment
d. comitment

With most office professionals today, management is not interested in simply hearing about problems. Professionals should of course recognize problems, but they should also seek out and offer solutions. When you see a problem in the workplace, think about how you might remedy the situation before you take the problem to your manager.

65. The paragraph best supports the statement that
a. managers will not listen to employees' problems
b. office professionals should recognize problems and offer solutions
c. it is easier to remedy a problem than to recognize its seriousness
d. most office professionals seek out several solutions to one problem

Desktop videoconferencing may be today's newest meeting technology, but it may not be for everyone. Before you recommend that your company buy a desktop videoconferencing system, you need to examine your goals and needs. New technologies need to complement how people operate within a company.

66. The paragraph best supports the statement that
a. desktop videoconferencing is the wave of the future for most businesses
b. before buying a new technology, a company should identify why and how it will be used
c. new technologies such as desktop videoconferencing are changing the role of the business meeting
d. how people operate within a company is one way of judging whether a company can afford a new technology

An organized desk will save many hours of time. Here are some ways to make your work flow more efficient: 1) Filing should be done often to keep papers from gathering on your desk. 2) Update your calendar and address book frequently. 3) Limit the number of papers and personal items on your desk top. 4) Keep a spiral notebook to record all phone messages. 5) Organize and clean up your desk each day before you leave the office.

67. The paragraph best supports the statement that in an office
a. an unorganized desk results in wasted time
b. all personal items should be placed inside desk drawers
c. people who are organized work fewer hours each day
d. organization is the key to job satisfaction

68. *Eternal* means most nearly
a. timeless
b. heavenly
c. loving
d. wealthy

69. *Hostel* means most nearly
a. turnstile
b. cot
c. trek
d. inn

70. To *stow* means most nearly to
a. pack
b. curtsy
c. fool
d. trample

For questions 71–74, choose the answer that is most clearly and correctly expressed.

71. a. Officer Alvarez was able to search the suspect's car, where she found $200,000 worth of stolen jewels. Because she had a warrant.
b. $200,000 worth of stolen jewels were found. The result of a search by Office Alvarez of the suspect's car, because she had a warrant.
c. Because of a warrant and a search of the suspect's car. $200,000 worth of stolen jewels were found by Officer Alvarez.
d. Because Officer Alvarez had a warrant, she was able to search the suspect's car, where she found $200,000 worth of stolen jewels.

72. a. The teacher, like the students, were sick of the food in the school cafeteria, and yesterday he went to the principal and complained.
b. The teacher, like the students, was sick of the food in the school cafeteria, and yesterday he goes to the principal and complains.
c. The teacher, like the students, was sick of the food in the school cafeteria, and yesterday he went to the principal and complained.
d. The teacher, like the students, were sick of the food in the school cafeteria, and yesterday he goes to the principal and complained.

73.
a. Mr. Love felt it was time to change jobs, but he was too cautious to do so.
b. Mr. Love felt it was time to change jobs, he was too cautious to do so.
c. Mr. Love felt it was time to change jobs he was too cautious to do so.
d. Mr. Love felt it was time. To change jobs, but he was too cautious to do so.

74.
a. Supervisor Wells knew that her typists were capable to excellent work.
b. Supervisor Wells knew that her typists were capable with excellent work.
c. Supervisor Wells knew that her typists were capable of excellent work.
d. Supervisor Wells knew that her typists were capable for excellent work.

75. PLAY is related to ACTOR as CONCERT is related to
a. symphony
b. musician
c. piano
d. percussion

76. PRIDE is related to LION as SCHOOL is related to
a. teacher
b. student
c. self-respect
d. fish

77. SPONGE is related to POROUS is as RUBBER is related to
a. massive
b. solid
c. elastic
d. inflexible

78. CANDID is related to INDIRECT as HONEST is related to
a. frank
b. wicked
c. truthful
d. devious

Secretaries are often asked to organize training sessions for other office workers. A quality training program will not be successful if the training takes place in a poor setting. For all-day training programs, a classroom setting with videotaping equipment and small circular tables is best.

79. The paragraph best supports the statement that
a. all-day training programs are more successful than other programs
b. secretaries should learn to operate videotaping equipment
c. a classroom is the best setting for an all-day training session
d. all office workers should receive periodic training

Handling computer repairs does not have to frustrate a well-organized office staff. Many office professionals have an in-house checklist for initially handling computer problems. The checklist consists of the common causes of computer down time: disconnected cables, competing electrical devices, dirty equipment, the wrong type of paper. By going through the checklist before phoning a computer technician, office assistants will often correct the problem quickly.

80. The paragraph best supports the statement that
   a. computer down time is usually the result of a mistake by an office worker
   b. a technician should be called in for computer repairs only after an office worker has completed an in-house checklist
   c. to avoid costly repairs, office workers should clean computer equipment several times each month
   d. computer breakdowns cause more frustration to office workers than other problems do

For questions 81–83, choose the correctly spelled word.

81. a. rediculous
   b. rediculus
   c. ridiculous
   d. ridiculus

82. a. prosecuted
   b. prossecuted
   c. prosecutted
   d. proseccuted

83. a. conspiccuous
   b. connspicuous
   c. conspicious
   d. conspicuous

Whether or not you can accomplish a specific goal or meet a specific deadline depends first on how much time you need to get the job done. What should you do when the demands of the job exceed the time you have available? The best approach is to divide the project into smaller pieces. Different goals will have to be divided in different ways, but one seemingly unrealistic goal can often be accomplished by working on several smaller, more reasonable goals.

84. The paragraph best supports the statement that
   a. demanding jobs often must remain only partially completed
   b. the best way to complete projects is not to have too many goals
   c. the best way to tackle a large project is to separate it into smaller parts
   d. the best approach to a demanding job is to assign portions to other employees

Members of your work team may have skills and abilities that you are not aware of, and they may be able to contribute to your team's as well as your own success. Whenever a new responsibility is given to your work team, it is usually a good idea to have all the members come up with ideas and suggestions about how to perform the new tasks. This way, you are likely to discover special work-related skills you never suspected they had. So take time to explore your work team's talents.

85. The paragraph best supports the statement that one member of a work team
   a. may have abilities that others on the team don't know about
   b. usually stands out as having more ideas than other members do
   c. should be assigned the task of discovering the whole team's talents
   d. should act as a leader for the entire team

CLERICAL APTITUDE

In questions 1–5, compare the three names and numbers, and select the answer from the five choices below:

a. if ALL THREE names or numbers are exactly ALIKE

b. if only the FIRST and SECOND names or numbers are exactly ALIKE

c. if only the FIRST and THIRD names or numbers are exactly ALIKE

d. if only the SECOND and THIRD names or numbers are exactly ALIKE

e. if ALL THREE names or numbers are DIFFERENT

1. Willam Donalds William Donalds William Donald

2. P. K. Windham R. K. Windham P. R. Windham

3. 4238907 4238907 4238907

4. 9786541 9785641 9785641

5. Abbey Grant Abbey Grant Abby Grant

6. Add:

   27
   +13

a. 34

b. 39

c. 40

d. 48

e. none of these

7. Subtract:

   69
   −12

a. 56

b. 57

c. 59

d. 60

e. none of these

8. Divide:

   14 ⟌ 28

a. 3

b. 4

c. 5

d. 7

e. none of these

9. Multiply:

   33
   ×3

a. 55

b. 66

c. 96

d. 99

e. none of these

10. Add:

   12
   +6

a. 7

b. 18

c. 20

d. 22

e. none of these

For questions 11–15, choose the correct place for the name in the box.

11. Hough, James P.
   a. →
      Houde, Jeremy
   b. →
      Hough, Henry L.
   c. →
      Hough, Kenneth
   d. →
      Houghton, Robert
   e. →

12. Lerner, Agnes H.
   a. →
      Lerner, Robert P.
   b. →
      Leroux, Charles A.
   c. →
      Leroy, Mary A.
   d. →
      Leshane, Rachel
   e. →

13. Paquin, M. J.
   a. →
      Paquet, L.T.
   b. →
      Paquette, Vera
   c. →
      Paquin, Douglas
   d. →
      Paquin, P.S.
   e. →

14. Carver, Allyn
   a. →
      Carver, Allen
   b. →
      Carver, Carl
   c. →
      Carver, Ellen
   d. →
      Carver, Francis
   e. →

15. Edison, Mikhail
   a. →
      Edison, M.K.
   b. →
      Edison, Nathan
   c. →
      Edson, Lawrence
   d. →
      Edson, Paula
   e. →

For questions 16–20, choose the suggested answer that contains numbers and letters all of which appear in that question.

16. 4 7 L 8 H C 3 D

17. J 5 3 G C 8 7 S

18. 8 F 3 X 9 2 N Q

19. L 1 C D M 5 9 4

20. S 5 F 8 U E 2 9

Suggested Answers
{
   a. = 2, 3, F, N
   b. = 5, 8, S, U
   c. = 4, 7, C, D
   d. = 5, 9, C, L
   e. = none of these
}

For questions 21–25, compare the three names and numbers, and select the answer from the five choices below:

a. if ALL THREE names or numbers are exactly ALIKE

b. if only the FIRST and SECOND names or numbers are exactly ALIKE

c. if only the FIRST and THIRD names or numbers are exactly ALIKE

d. if only the SECOND and THIRD names or numbers are exactly ALIKE

e. if ALL THREE names or numbers are DIFFERENT

21. Raymond L. Goyet   Raymond L. Goyat   Raymond L. Goyet

22. Leslie Peters   Leslie Peters   Leslie Peters

23. 1145670   1144670   1145670

24. 6903742   6093742   6907342

25. Melvoin Ashford   Melvin Ashford   Melvin Ashford

For questions 26–30, choose the correct place for the name in the box.

26. | Potter, Barry |
a. →
Potray, Alan
b. →
Potser, G.H.
c. →
Pottan, David
d. →
Potter, Barbara
e. →

27. | Lever, Sally Q. |
a. →
Lever, Samuel
b. →
Levere, Robert
c. →
Levere, Tess
d. →
Leveris, Justin
e. →

28. | Cohn, Anthony |
a. →
Cohen, Mildred
b. →
Cohen, Quentin P.
c. →
Cohn, Margaret
d. →
Cohn, Oscar
e. →

29. | Naddif, Omar |
a. →
Nacsin, Melody
b. →
Nactman, A.J.
c. →
Nadage, Moe
d. →
Nadeau, Susan
e. →

30. | Thorne, Mabel |

   a. →

     Thorn, Arthur

   b. →

     Thorn, B. L.

   c. →

     Thorn, Felipe

   d. →

     Thorn, Nancy

   e. →

For questions 31–35, choose the suggested answer that contains numbers and letters all of which appear in that question.

31. 4   G   R   D   6   5   S   W

32. 2   F   9   D   5   P   S   8

33. 6   T   P   5   D   3   G   2

34. 3   8   P   5   S   W   T   4

35. 2   P   8   S   F   9   5   W

Suggested Answers
  a. = 2, 5, F, P
  b. = 6, 9, T, W
  c. = 3, 5, P, S
  d. = 4, 6, D, G
  e. = none of these

36. Multiply:

   16
   ×2

  a. 30
  b. 31
  c. 32
  d. 33
  e. none of these

37. Add:

   18
  +17

  a. 35
  b. 36
  c. 37
  d. 38
  e. none of these

38. Subtract:

   22
  −16

  a. 9
  b. 8
  c. 7
  d. 6
  e. none of these

39. Divide:

  $12\overline{)60}$

  a. 4
  b. 7
  c. 9
  d. 11
  e. none of these

40. Subtract:

   21
  −13

  a. 6
  b. 7
  c. 8
  d. 9
  e. none of these

For questions 41–45, compare the three names and numbers, and select the answer from the five choices below:

a. if ALL THREE names or numbers are exactly ALIKE
b. if only the FIRST and SECOND names or numbers are exactly ALIKE
c. if only the FIRST and THIRD names or numbers are exactly ALIKE
d. if only the SECOND and THIRD names or numbers are exactly ALIKE
e. if ALL THREE names or numbers are DIFFERENT

41. Michael   Michael   Michael
         Pethick   Pethick   Petrick

42. Alice B.   Alice B.   Alice B.
         Philbrick   Philbrick   Philbrick

43. 0410157   0410157   0410157

44. Thomas   Tomas   Thomas
         Deltorchio   Deltorchio   Deltochio

45. 4817448   4817443   4817448

For questions 46–50, choose the correct place for the name in the box.

46. | Sliger, Maxwell |
- a. →
  Sligar, Patience
- b. →
  Sliger, Patrice
- c. →
  Sliger, Patrick
- d. →
  Sliger, Paul
- e. →

47. | Herring, Maurice |
- a. →
  Herring, Mavis
- b. →
  Herring, Maxwell
- c. →
  Herst, Michael
- d. →
  Herst, Michelle
- e. →

48. | Milligan, Edwin |
- a. →
  Millick, Pearl
- b. →
  Millider, Hallie
- c. →
  Milligan, Edward
- d. →
  Milligan, Elizabeth
- e. →

49. | Wallach, Lee |
- a. →
  Wallach, Burt
- b. →
  Wallach, Frank
- c. →
  Wallach, Morris
- d. →
  Wallach, Roger
- e. →

50. | Zaharis, Wendy |

   a. →

     Zaharas, Sandra

   b. →

     Zaharas, Vanna

   c. →

     Zahares, Vera

   d. →

     Zahares, Wanda

   e. →

51. Add:

    14

   +18

   a. 31

   b. 32

   c. 33

   d. 34

   e. none of these

52. Multiply:

    17

   ×3

   a. 30

   b. 41

   c. 50

   d. 51

   e. none of these

53. Divide:

   $3\overline{)27}$

   a. 18

   b. 12

   c. 8

   d. 7

   e. none of these

54. Divide:

   $8\overline{)56}$

   a. 7

   b. 8

   c. 12

   d. 18

   e. none of these

55. Subtract:

    29

   −13

   a. 6

   b. 7

   c. 11

   d. 16

   e. none of these

For questions 56–60, choose the suggested answer that contains numbers and letters all of which appear in that question.

56. X S 7 9 L 3 2 H

57. 2 S V 5 3 D 8 E

58. 6 E X 2 L S 5 H

59. H 3 D V 7 E S 5

60. 5 X D 6 H 8 L V

Suggested Answers

   a. = 5, 8, D, H

   b. = 3, 7, S, X

   c. = 2, 6, E, L

   d. = 2, 5, S, V

   e. = none of these

For questions 61–65, compare the three names and numbers, and select the answer from the five choices below:

a. if ALL THREE names or numbers are exactly ALIKE

b. if only the FIRST and SECOND names or numbers are exactly ALIKE

c. if only the FIRST and THIRD names or numbers are exactly ALIKE

d. if only the SECOND and THIRD names or numbers are exactly ALIKE

e. if ALL THREE names or numbers are DIFFERENT

61. 9765213   9765213   9675213

62. May   May   May
Farrally-Plourde   Farally-Plourde   Farally-Plourde

63. Archibald   Archibald   Archibald
Sumner   Sumner   Summer

64. 6856549   6855649   6856549

65. 3346613   3346613   3346613

For questions 66–70, choose the suggested answer that contains numbers and letters all of which appear in that question.

66. 4   P   Q   9   7   T   M   5

67. M   T   3   A   G   9   4   7

68. 2   6   M   5   A   3   G   4

69. T   7   4   R   P   6   2   M

70. A   2   R   5   6   G   M   7

Suggested Answers
{
  a. = 4, 6, P, R
  b. = 3, 9, G, M
  c. = 2, 5, A, G
  d. = 4, 7, Q, T
  e. = none of these
}

71. Multiply:

15
×4

a. 50
b. 60
c. 69
d. 73
e. none of these

72. Divide:

2 | 60

a. 20
b. 30
c. 35
d. 36
e. none of these

73. Add:

14
+17

a. 39
b. 35
c. 31
d. 30
e. none of these

74. Subtract:

98
−13

a. 85
b. 87
c. 90
d. 92
e. none of these

75. Multiply:

18
×3

a. 67
b. 64
c. 55
d. 54
e. none of these

For questions 76–80, choose the correct place for the name in the box.

76. | Oliver, W. W. |

a. →
Olivier, Alexander
b. →
Olivier, Gary
c. →
Olivier, Kathy
d. →
Olivier, Rachel
e. →

77. | Thatcher, J. C. |

a. →
Thacher, B. L.
b. →
Thacher, W. P.
c. →
Thatcher, L. B.
d. →
Thatcher, N. Y.
e. →

78. | Ivers, Maeve |

a. →
Ivers, Mabel
b. →
Ivers, Maggie
c. →
Ivers, Malvina
d. →
Ivers, Marsha
e. →

79. | Milloy, Jacques |

a. →
Millay, Edna
b. →
Millay, Leonard
c. →
Milloy, Ingrid
d. →
Milloy, Jackie
e. →

80. | Perez, Salvador |

a. →
Peretti, Phyllis
b. →
Pereve, Rose Marie
c. →
Perez, Jonathan
d. →
Perez, Raymond
e. →

For questions 81–85, compare the three names and numbers, and select the answer from the five choices below:

a. if ALL THREE names or numbers are exactly ALIKE

b. if only the FIRST and SECOND names or numbers are exactly ALIKE

c. if only the FIRST and THIRD names or numbers are exactly ALIKE

d. if only the SECOND and THIRD names or numbers are exactly ALIKE

e. if ALL THREE names or numbers are DIFFERENT

81. Francis Lemoine   Frances Lemoine   Francie Lemoine

82. 3355366   3535366   3535366

83. 8802040   8082040   8804020

84. Margaret M. Meyer   Margaret M. Meyer   Margaret M. Mayer

85. Curtis Osborne   Curtis Osborn   Curtis Osborne

For questions 86–90, choose the correct place for the name in the box.

86. | Robins, Stanley |

a. →

Robbins, Marshall

b. →

Robbins, Wendy

c. →

Robins, Karen

d. →

Robins, Victor

e. →

87. | Wallin, Leslie |

a. →

Walling, Allan

b. →

Walling, Derrick

c. →

Walling, Galen

d. →

Walling, Kevin

e. →

88. | Aceto, Rose |

a. →

Aceto, Roberta

b. →

Aceto, Rodney

c. →

Aceto, Roger

d. →

Aceto, Roy

e. →

89. | Schrage, D. G. |

a. →

Schraeter, David

b. →

Schraft, Millicent

c. →

Schralt, Kelly

d. →

Schram, Calvin

e. →

90. | Huntress, Ethel |

    a. →

       Hunter, Beryl

    b. →

       Huntress, Lani

    c. →

       Huntsinger, Brad

    d. →

       Huntsman, Jane

    e. →

For questions 91–95, choose the suggested answer that contains numbers and letters all of which appear in that question.

91. L M 5 3 8 N 7 R

92. 3 R L 4 M 7 S T

93. 4 M 7 L T 8 N 5

94. P 7 M 5 4 S L 3

95. S 8 P M 3 2 R 5

Suggested Answers
    a. = 4, 7, L, P
    b. = 3, 4, M, R
    c. = 2, 5, M, S
    d. = 4, 8, N, T
    e. = none of these

96. Subtract:

    22
   −17

    a. 8
    b. 6
    c. 5
    d. 3
    e. none of these

97. Multiply:

    14
  ×14

    a. 186
    b. 153
    c. 146
    d. 139
    e. none of these

98. Divide:

  6 | 36

    a. 4
    b. 6
    c. 8
    d. 9
    e. none of these

99. Add:

    12
  +15

    a. 27
    b. 25
    c. 29
    d. 21
    e. none of these

100. Subtract:

    33
  −11

    a. 12
    b. 14
    c. 20
    d. 22
    e. none of these

For questions 101–105, compare the three names and numbers, and select the answer from the five choices below:

a. if ALL THREE names or numbers are exactly ALIKE

b. if only the FIRST and SECOND names or numbers are exactly ALIKE

c. if only the FIRST and THIRD names or numbers are exactly ALIKE

d. if only the SECOND and THIRD names or numbers are exactly ALIKE

e. if ALL THREE names or numbers are DIFFERENT

101. 3524628   3524682   3524682

102. Marcus P.   Marcus P.   Marcus P.
Webber   Webber   Webber

103. 1249125   1429125   1249152

104. Gerald Franck   Gerald Frank   Gerald Frank

105. L. D. Payeur   L. D. Payer   L. D. Payeur

For questions 106–110, choose the suggested answer that contains numbers and letters all of which appear in that question.

106. H 3 W 5 Y E 4 5

107. 9 E Y 4 F 5 D 6

108. R 9 2 D 3 7 Y E

109. F 4 D 6 5 9 W R

110. 9 5 W Y 2 4 R D

Suggested Answers
{
a. = 6, 9, D, F
b. = 3, 4, E, H
c. = 2, 5, R, Y
d. = 4, 9, E, W
e. = none of these
}

For questions 111–115, choose the correct place for the name in the box.

111. | McDonnell, Jennifer |

a. →
   McDonough, Farley
b. →
   McDougal, Chandler
c. →
   McDougall, Alvin
d. →
   McDowell, Marvin
e. →

112. | Perla, Richard |

a. →
   Perl, Rick
b. →
   Perl, Samuel
c. →
   Perla, Aaron
d. →
   Perla, Norman
e. →

113. | Sherman, Thomas |

a. →
   Sherman, Edna
b. →
   Sherman, Martin
c. →
   Sherman, Philip
d. →
   Sherman, Stephen
e. →

114. | Winger, Melanie |

   a. →

      Wingert, Suzanne

   b. →

      Wingfield, Melinda

   c. →

      Wingren, Lisa

   d. →

      Wingrent, Evelyn

   e. →

115. | DeVito, Janet |

   a. →

      DeVane, William

   b. →

      DeVine, Christine

   c. →

      DeVito, Peter

   d. →

      DeVry, Michelle

   e. →

116. Multiply:

    14

    ×12

   a. 124

   b. 132

   c. 168

   d. 176

   e. none of these

117. Divide:

   3 ⟌ 18

   a. 9

   b. 8

   c. 7

   d. 6

   e. none of these

118. Subtract:

    28

    −17

   a. 8

   b. 11

   c. 16

   d. 17

   e. none of these

119. Add:

    17

    +13

   a. 31

   b. 32

   c. 39

   d. 44

   e. none of these

120. Multiply:

    15

    ×7

   a. 101

   b. 103

   c. 105

   d. 111

   e. none of these

ANSWERS

VERBAL ABILITIES

Answer explanations are given for all questions except spelling. If you are not sure why the designated answer is correct for a spelling question, consult a dictionary.

1. **b.** The third sentence shows that an index system is needed to schedule reminders. Choices **a** and **d** are not mentioned in the passage. Choice **c** is wrong because the paragraph says that reminders should be reviewed in the morning, not filed in the morning.

2. **c.** The answer is found in the last sentence of the paragraph. Choice **a** is not mentioned. Choice **b** is wrong because although the paragraph mentions phone calls, it does not say how many calls a secretary may or may not make. Choice **d** is not mentioned.

3. **b.** Coffee goes into a cup and soup goes into an bowl. Choices **a** and **c** are incorrect because they are other utensils. The answer is not **d** because the word *food* is too general.

4. **c.** A mouse is a type of rodent, and an elm is a type of tree. The answer is not **a** or **b** because leaf and trunk are parts of the tree, not types of trees. Choice **d** is incorrect because a squirrel is another rodent.

5. **a.** A marathon is a long race and hibernation is a lengthy period of sleep. The answer is not **b** or **d** because even though bear and winter have a relationship with the word *hibernation,* neither of these completes the analogy. Choice **c** is incorrect because a nap is a short period of sleep.

6. **b.** *Elated* is the opposite of *despondent; enlightened* is the opposite of *ignorant.* The answer is not **a** because *aware* is a synonym for *enlightened.* The answer is not **c** or **d** because neither of these is the opposite of *enlightened.*

7. **c.**

8. **d.**

9. **d.** This choice establishes the causal relationship between the two ideas.

10. **b.** The transitional word *whereas* correctly establishes a contrast.

11. **d.** The modifier *with a sneer* should be placed next to *the auditor.*

12. **b.** To *croon* and to *vocalize* both mean to sing.

13. **a.** To *humidify* and to *moisten* both mean to make damp.

14. **b.** *Philosophy* means a system of motivating principles.

15. **b.**

16. **d.**

17. **c.** The phrase *just a few minutes each day* in the last sentence points to the answer. Choice **a** is incorrect because even though verbal skills are mentioned as being important to a secretary's job, it does not say that secretaries have above-average skills. Choice **b** is wrong because even though dictionaries are mentioned, the paragraph does not say they should be carried around. Choice **d** is not mentioned.

18. **a.** The first sentence points to the need for planning a business letter. Choice **b** is incorrect because even though complaint letters are mentioned, the paragraph does not say they are frequent. Choices **c** and **d** are not mentioned.

19. **c.** *Sphere* and *globe* both mean ball or orb.

20. **a.** The verbs *got* and *sharpened* agree in tense.

21. **a.**

22. **c.**

23. a.

24. d. The verbs *liked* and *got* agree in tense.

25. a. The transitional word *however* correctly establishes a contrast.

26. d. The introductory word *because* correctly links the work's being *boring* with *I do not like my job.* Choices **a**, **b**, and **c** are incorrect because they do not make that link.

27. d. This is a complete sentence; the others are fragments.

28. d. To *refine* and to *purify* both mean to remove impurities.

29. b. To *muse* and to *ponder* both mean to consider carefully or at length.

30. d. *Gangly* and *lanky* both mean tall, thin, and awkward.

31. d. The phrase *job rotation also reduces boredom* in the last sentence provides the answer. Choice **a** is incorrect because there is no indication that most organizations rotate employees. Choice **b** is obviously false. Choice **c** is not mentioned in the paragraph.

32. c. The last sentence indicates that tailored clothing shows professionalism. Choice **a** is wrong because the first sentence says that secretaries only occasionally fight stereotypes. Choice **b** is incorrect because even though the paragraph mentions that casual dress is acceptable, it does not say it is acceptable in most offices. Choice **d** is not mentioned.

33. a. The answer can be found in the first three sentences: technology has brought changes to secretarial roles, and these changes have brought new responsibilities. Choices **b**, **c**, and **d** are not mentioned in the paragraph.

34. d. The telephone is a means of communication. The bus is a means of transportation. Aviation (choice **a**) is not the answer because it is a type of transportation, not a means. The answer is not **b** or **c** because neither of these represents a means of transportation.

35. a. *Tactful* and *diplomatic* are synonyms (they mean about the same thing). *Bashful* and *timid* are also synonyms. The answer is not **b** or **c** because neither of these means the same as *bashful*. *Bold* (choice **d**) is incorrect because it means the opposite of *bashful*.

36. d. A window is made up of panes, and a book is made up of pages. The answer is not **a**, because a novel is a type of book. The answer is not **b**, because glass has no relationship to a book. Choice **c** is incorrect because a reader is a person related to a book; a book is not made up of readers.

37. b. A yard is a larger measure than an inch (a yard contains 36 inches). A quart is a larger measure than an ounce (a quart contains 32 ounces). Choice **a** is incorrect because a gallon is larger than a quart. Choices **c** and **d** are incorrect because they are not units of measurement.

38. d.

39. c.

40. b.

41. b. This is a complete sentence; choices **c** and **d** are fragments; in choice **a**, the verb does not agree in number with its subject, *one*.

42. d. Choices **a** and **b** contain sentence fragments. Choice **c** has a comma between subject and verb.

43. c. *Sage* and *wise* both mean intelligent, perceptive.

44. c. To *navigate* and to *steer* both mean to direct a course.

45. b. *Dormant* and *slumbering* both mean sleeping.

46. c. *Scarcely* is the opposite of *mostly*, and *quietly* is the opposite of *loudly*. Choices **a** and **b** are clearly not opposites of *quietly*. Choice **d** means the same as *quietly*.

47. b. A baker makes bread; a congressman makes laws. The answer is not choice **a** because a senator and a congressman both make laws. Choice **c** is incorrect because a congressman does not make a state. Politician (choice **d**) is also incorrect because a congressman is a politician.

48. d. The answer is clearly stated in the second sentence. Choice **a** is incorrect because even though memos and letters are similar, the paragraph does not say they have the same function. Choice **b** is not mentioned. Choice **c** is wrong because memos have two functions; the paragraph doesn't say they have two pieces of information.

49. d. The second sentence indicates that looking for simple answers is a productive way to solve problems. Choice **a** is not mentioned. Choice **b** is wrong because the opposite is asserted in the paragraph. Choice **c** is not mentioned in the paragraph.

50. c. The answer is clearly stated in the second sentence. Choice **a** is not mentioned. Although choice **b** may be true for some people, it is not stated in the paragraph. The paragraph indicates that placing a napkin inside a shirt, choice **d**, is a serious mistake, not a simple one.

51. a. If someone has been humiliated, they have been greatly embarrassed. If someone is terrified, they are extremely frightened. The answer is not **b** because an agitated person is not necessarily frightened. Choices **c** and **d** are incorrect because neither word expresses a state of being frightened.

52. d. An odometer is an instrument used to measure mileage. A compass is an instrument used to determine direction. Choices **a**, **b** and **c** are incorrect because none describe what a compass measures.

53. a. *Control* and *dominate* are synonyms, and *magnify* and *enlarge* are synonyms. The answer is not **b** or **d** because neither of these means the same as

enlarge. Choice **c** is incorrect because *decrease* is the opposite of *enlarge.*

54. a. To *banish* and to *exile* both mean to force to leave.

55. d. To *tailor* and to *alter* both mean to make something fit.

56. b. To *yield* and to *relinquish* both mean to give up.

57. c. A *journal* and a *diary* are both records of daily happenings.

58. c. The word *returned* is in the past tense, as are *finished* and *left* in the first part of the sentence, so this sentence is the only one that uses proper parallel structure.

59. d. Choices **b** and **c** contain sentence fragments. The first part of choice **a** is a dangling modifier; in addition, no comma should separate *police officers* from *must.*

60. b. Choices **a** and **d** are run-on sentences; choice **c** contains a sentence fragment.

61. a.

62. c.

63. b.

64. a.

65. b. The second sentence points to the need for both recognizing problems and offering solutions. Choice **a** is incorrect because the first sentence implies that management will hear about problems if solutions are offered, too. Choice **c** is not stated in the paragraph. Choice **d** may be true, but it is not mentioned in this paragraph.

66. b. The second sentence points out that goals and needs should be established before a company purchases a new technology such as videoconferencing. Choice **a** is incorrect because the paragraph indicates that videoconferencing is happening now; it is not necessarily the wave of the future. Choices **c** and **d** are incorrect because neither of these is mentioned in the paragraph.

67. a. The first sentence points to the relationship between organization and time saved, so a lack of organization would be time wasted. Choice **b** is wrong because the paragraph indicates that personal items on desktops should be limited, not eliminated. Choices **c** and **d** are not mentioned.

68. a. *Eternal* and *timeless* both mean without end.

69. d. A *hostel* and an *inn* are both lodging places.

70. a. To *stow* and to *pack* both mean to store away.

71. d. Each of the other choices includes a sentence fragment.

72. c. The verb must be *was* (not *were*), to agree with the subject, *the teacher*. The verbs in the second half of the sentence must be in the past tense, consistent with the verbs in the first half of the sentence.

73. a. This is a complete sentence. Choice **b** is a comma splice; choice **c** is a run-on sentence; choice **d** contains a sentence fragment.

74. c. The correct preposition is *of* rather than *to*, *with*, or *for*, so the choices **a**, **b**, and **d** are incorrect.

75. b. An actor performs in a play. A musician performs at a concert. Choices **a**, **c**, and **d** are incorrect because none are people who perform.

76. d. A group of lions is called a pride. A group of fish swim in a school. Teacher (choice **a**) and student (choice **b**) refer to another meaning of the word *school*. The answer is not **c** because self-respect has no obvious relationship to this particular meaning of *school*.

77. c. A sponge is a porous material. Rubber is an elastic material. Choice **a** is incorrect because rubber would not generally be referred to as massive. The answer is not **b** because even though rubber is a solid, its most noticeable characteristic is its elasticity. Choice **d** is incorrect because rubber has flexibility.

78. d. *Candid* and *indirect* describe opposing traits. *Honest* and *devious* describe opposing traits. The answer is not **a**, because *frank* means the same thing as *candid*. *Wicked* (choice **b**) is incorrect because even though it is a negative trait, it does not mean the opposite of *honest*. Choice **c** is incorrect because *truthful* and *honest* mean the same thing.

79. c. The last sentence states that classroom settings are best for all-day training. Choice **a** is wrong because it is not mentioned in the paragraph. Choice **b** may be a goal for some secretaries, but the paragraph does not suggest this. Choice **d** may be a goal for many businesses, but, again, the paragraph does not mention this.

80. b. The fourth sentence points to the idea of completing a checklist before phoning for a repair person. Choice **a** is not stated in the paragraph. Choice **c** may be a good idea, but it is not in the paragraph. The first sentence refutes choice **d**.

81. c.

82. a.

83. d.

84. c. The answer is clearly stated in the third sentence. Choice **a** is incorrect because the entire paragraph suggests otherwise. Choice **b** is not mentioned. Choice **d** looks attractive, but the idea of dividing jobs among several people is not mentioned in the paragraph.

85. a. The first sentence states that skills and abilities of one member may not be known by another. Choice **b** is not mentioned. Choice **c** is incorrect because even though the paragraph seems to be addressed to one individual reader, it does not say that one member should be assigned the task of discovering everyone's talents. Choice **d** is incorrect for that same reason.

CLERICAL APTITUDE

No answer explanations are given in this section. Once you know the correct answer, you should be able to go back to the question and see why it is right. Most mistakes in this section are the result of having to work quickly.

1. b.		33. e.	
2. e.		34. c.	
3. a.		35. a.	
4. d.		36. c.	
5. b.		37. a.	
6. c.		38. d.	
7. b.		39. e.	
8. e.		40. c.	
9. d.		41. b.	
10. b.		42. a.	
11. c.		43. a.	
12. a.		44. e.	
13. d.		45. c.	
14. b.		46. b.	
15. b.		47. a.	
16. c.		48. d.	
17. e.		49. c.	
18. a.		50. e.	
19. d.		51. b.	
20. b.		52. d.	
21. c.		53. e.	
22. a.		54. a.	
23. c.		55. d.	
24. e.		56. b.	
25. d.		57. d.	
26. e.		58. c.	
27. a.		59. e.	
28. c.		60. a.	
29. d.		61. b.	
30. e.		62. d.	
31. d.		63. b.	
32. a.		64. c.	

65. a.
66. d.
67. b.
68. c.
69. a.
70. c.
71. b.
72. b.
73. c.
74. a.
75. d.
76. a.
77. c.
78. b.
79. e.
80. e.
81. e.
82. d.
83. e.
84. b.
85. c.
86. d.
87. a.
88. d.
89. c.
90. b.
91. e.
92. b.

93. d.
94. a.
95. c.
96. c.
97. e.
98. b.
99. a.
100. d.
101. d.
102. a.
103. e.
104. d.
105. c.
106. b.
107. a.
108. e.
109. a.
110. c.
111. a.
112. e.
113. e.
114. a.
115. c.
116. c.
117. d.
118. b.
119. e.
120. c.

SCORING

In order to figure your total score on this exam, you'll need to figure your score for the Verbal Abilities and Clerical Aptitude sections separately. For the Verbal Abilities section, simply count up the number you got right. Questions you didn't answer or got wrong don't count.

1. Number of questions right: _____

For the Clerical Aptitude section, the scoring is a little more complicated. First, count up your right answers. Then count your wrong answers separately. Do not count questions you skipped. In order to figure the penalty for your wrong answers, divide your number of wrong answers by four, and then subtract the result from your total number of right answers.

2. Number of questions right: _____

3. Number of questions wrong: _____

4. Divide number 3 by 4: _____

5. Subtract number 4 from number 2: _____

Now you have your total raw score for both the Verbal Abilities and Clerical Aptitude sections. Add them together, and then divide by 205 to determine your total percentage score.

6. Add numbers 1 and 5 together: _____

7. Divide number 6 by 205: _____

The table on this page will help you check your math by giving you percentage equivalents for some possible scores. Use this percentage score to compare your score on this exam to your scores on the other exams in this book. This percentage score may not be equivalent to the kind of score that will be reported to you on your Notification of Results when you take the real Clerical and Administrative Support Exam.

Number of questions right	Approximate percentage
205	100%
190	93%
176	86%
161	79%
145	71%
131	64%
116	57%
102	50%

You need a score of at least 80 percent to pass, but you should strive for the best score you can achieve, since a higher score may give you a shot at a wider range of good jobs. You have probably seen improvement between your first two practice exam scores and this one; however, if you improved less than you would like, remember these options:

- **If you scored below 60 percent,** you should seriously consider whether you're ready for the Federal Clerical Exam right now. You may need to take courses in reading, writing, or clerical abilities, or find a friend who can tutor you.

- **If your score is in the 60 to 80 percent range,** you need to work as hard as you can to improve your skills. Re-read the advice in Chapters 4–11 of this book in order to improve your score. Ask friends and family to make up mock test questions and quiz you on them.

- **If your score is between 80 and 90 percent,** you could still benefit from doing some extra work by going back to Chapters 4–11 and by brushing up your reading comprehension and general math skills before the exam.

- **If you scored above 90 percent,** that's terrific! This kind of score should make you a good candidate in the eyes of the federal government; however, be sure to keep studying right up to the day before the exam so as not to lose your advantage.

If you didn't score as well as you would like, try to figure out the reasons why. Did you run out of time before you could answer all the questions? Did you go back and change your answers from right to wrong, or get flustered and sit staring at a hard question for what seemed like an eternity? If you had any of these problems, be sure to take another look at the EasySmart Test Preparation System in Chapter 2 again to learn how to avoid them.

Finally, examine how you did on each kind of question, and analyze where your strengths and weak-

nesses lie. That way you'll know which areas require special effort in the time you have left before the exam. The table on the next page identifies which questions on this third practice exam fall into which categories and lets you know which chapters to review if you had trouble with a particular type.

Remember, one of the biggest factors in your success on the exam is self-confidence. You've studied hard and you know where your strengths and weaknesses lie, so half the battle is won. Use the time you have left before the exam to brush up the problem areas that remain, and also to look over the chapters that deal with your strengths. Then go to the exam with every confidence that you'll do well.

VERBAL ABILITIES

Question Type	Question Numbers	Chapter
Vocabulary	12–14, 19, 28–30, 43–45, 54–57, 68–70	Chapter 4, Vocabulary and Spelling
Spelling	7, 8, 15, 16, 21–23, 38–40, 61–64, 81–83	Chapter 4, Vocabulary and Spelling
Grammar	9–11, 20, 24–27, 41, 42, 58–60, 71–74	Chapter 5, Grammar
Reading Comprehension	1, 2, 17, 18, 31–33, 48–50, 65–67, 79, 80, 84, 85	Chapter 6, Reading Comprehension
Word Relations (Analogies)	3–6, 34–37, 46, 47, 51–53, 75–78	Chapter 7, Word Relations

CLERICAL APTITUDE

Question Type	Question Numbers	Chapter
Name and Number Comparisons	1–5, 21–25, 41–45, 61–65, 81–85, 101–105	Chapter 8, Name and Number Comparisons
Alphabetizing	11–15, 26–30, 46–50, 76–80, 86–90, 111–115	Chapter 9, Alphabetizing
Arithmetic	6–10, 36–40, 51–55, 71–75, 96–100, 115–120	Chapter 10, Arithmetic
Number & Letter Matching	16–20, 31–35, 56–60, 66–70, 91–95, 106–110	Chapter 11, Number and Letter Matching

C·H·A·P·T·E·R

TYPING PROFICIENCY EXAM

14

CHAPTER SUMMARY

This chapter includes a timed exercise to test your typing skill level, timed practice sessions and tips to help you develop speed and accuracy, tips on dealing with the stress of typing in a timed situation, and a brief discussion of the differences between being tested on a computer and a typewriter.

Being able to type is no longer a requirement limited to secretaries and novelists. Thanks to the computer, anyone who wants to enter the working world needs to be familiar with a keyboard. Just knowing your way around a keyboard doesn't mean that you can use one efficiently, though. Although you may have progressed beyond the "hunt and peck" method, you may need help in increasing your speed and accuracy. Being able to type quickly with few errors not only will ensure that you pass the typing proficiency portion of the Clerical and Administrative Support Exam, but will also help you advance your career in any number of fields.

This chapter assumes that you are familiar enough with a standard keyboard to be able to use it without looking at the keys, which is the first step in learning to type, and that you are aware of the proper fingering. The following information will help you to increase your speed and accuracy, and to do your best when being tested on timed writing passages.

GETTING READY FOR THE TYPING PROFICIENCY EXAM

If you want to be sure to pass the typing proficiency exam, you will need to practice for it specifically. Even if you operate a typewriter or a computer for a living or have had keyboard training in the past, you will need to evaluate your speed and accuracy in preparation for the exam, and improve in both of these areas if necessary.

EVALUATING YOUR CURRENT SKILL LEVEL

The first step is to evaluate how fast and how accurately you can type at the present time. In order to do so, you will need the following tools:

- An electric typewriter, word processor, or computer
- A kitchen timer
- A document holder, if possible (available in business supply stores)

If you don't have your own typewriter, word processor, or computer, any of these can be rented by the month and used in your own home, or rented by the hour at many libraries and copy stores.

Of course, in addition, you will need:

- A comfortable chair that enables you to keep forearms straight with fingers hovering above the typewriter or computer keys
- A table or desk that is the right height to accomplish the above
- Good light that does not cause screen glare (if you use a computer)
- A wrist rest

Because you will need to practice at least 30 minutes a day, and preferably longer, it is important that you are comfortable while doing so. Typing for long periods of time while sitting incorrectly can cause stress injuries of the wrist and stiffness in the neck and the lower back. If you are using a monitor, make sure it is at eye level. If you are using a computer keyboard, be sure you have wrist supports (available in many computer and office supply stores) for both the keyboard and the mouse.

No matter what type of machine you are using, your forearms should be held at a 45-degree angle. If you are using a computer keyboard, your wrists should **not** rest on the wrist support while you are typing, but you should have a wrist support so that you can rest your wrists between typing sessions. Use the document holder to elevate this book at an angle next to the typewriter or monitor, and make sure the light is bright enough to prevent eye strain, but that no light glares on the computer screen.

TESTING YOUR CURRENT SKILL LEVEL

Set the margins of your typewriter or computer for a 60-character line, with 1-1/2 spaces between lines. On a typewriter, use pica spacing; on a computer, use a 12-point serif typeface such as Times or Palatino.

Type the passage on the next page as quickly as you can while trying to work as accurately as possible. Remember: Accuracy is more important than speed.

Whether you are using a typewriter or computer, if you see that you have made an error, *do not* take the time to correct it. (If you take the test on a computer, the chances are good that you will not be allowed to correct your errors.) If you finish the passage before the timer rings, begin again at the beginning and type until the timer rings. Now, set the timer for 4 minutes and begin.

SKILL-LEVEL TEST (4 MINUTES)

Dear Mayor Green:

I am writing to discuss an incident that occurred on the afternoon of June 30, 1998. As I was waiting on the street corner, holding an umbrella and a bag of groceries, a city bus came by and splashed my clothes with muddy water from a clogged drain. The next thing I knew, the bottom of my grocery bag fell out, and all my groceries fell into the flooded gutter at my feet. When I bent over to pick up my groceries, someone brushed against me from behind and knocked me over, so that I landed in the pool of water, along with my groceries. It took me some time to pick myself up and gather all my mud-soaked groceries (a kindly

passing woman did help me). In the process, I sustained a	35
knee, a torn sleeve, ruined groceries (the oranges	38
and lemons were okay, but the bag of sugar was a total	41
loss), and mud-stained clothes (my best suit!).	43
I realize that I have probably have no recourse against the	46
city, and in any event, I don't want to go to all the	49
trouble to discuss this with counsel and I do not consider	52
myself a litigious person, but I would like you to know	55
that you do a great disservice to the public by not keeping	58
gutters and storm drains clear of debris. It seems to me	61
that in a city of this size, with a huge tax base and an	64
affluent population, the least the city could do would be	67
to keep the streets clean. I have lived here since 1970,	69
and I must say that I consider myself a model resident. I	72
would appreciate it if the city would try a little harder	75
to keep the streets clean for its hard-working taxpayers.	78
Yours very sincerely,	79
A Concerned Citizen	80

Now, read through the passage and count up any errors you may have made. The numbers at the end of the lines will show you how many words you typed per minute for each line after reaching the speed of 35 words per minute.

IMPROVING YOUR TYPING SPEED AND ACCURACY

There is no magic solution to learning to type well. *Only consistent daily practice over a period of time will improve your speed and accuracy.* If you typed fewer than 35 words per minute in the preceding test passage and/or had more than six errors, you will need to practice over a longer period of time, and you should buy a book devoted to improving your typing, as you probably need to thoroughly memorize the keyboard and learn proper fingering. If you typed more than 35 words a minute and with six or fewer errors, you will still need to practice, both to increase your speed and accuracy to the highest level you have time for, and to gain the confidence you will need to perform well in a test situation.

First, you will need to set yourself a practice schedule. Typing in the course of your regular job will not give you the kind of focused attention necessary to increase your speed and accuracy. To prepare adequately for the text, you should do the following:

- Give yourself a minimum of two weeks to prepare for the exam—but one month is much better.
- Practice at approximately the same time every day.
- Begin with a 30-minute daily practice period; if you need a great deal of improvement, or if the test is coming up quickly, add 10 minutes a day until you are typing one hour a day.
- Try to practice every day—consistent practice is the key both to improvement and to testing well.

TYPEWRITERS VS. COMPUTERS

Although they have essentially the same keyboard, there are some important differences between typewriters and computers. Because computer keys require less pressure than those of a typewriter, you will be able to type faster on a computer. Correction is also much simpler on a computer and a word processor, as the delete key is used to erase any mistakes. (As was pointed out above, however, the chances are good that, if you take the test on a computer, you will not be allowed to correct your mistakes.) One other difference between the two machines: You should hit the space bar twice after all punctuation marks at the end of a sentence when using a typewriter, but only once when using a computer. The characters on a computer are spaced proportionally, so no extra space is needed to divide sentences.

KEYBOARD FORM

The way you hold and move your hands and fingers affects your speed and accuracy. Before beginning the following practice sessions, review the proper body, hand, and finger positions and keystroking movements:

- Sit with both feet on the floor, one slightly in front of the other, and your body about 8 inches from the center of the keyboard.
- If using a computer keyboard, your wrists should rest on the wrist support *between* typing sessions—do NOT rest your wrists as you type, however.
- Keep your hands flat, your fingers curved and fingertips lightly resting on the home keys, and your thumb above the center of the space bar.
- The keys should not be *struck,* but instead *stroked,* by lightly pulling the fingers toward you without moving your wrists or arms.
- Do not look at the keyboard, as this will inevitably slow you down.

PRACTICE SESSION NO. 1 (3 MINUTES)   WPM

Gina was late for work: It was already 9:15, and she
was more than three blocks from her office. (She was walking
today, as her car was in the garage.) She hurried along,
concerned. Her boss was irritated when people were late.
Although she was rushing, out of the corner of her eye she
noticed a jacket in a store window that made her stop
momentarily; it was just what she had been looking for, and
since it was on sale, it was $20 off! She noted the name of
the store, Winthrop & Sons, and hurried on toward her
office.   35

As it happened, her boss was late himself and hadn't   39
arrived yet. Gina gave a sigh of relief and sat down at her   43
desk. Now, she had a few minutes to settle herself before   46
the day began. She looked through one of the folders on her   50
desk to remind herself of what she had to do that day. But   54
the image of the jacket stayed in her mind. Quickly, she   58
looked up the phone number of the store in the Yellow Pages   62
and wrote it down: 835-2211. She would call the store on   66
her lunch hour, she decided, and ask them to hold the   70
jacket for her until she could come in and try it on. Just   73
then, her boss came through the door, smiling to see all   77
his employees present and working hard.   80

IMPROVING YOUR ACCURACY

If you find that you regularly make *more* than two errors for each minute typed on the practice sessions, slow your pace and practice diligently until your errors decrease. Your ultimate goal is to make one error or fewer for each 2 minutes typed, or two errors per 4-minute session. Please note that some of the practice sessions in this chapter are more difficult than others, because they contain more numbers and symbols. Pay particular attention to Practice Session No. 3 and to the accuracy drills in Practice Session No. 4. If you need new passages to practice, buy a book devoted to improving your typing, or copy passages from newspaper and magazines. Be sure to monitor yourself, proofreading your typing against the original copy carefully and counting your errors so that you will know how well you are doing.

PRACTICE SESSION NO. 2 (4 MINUTES)

WPM

The typewriter was invented in 1867; in 1874 the first
models were manufactured by Philo Remington, a gunsmith.
This machine had only capital letters, but machines with
shift keys were available by 1878.

The invention of the typewriter and the entry of women into
the workforce paralleled each other, and soon secretarial
academies were set up to teach young women how to operate
the typewriter. The early models were large and heavy, and
required strong pressure to operate the keys, which were
quite noisy. But secretarial work became a respectable
occupation that allowed young women to leave home and
support themselves, and was significant in the movement
toward the emancipation of women.   35

In later years, the ability to type became instead a kind   38
of trap for women: They had to learn to type in order to   41
enter the workforce, and once there they were kept at a   44
secretarial level, unable to rise in the ranks to executive 46
positions.   47

The invention of the computer, which uses virtually the   50
same keyboard as the typewriter, changed everything. Now,   53
male executives who did not know how to type were left   56
behind in the technological revolution, while young   58
programmers, software developers, and computer whizzes were 61
busily inputting information using keyboards.   63

Today, with children taking computer classes in grade   66
school, the ability to use a keyboard is beginning to seem   69
almost second nature. In a cultural change that could be   72
called "the secretary's revenge," typing has become a skill 75
that almost anyone who wants to be part of the working   78
world must learn to the best of his or her ability.   80

INCREASING YOUR SPEED

Once you have improved your level of accuracy, you can concentrate on increasing your speed. Go back to the practice sessions in this chapter that you have already typed (including the skill test), and type them at a pace just slightly faster than you are comfortable with. Concentrate on trying to establish a regular rhythm of stroking the keys. Continue to force yourself to type at a faster pace until you are comfortable with that pace, then push yourself to the next level by repeating this pattern. Intersperse these sessions with brief "typing sprints": typing several short sentences *as fast as you can* (see Practice Session No. 4, Section 3). Like the brief sprints runners use to increase their speed, these typing sprints will help to make your overall pace faster. Keep working at improving your speed until you are typing *slightly faster* than your goal, with a maximum of two errors for each three-minute session.

PRACTICE SESSION NO. 3 (3 MINUTES)   WPM

November 17, 1998

Dear Sir or Madam:

I recently visited your store during the fall sale and
purchased a coverlet that was advertised at a sale price
of 20 percent off the regular price. (The only reason I
went to the store was that I repeatedly tried and failed
to order this coverlet by phone: Although I tried dialing
the 800 number, I never got an answer, only a busy
signal.)

Once I found a sales clerk and the coverlet was located, I
purchased it and went home. Imagine my surprise on checking
my receipt to find this: 35

"Coverlet, QTY 1, @ $49.95, @ 10% discount = $46.50."   39

Not only is the sale discount wrong, the math is incorrect!   43
This means that not only was the wrong sale discount   46
entered into the computer, but that the computer has   50
figured the amount wrong! I am reluctant to try to solve   54
this by phone, given my problems with the 800 number. I am   58
also reluctant to make trip back into the store again, as   62
that is time-consuming for me. I hope that this letter will   66
receive prompt attention, and that the amount owed me   69
(which, by my calculations, is $7.13) will be credited to   73
my account, #387-439-1190. Please let me know.   76

Thank you for your attention to this matter.   79

A. S. Ballou   80

TIPS ON TESTING WELL

Being tested in a timed situation is always stressful; we are inevitably nervous and ill at ease, which can cause us to make more mistakes than we would ordinarily. There are several things you can do to cut down on the stress of being tested.

- The first, and by far the most important, is to *be well prepared for the test.* Some people tend to test well naturally, but nothing can replace the confidence that comes from knowing that you have done your best to prepare for a test.
- Make sure you've have a good night's sleep and a good breakfast.
- Arrive for the exam with plenty of time to spare. Take the time to go to a private place to stretch for a few minutes, especially your arms, hands, and fingers.
- When you are seated and ready for the test, take some time to focus yourself by closing your eyes and breathing deeply for a few minutes.
- Envision yourself taking the test and typing quickly and accurately, confident that all your practice has allowed you to perform well.
- Remember that accuracy is your first goal, and speed your second. When you begin the test, proceed at a pace that is slightly *less* than your top speed.

PRACTICE SESSION NO. 4 (UNTIMED)

Sections 1 and 2 are made up of words that are difficult to type. Begin by typing these slowly, repeating them until you show significant improvement in the number of errors you make.

Section 1: Accuracy Drill

```
believe  receive  you  your  mistake  attacking  grieve
freshest  efficient  situation  population  nocturnal
diurnal  elemental  motorcycle  understanding  withholding
personnel  department  borne  discipline  huddle  credit
auxiliary  require  their  there  millennium  eighteen
alleviate  tired  tried  instantaneously  attached
belatedly  eligible  risible  tangoed  philanthropy
dogsbody  dog-eared  longitudinal  lithograph  chronological
```

Section 2: Accuracy Drill

```
Suddenly, quietly, the immense moose rose to his feet. His
haughty profile stood out against the dark pine trees. Now,
he would follow his daily routine of walking to the lake at
his leisure. He was not impatient; he had all day to make
his way through the limpid sunlight. He required nothing but
a forest floor of moss, a fresh breeze, and time to graze.
And so, once he had arrived, he drank from the cool, lucid
pool.
```

Section 3: Speed Drill

Type the following short sentences several times as fast as you can. Repeat this speed drill periodically, in between typing the longer practice sessions.

```
Very truly yours,
I remain, yours sincerely, Gerald Finstermaker
At your earliest convenience
Let me know as soon as you can.
What else can we do to help you?
I apologize for any inconvenience you may have experienced.
I am sorry that you did not receive adequate compensation.
It is expedient that our service be the best that it can be.
```

PRACTICE SESSION NO. 5 (4 MINUTES)

WPM

In the old days, in the dark ages before the invention of
the electric typewriter, typing was a real trial for people
who were not skilled typists. You had to really push on the
keys, which were arranged in steeply raked rows. Each key
was elevated on metal prongs, and when you pushed one down,
the whole machine rattled and clanged and shuddered, and
the key itself made a sharp clacking sound.

There was no way to correct mistakes automatically in those
days. In fact, before correction fluid was invented, it was
difficult to correct mistakes at all: The only method was
by using a round typewriter eraser with a little brush at
one end. You had to take the paper out of the typewriter   35
(with a great noise as the cylinder turned), then try to   37
erase your error. This process was never more than   40
partially successful, leaving a ghostly trace of the error   43
along with erasure marks, worn spots on the paper, and   46
little gray shreds of eraser.   47

To make your correction, you had to reinsert the paper into   50
the machine, only to find that there was no way to return   53
the paper to the exact same place. Inevitably, the letters   56
that you typed to try to correct your error would be either   59
higher or lower than the letters immediately before and   62
after it, giving the line an antic look.   64

And making copies was a nightmare, because you had to use   67
carbon paper interleaved with sheets of typing paper. This   70
meant you had to erase both sheets of paper, then reinsert   73
both along with the carbon paper, making your chances of   76
getting the sheets of paper aligned with the original line   79
of letters twice as slim.   80

PRACTICE SESSION NO. 6 (4 MINUTES)

WPM

Have you ever read the writings of archy, the cockroach who
wrote to his friend, the cat mehitabel? Several volumes of
archy's letters, which were composed in an empty office at
night, were published from 1927 to 1940. It's not clear how
archy had the strength to push down those heavy-actioned
typewriter keys (and of course he couldn't use the shift
key at the same time, which accounts for the lower-cased
first names), but his missives reflected the miseries of
manual typewriters, complete with broken letters and
strike-throughs.

Electronic typewriters with correction keys were a dream
come true for the less-than-perfect typist, and the modern
computer keyboard, with its ease of action, immediate   35
deletion of errors, and near-silent operation, has taken   38
the task of communicating and recording information to a   41
new level.   42

To anyone who once had to use carbon paper to make copies,   45
the memory capability of computers is a miracle: It means   48
everything you input can be saved, changed almost instantly   51
at a later date, cut and pasted into other documents, and   54
copied an almost infinite number of times.   56

Like the printing press, which made it possible, for the   59
first time, for the ordinary person to possess a book, the   62
computer has made a revolutionary change in the way   64
information is communicated. Now, anyone with a computer   67
and the ability to use a keyboard can write his or her own   70
book, and, at the same time, illustrate it, format it, and   73
print it as well. The power of the press is a personal   76
possession today, which is a true revolution in the largest   79
sense of the word.   80

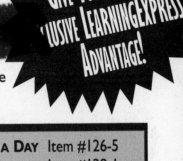